Communes in America, 1975–2000

Previous volumes in this trilogy

The Quest for Utopia in Twentieth-Century America, Volume 1: 1900–1960
The 60s Communes: Hippies and Beyond

Communes in America, 1975–2000

Timothy Miller

SU

Syracuse University Press

Syracuse, New York 13244-5290

First Edition 2019

19 20 21 22 23 24 6 5 4 3 2 1

∞ The paper used in this publication meets the minimum requirements of the American National Standard for Information Sciences—Permanence of Paper for Printed Library Materials, ANSI Z39.48-1992.

For a listing of books published and distributed by Syracuse University Press, visit www.SyracuseUniversityPress.syr.edu.

ISBN: 978-0-8156-3630-4 (hardcover)
978-0-8156-3648-9 (paperback)
978-0-8156-5476-6 (e-book)

Library of Congress Cataloging-in-Publication Data (for vol. 1)

Miller, Timothy, 1944–
The quest for utopia in twentieth century America / Timothy Miller.
p. cm.
Includes bibliographical references and index.
Contents: Vol. 1. 1900–1960
ISBN 0-8156-2775-0 (v. 1 : alk. paper)
1. Collective settlements—United States—History—20th century. 2. Utopias—History—20th century. I. Title
HX653.M55 1998
335'.12'09730904—dc21 97-48903

Manufactured in the United States of America

SUPPORTED BY A GRANT FROM
A SMALL, ANONYMOUS COMMUNITY

For Tamara, Jesse, and Aber

A map of the world that does not include Utopia is not worth even glancing at, for it leaves out the one country at which Humanity is always landing. And when Humanity lands there, it looks out, and, seeing a better country, sets sail. Progress is the realisation of Utopias.

—Oscar Wilde

Contents

Tables

Preface

A Century of American Intentional Communities

Nearly two decades ago I set out to compile a survey history of communal living in the United States in the twentieth century. The first two volumes carry the story up to 1975; the present volume covers the last quarter of the century and tries to do some summing up, some reflecting on this small but optimistic part of the human experience. As in the first two volumes, my focus is on communities founded during the time period in question, but if the community survives the cutoff date (in this case, the year 2000), I provide a bit of the ongoing story as well.

First, a matter of definition: in the first volume in this series I provided a seven-point definition of intentional community, and I still think it represents my thinking well enough.[1] More recently I have condensed it a bit; here is the rendition I used in my most recent book, *The Encyclopedic Guide to American Intentional Communities*. It guides this volume as well, so I will simply repeat it (slightly edited) here:

> I would contend that it is easier to recognize an intentional community than it is to define the term. However, some standard had to be developed for this work to proceed. The definition I am using, which I believe represents the mainstream of scholarly thought on the matter, has four components:
>
> 1. The group in question must be gathered on the basis of some kind of purpose or vision. Intentional communities are not simply group living situations; they are group living situations centered on specific causes and visions. That purpose might be

religious, as in the case of Christian communities built on the precept that the descriptions of early Christian church life in Acts 2 and 4 are timeless mandates for Christians. The purpose might be secular, as in the case of an egalitarian community striving to create a model of a just society or a community of environmentalists dedicated to reducing their carbon footprints. Communities can gather for contemplation and withdrawal, or for service to the larger world. Somehow the group must have a sense of being withdrawn or set apart from conventional society and operating in pursuit of a goal that transcends simply living together. Perdita Buchan's observation that "moral energy" is the distinctive identifier of an intentional community is on the mark.[2]

2. The group in question must live together on property that has some clear physical commonality to it. The group may live on commonly owned or rented land, or it may live on privately owned parcels that are in close proximity (normally adjacent) to each other. Its members may live in one unitary dwelling or in separate homes, but physical closeness of residence is required.
3. The group must have some kind of financial or material sharing, some kind of economic commonality. That does not mean that all income and assets must be pooled; indeed, that pattern is the exception rather than the rule in American communities. But some common economic involvement, some joint use of resources, needs to be present. That may mean that some or all of the real estate of the community is owned in common, or that community members contribute to a common pool for paying expenses.
4. The group must have a membership of at least five adults, not all of whom are related by blood or marriage. That standard is the one most frequently proposed by communal studies scholars, and therefore is employed here. (However, the minimum-size rule is bent slightly in a few cases, as long as the other elements of the definition are met. Some groups might fall slightly short of five permanent adult members yet operate as cultural magnets, with many like-minded short-term members or visitors present at certain times, often attending purpose-driven events [festivals,

> workshops, seminars, concerts]. Some religious communities, and a few gay and lesbian communities, fit this pattern.)[3]

And beyond all formal elements of any definition, I have tried to respect the communal intentions of the communitarians themselves. Intentions are vital here, and I do not want to exclude any who sincerely make common cause in their collective lives.

That might seem clear enough, but there remain all kinds of gray areas that defy easy solution. What about prisons? What about organized-crime syndicates? I have excluded both of these examples, and many others, rather arbitrarily, perhaps. I have also excluded traditional American Indian tribes on the grounds that they were not "withdrawn or set apart from conventional society," to quote my own definition above; instead, they *are* (or *were*) the conventional society of their time and place. I have excluded college fraternities and sororities, which provide common housing but seem to me not to embody the visionary purpose I am looking for; but I have included student housing cooperatives, which often see themselves as important vehicles of social change. I have not set any minimum duration for a group to qualify; if we were to exclude those that last less than a year, say, our list of American communities would be enormously shorter. Simply to keep the project manageable, I have also excluded from consideration—both in the text and in the lists that comprise appendix B—the thousand or more monasteries and convents of the Catholic and other hierarchical churches, institutions that would certainly meet my definition. I refer readers interested in further musings on the matter of definition to my earlier books, cited in notes 1 and 3 at the end of this preface.

The American communal experience has evolved considerably over the four centuries it has been with us. Many earlier communitarian ventures involved full economic sharing, with all assets held by the group. That model persists; the largest contemporary movement in North America today that practices communal living, apart from Catholic religious communities, is that of the Hutterites, who hold everything but a few personal effects in common. Far more communities today are economically mixed: some assets (especially real estate) are held in common, while members otherwise keep their own money. As a result, perhaps, members often seem to have lower levels of commitment to the group than might have been the case in earlier times. Things do change, and contemporary intentional communities have more diverse forms than they once did.

More significantly, perhaps, the quarter-century under observation here, 1975–2000, saw substantial evolution in communal forms in large part because of social and environmental challenges that confronted not just communitarian experiments but American society as a whole. The decade and a half before the time we are considering here, what I call the 1960s era, was a time of great social innovation and upheaval. Long-accepted social institutions—family, religion, medicine, politics, and many more—were challenged directly, sometimes harshly. New concern with health and well-being spurred a new public interest in natural foods. Stable lifelong heterosexual marriages were no longer the norm; instead, half of marriages ended in divorce, sexual activity outside of marriage became commonplace, and the emergence of a gay-rights movement put America on the path toward gay marriage—where it was once unthinkable to discuss homosexuality openly, it became an inescapable presence among us and experienced an accelerating curve of acceptance. The cultural domination of Protestantism, Catholicism, and Judaism was challenged by the arrival of spiritual teachers from Asia and other religious innovators. Alternative medical practices found followings as never before. New drugs and psychedelics pointed toward pleasure-seeking, challenging the heritage of a Protestant ethic of hard work. The unpopular war in Vietnam was just ending in 1975, and disgust with that war, especially among the young, fueled questioning of the received truth that had long been handed down by the country's ruling class. Steadily rising income inequality helped foster widespread skepticism that the American dream was still possible.

And, perhaps most important of all, it has only been in the last few decades that preservation of the environment has become a leading commitment of tens of millions of Americans. A world that once seemed like a cornucopia, furnishing us with endless resources and effortlessly absorbing and discarding our wastes, began to cloud over, literally and figuratively. Somehow in our headlong rush for more comfortable material lives we hadn't noticed that minerals extracted from the earth were not infinite, and that the byproducts being dumped into rivers and landfills and blasted into the sky just might cause trouble down the road.

How did these changes in society affect communal living, which has been continuously present in America since the seventeenth century? They brought about a back-to-the-land movement in which the new pioneers sought to grow much of their own food, and grow it organically. They saw the coming of intentional communities rooted in sexual politics—LGBTQ, polyamorous communities, serially monogamous communities, and the occasional celibate community. New religious communes were founded by the hundreds, even thousands—new radical Christian communities, settlements of adherents of a variety of Asian traditions, Pagan communities, and New Age communities of bewildering diversity. Communities of young political radicals kept the antiwar torch burning. Communities dedicated to meeting the needs of the poor, the disabled, the homeless, and the misfits of society, some following long-established models, as in the case of the Catholic Worker and the Camphill communities, continued to expand. Finally, environmental concern came to permeate the communal world, even more thoroughly than it did the world at large. Some communities were built around ecological projects, and most of them tried to play their parts in slowing the already far advanced environmental damage.

For all of the changes, what might be considered the centerpiece of communal living remains intact. Joining with others to live together in pursuit of a high purpose is applied idealism of the first order, and a dedicated minority of human beings at any time or place still seeks to make a difference—together, because many are stronger than one.

Just as scholars and the public do not share a precise definition of "intentional community," they also lack agreement on terminology more broadly. Terms such as commune, community, intentional community, colony, enclave, utopian community, collective settlement, and cooperative colony are sprinkled throughout the extensive literature on the topic. Moreover, different authors use such terms with somewhat different shades of meaning. Perhaps someday a consensus on terminology will appear, but that has not happened yet. I will not follow any strict system of nomenclature in the following pages, but will use such terms more or less interchangeably. Similarly, various authors have used such terms as "communal movement" and "communitarianism" in somewhat different ways, and, again, I am not going to dwell on precise usage. There is arguably no single "communal movement," after all, although some use that term to refer, collectively, to all kinds of groups practicing communal living. Among America's communitarians, or communards, there are some who are truly dedicated to the idea of communal living for its own inherent virtues, even though they have other commitments as well. That is often the case among the activists of the Fellowship for Intentional Community, for example, or the Christian communitarians who label their collective faith-based lifestyle the New Monasticism. But many more who have adopted communal living have done so not because that is itself a goal, but rather because it is a means to an end, a useful way of structuring their lives in pursuit of an entirely separate goal or a vision—a religious commitment, in many cases, or a dedication to serving others, or a belief that communal living arrangements, which tend to reduce carbon footprints, are environmentally valuable. For some communitarianism itself is an important goal, but for others it is simply a tool. Donald Pitzer has created the term "developmental communalism" to describe the type of communitarianism that regards communal arrangements not as an end but as a means that may well drop away when the group no longer needs such arrangements.[4] This volume will consider all kinds of groups and movements that practice communal living, whatever role communitarianism plays for them.

The chapters that follow are topical, not chronological, in orientation. In each case they provide basic information about the type of community in question, and then provide some examples of that type. Inevitably those examples provide only a sampling of specific communities, given the fact that providing a profile for every community founded during the last quarter of the twentieth century would mean producing an encyclopedia, not a monograph—and, for that matter, an incomplete encyclopedia, because locating every intentional community at a given time or in a given territory is an impossible task. I have tried in my choices to show the remarkable diversity of the communal universe and to tell some good and memorable stories.

Chapter 1 provides a bridge between earlier communitarianism and the period under examination in this volume. It demonstrates that more than a few communities from the past were still present by 1975, in some cases providing models for new community-builders and in others simply abiding quietly out of any spotlight, continuing the venerable tradition of communal living without fanfare. Then we proceed to an examination of cohousing, which has mixed some well-established communitarian ideas with modern technology as well as building design that promotes social interaction. Cohousing has produced hundreds of projects housing many thousands of members in the United States and several other countries, and at this writing it appears to have a bright future as a model for retirement living. Next follows a chapter on the new ecovillages, a communal type whose time has surely arrived. The continued degradation of the environment and the neverending extraction of nonrenewable minerals from the earth is inescapably a worldwide social crisis, and the ecovillagers are trying to do something about it. They are building model structures from sustainably sourced materials, powering themselves with renewable energy, developing new types of sustainable agriculture, and lowering their carbon footprints to a small fraction of what most people in the developed world are producing. The concept of building environmental responsibility into a communitarian housing project is not exactly new, but the ecovillagers have taken the concept to a new level and are showing the world, or at least their neighbors, that one can live comfortably without taking a high toll on the earth and its resources.

Spiritual communities have always been a large part—sometimes a dominant one—of the world of cooperative living, and that was as true after 1975 as it had been before. They were so abundant in the late twentieth century that they merit two chapters here. Some were situated in the long-dominant institutions of Christianity and Judaism, but often with a twist—perhaps a new and updated take on the old ways, or even something that followed divergent paths, as in the case of new movements that added new scriptures and theological principles to the accepted orthodoxy. Others were outside the old mainstream altogether—for example, with new Hindu and Buddhist communities slowly but steadily appearing in towns and villages and the countryside across the land. Even more surprising, perhaps, was the rise and spread of Paganism (or neo-Paganism, as some have called it), a recreation of what were believed to be the feminine and earth-centered spiritual paths of older times, and in several cases Pagans also settled into communal havens. The American religious landscape was far more diverse than it had ever been, and communal encampments of people adhering to religions of many different types proliferated.

Communities devoted to human services and other specific commitments, some of them based in religious traditions and some not, have been a part of the communitarian scene all along, but seemed to be on an upward trajectory during the last quarter of the century. Quite a few communities that were focused on activism for peace and justice, many of them short-lived but some quite durable, appeared and often presented new approaches to the work they undertook. Religious communities serving the poor, the hungry, and the homeless have long been with us, but the New Monastics, for instance, brought forward a powerful new model. Evangelical Christians of a new breed, they moved in amid the poor they served and lived a lifestyle of committed sharing in what they called the abandoned places of empire. Beyond that lay other purpose-driven communities. Artists have long congregated in congenial places, and communal forms have often served them well, as they have found that most kinds of art—visual arts, theater, music, and the rest—can be pursued creatively in collaborative residential spaces. And as gay men and lesbians emerged from their closets, intentional communities of those with same-sex orientations became valuable enclaves of safety and identity.

After several chapters of surveys of the communal world of the late twentieth century, the book nears a close with a chapter on situations in which communities were thrust prominently into public view either because of their own excesses and misdeeds or because prejudice from the outside world boiled over, or some combination of the two. Mass suicides, murders, and government raids all commanded headlines and stories that tended to reproduce stereotypes of mad "cult" leaders, brainwashed zombie followers, sexual perversions, financial malfeasance, and much more. In fact, things rarely follow the patterns of any stereotype, and unraveling the sensational media coverage from the real facts is an important purpose of that chapter.

Because this book concludes a series spanning the whole twentieth century, the main text ends with a look at the prevalence of community in American life, which transcends the time period that frames this volume alone. How many communities have there been in our collective past and present? Are there any patterns to communal longevity? The point here is to step back and look at the larger setting—the way the quarter-century we have surveyed fits the much larger matrix of American communal living. The chapter also provides some musing on methodological limitations that historians of communal life face. We will never be able to count, much less describe, all of the thousands of communal enterprises in American life, but understanding this undying strain of applied idealism in our culture makes it all worthwhile.

The book closes with two appendices. The first examines the prevalence of intentional communities in American life. Various observers have perceived "waves" of communal activity, most typically in the early to mid-nineteenth century, in the 1960s era, and in some cases at other times as well. This appendix analyzes my extensive database of American communities and, while recognizing that exact measurements of communal activity are impossibly difficult, there have indeed been some waves, the most substantial of which came in the 1970s. The second appendix is a list of all the communities I can identify that were active in the twentieth century.

Acknowledgments

This volume incorporates the fruits of research of three decades, and listing all of the generous scholars and communitarians who have contributed to my work would be impossible. So let me thank a few who helped by category: my excellent colleagues in the Communal Studies Association, the International Communal Studies Association, the two Utopian Studies societies (the US-based Society for Utopian Studies and the Europe-based Utopian Studies Society), and the American Academy of Religion (especially the New Religious Movements Group); the helpful editors and staff members at the presses that published my earlier communal and countercultural works (Syracuse University Press, the Richard W. Couper Press, Ashgate Publishing, Garland Publishing, and the University of Tennessee Press); my colleagues in the Department of Religious Studies; the Hall Center for the Humanities and the College of Liberal Arts and Sciences at the University of Kansas, both of which provided research support; the current and former members of communal societies and the Fellowship for Intentional Community, whose passion has been an inspiration; my students, many of whom have shared my passion for finding and documenting communities, and in several cases have introduced me to communities that I had not previously known; the anonymous referees for the press, whose critiques were most helpful; and my family, Tamara, Jesse, and Aber, plus my parents and siblings. With that, I haven't overlooked anyone (at least any individual), because I haven't named anyone beyond my own immediate family. Please, all, know how deep my gratitude is. How sweet and fitting it is that my studies of human cooperation have been supported by such a far-flung web of people of assistance and good will.

Communes in America, 1975–2000

1

The Century Winds Down, and Communities Thrive

By the mid-1970s the fantastic communal surge of the previous decade seemed to be winding down. Of the tens of thousands of communitarian experiments started between 1960 and 1975, a solid majority were already defunct.[1] In fact, more communes were active in the 1970s and 1980s (and beyond) than in the 1960s, but the flamboyant, hip enclaves, at least, were receiving less public attention than they had earlier, and the ones that survived were settling down and no longer generating much controversy. During the rush to the countryside in the late 1960s, in too many cases the communal enterprise had been undertaken without much preparation, financial backing, or a clear course of action. A great cultural convergence had been in full swing: the back-to-the-land impulse that sweeps the country now and then was having one of its periodic resurgences, and a blossoming counterculture was questioning conventional ways of living. Moreover, self-sufficiency and sustainability were just entering public consciousness. Although some of those themes persevered, others did not. Communes did not disappear from the landscape, but their presence in the public eye dimmed.

Farming had long been integral to the communal vision. Most of the new communards, however, were urban young people, and they knew little about farming. Although handy guidebooks appeared in abundance, and the amazing compendium the *Whole Earth Catalog* pointed to the many kinds of agricultural resources the new pioneers sorely needed, it turned out that, for many, farming was an art and a science for which they were simply not prepared. Other problems loomed as well, including the fact that, in many cases, an open-door membership policy attracted a lot of dead weight. And so the dream was abandoned, in case after case, and the dreamers moved on to the next stage of life, whatever that might have been.

Communal dissolution, however, is hardly the whole story. While some of the communes founded in the 1960s closed within a few years, others survived—hundreds at least. Surprisingly many are still alive and relatively well today. And several venerable communities from earlier times have also survived. The sketches below are not comprehensive; many other communities have similarly persevered for many years. The ones featured here may be taken as exemplars; their paths were duplicated, with variations, by many others.

Communities that survive for several decades manage to work out a transition between generations. There is no one formula for success in making that transition, however. Some long-lived communities, such as the Hutterites, have high birth rates and low attrition rates, leading to stable or increasing populations. Some communities manage to appeal to new and younger residents: the Catholic Worker and the Camphill communities, for example, have endured for many decades, attracting a stream of new members interested in the human service work that both movements provide and, in the case of the Catholic Worker, faith-based radical activism. The Farm community in Tennessee lost over a thousand members in the 1980s, but it seems to have reached a fairly solid bedrock membership in the low hundreds. Twin Oaks, the egalitarian income-sharing community in Virginia, came to accept substantial turnover in membership as an ongoing reality but attracted enough newcomers to, at times, relegate some would-be members to a waiting list. As with so many things in the communal world, there is no single answer to the question of longevity.

The Survivors from Earlier Times

The Hutterites and the Bruderhof

To begin with, the biggest group of communes in North America, apart from the religious communities of the Catholic Church, remains the Hutterites, whose presence long pre-dates the 1970s. Coming here from Russia in 1874, the numbers of these communitarian Anabaptists have increased over one-hundred-fold, to some fifty thousand members in about five hundred colonies, one-third or so of each in the United States and the rest in Canada. The Hutterites present the greatest independent communal success story in history—larger and longer-lived than any other communal movement not anchored in some larger religious tradition, such as a branch of Buddhism or Christianity.

That said, the latter years of the twentieth century were a time of change for the Hutterites. The most prominent change was the division of the Schmiedeleut, one of the movement's three branches. In 1992 an unexpected vote of the assembled Schmiedeleut ministers showed deep division over the leadership of Jacob Kleinsasser, the Schmiedeleut presiding elder. It was in part a classic liberal-conservative conflict: Kleinsasser had supported several controversial innovations in Hutterite life—the widespread use of English (as opposed to the traditional Hutterisch dialect of German), openness to education beyond middle school, and fostering fellowship with nonhutterites (and especially with the Bruderhof, about which more presently), to name only three. He had also been heavy-handed, his opponents maintained, with the internal affairs of some colonies. A majority of the ministers voted to depose Kleinsasser; but a significant minority supported him. Thus where there once were three main Hutterite "peoples"—Lehrerleut, Dariusleut, and Schmiedeleut—there now were four. Although reunion remains possible, the two Schmiedeleut groups have gone their separate ways, and not amicably.

Beyond that familial dispute the Hutterites faced other challenges as the century moved toward its conclusion. The Hutterites have valiantly tried to keep modern society at bay, although that is hard to do in today's interconnected world. Cell phones may be formally forbidden by Hutterites, but many, especially young ones, do have them. Computers, introduced in the colonies to support their agricultural businesses, have brought the outside world streaming in. So greatly has modernity penetrated the movement, especially the more liberal of the Schmiedeleut, that a key website on Hutterism, www.hutterite.org, is maintained by Hutterite youth—some of whom go to high school! Meanwhile, other changes are also having their effects. Birth control, always officially forbidden, is now a fact of life, as women get it from their doctors, which has reduced the birth rate dramatically, producing cultural changes that are yet to be worked out fully. Another very real inroad is the presence of evangelical Protestantism. Hutterites have traditionally had their own version of Christianity, one that rejects such things as missions, musical instruments, and personal, as opposed to communal, piety. Now, spurred by Christian radio broadcasts (radios remain nominally forbidden to Hutterites, but once again the traditional ban is failing), some Hutterites want a more satisfying religious culture, and more than a few have left the colonies to find it (or have been expelled).

No one should conclude that this giant of North American communitarianism is on the ropes. The movement is economically healthy, largely spiritually intact, and satisfying to most of its members, who have been socialized into Hutterism from infancy. The late twentieth century did present the Hutterites with their largest challenges in over a hundred years, however, and more change seemed inevitable.[2]

Another long-surviving Christian communal group deserves attention, in large part because of its interactions with the Hutterites. The Bruderhof was founded by Eberhard Arnold in Germany in 1920 as a communal youth movement. Arnold learned of the existence of the Hutterites in North America a few years later and traveled to meet these people he had only known through history books. The two groups since have had an up-and-down relationship, cordially declaring themselves allies at one time and severing contact at another. Although the Bruderhof adopted Hutterite dress and for a time called itself "Hutterian Brethren," gradually the majority of the Hutterites rejected the Bruderhof connection as undermining traditional Hutterite ways, given the cultural differences between the two. Bruderhof members were simply more worldly than Hutterites, much more connected to the outside world; they played musical instruments and even sometimes smoked cigarettes!

The Bruderhof, for its part, seems to be thriving despite occasional conflicts. Its early history saw the group flee from the Nazis and wartime conflict, moving from Germany to Liechtenstein, to England, to Paraguay, and finally to the United States in 1954. Arnold's son Heinrich, and then his grandson Christoph, became his successors as leader, and there have been conflicts about both of them, in part because they have overseen repeated expulsions of members. A group of ex-members keeps up a lively conversation accusing the movement of all kinds of shameful behavior. For all of that the Bruderhof has grown and, with its businesses (especially as a successful manufacturer of sturdy children's playthings) has been economically robust. Members continue, as do the Hutterites, to hold all things in common and pursue a way of life substantially removed from the corruptions of the outside world.[3]

Other Pre-1960 Survivors

Many other communities with pre-1960s origins survived through the end of the century as well, although in varying states of health. The Catholic Worker, that venerable movement of independent local houses that combine direct service to people in need with radical social and political activism, continues with its original vision and mission largely intact, and it still publishes its newspaper, the *Catholic Worker*, selling it for a penny a copy. Hundreds of the movement's Houses of Hospitality continue their work, with new ones founded every year.[4]

Another service-oriented communal network, Camphill, which was founded in Scotland in 1939 and arrived in the United States in 1961, is similarly hewing to its original purpose. Camphill communities take in the physically and mentally disabled, integrating them into the community with those serving and assisting them.[5] A similar network of service communities, L'Arche (The Ark), is newer than either the Catholic Worker or Camphill, but it also seems to have remained well. The movement, which was founded by Jean Vanier in France in 1964, is dedicated to supporting developmentally disabled persons in a fashion reminiscent of Camphill. L'Arche quickly spread worldwide, opening its first community in the United States in 1972. It has grown steadily since then.[6]

Koinonia Farm, founded in 1942, continues its work for peace and justice in south Georgia. In its first two decades it was bitterly opposed, sometimes violently, by many of its neighbors for its policy of racial equality and integration, but as times have changed it has been able to do its work in relative peace. Perhaps its largest enduring monument is Habitat for Humanity, which builds affordable low-income housing; Habitat grew out of, and still strongly resembles, a housing program that started at Koinonia.[7]

Still other communities managed to survive through the century and beyond, although not necessarily in robust health. Father Divine's Peace Mission Movement was declining even before his abandonment of his physical body (he had said he would never die) in 1965, and at the end of the century was selling property to support its few aging members. The House of David, which endured a major schism following the death of its founder, Benjamin Purnell, continued in two branches, but neither attracted many new members and each was reduced to a handful of survivors by the year 2000.[8]

One other group of communities with roots in the past seemed to be thriving through the last quarter of the century. The Latter-day Saints (LDS), or Mormons, had several waves of communal activity in their first several decades, especially during the 1870s, when dozens of United Order communities, as they were known, embraced varying degrees and styles of communitarianism. They soon waned, but after the main Mormon church abandoned its practice of polygamy, new splinter groups devoted to maintaining "the Principle," as they referred to plural marriage, sprouted up, often in enclaves that featured communal living. The largest of them planted a community at what was then called Short Creek, Arizona, beginning in the early twentieth century. Their numbers grew steadily, despite three major government raids that failed to deter the practice of the Principle, and by the end of the century stood at around five thousand, including many just over the state line in Hildale, Utah (effectively a part of Colorado City, as Short Creek had been renamed). Other LDS polygamists lived in intentional communities here and there around the American West as well as in Canada and Mexico. Although problems would wrack the Fundamentalist LDS Church, as the ecclesiastical organization was called early in the twenty-first century, its members appeared to be thriving as they approached the year 2000.[9]

1960s-Era Communities Still Alive and Well at the End of the Century

Several of the communes of the 1960s era have also survived, in one form or another. These five all had their stories related in volume 2 of this series, but they deserve brief recapitulations and updates here as exemplars of the ongoing communitarian spirit and the perseverance of communal life after 1975.

The Farm

Hundreds of intentional communities of more recent vintage than the Hutterites and Bruderhof survived through the last quarter of the twentieth century. Perhaps none of them has been more prominent than the Farm, the archetypal 1960s-era commune in Tennessee. Its roots were in San Francisco in the late 1960s, where the hippie philosopher Stephen Gaskin gathered a devoted following for his eclectic spiritual teachings. When Stephen, as he was always called, undertook a speaking tour, hundreds of his young compatriots accompanied him on a circuitous journey in a motley fleet of school buses, vans, and trucks. Landing in Tennessee in 1971, their numbers rose to about 1500 over a decade; members built the physical infrastructure of the Farm, pioneered vegan foods (including soy ice cream), developed a crackerjack corps of midwives, did disaster relief in the United States and abroad, and lived in relative poverty that was completely economically communal. The Farm's story has been recounted in the predecessor to this volume as well as many other books and articles.[10]

An abrupt change occurred in the early 1980s, when severe economic problems together with some loss of confidence in Stephen's temporal leadership brought a major restructuring of the Farm. No longer did the community meet everyone's needs; now all members needed to be self-sufficient—to have a job and pay dues. The Farm did have several good businesses and a well-regarded charitable organization known as Plenty, so some jobs were available—but not enough for everyone. People left in large numbers. A few years later the population dropped to about two hundred.

But at that level the Farm has recovered, at least to some degree. Small businesses purvey a range of products including vegetarian foods, radiation detectors, and mail-order books. Several nonprofits offer courses and workshops in sustainable living; the Ecovillage Training Center draws students from around the world. To a remarkable degree the communitarian ideals of the Farm remain intact. A younger generation is thriving and stands to keep the Farm vital for some time to come.

Twelve Tribes

The Twelve Tribes provide a story of ongoing development and considerable growth. Again, its early story was sketched briefly in volume 2 of this work, but so much happened after 1975 that the movement deserves an update here. From its beginnings in Chattanooga, Tennessee, the movement relocated to the small town of Island Pond, Vermont, where it burst suddenly into prominence. In 1984 a battalion of over 100 state troopers and social workers swept down on the community and seized 112 community children. Apparently a disaffected ex-member, supported by anticult activists, had complained to the authorities of child abuse, and thus a raid was triggered. But what a fiasco! The Twelve Tribes unapologetically practices stern discipline of its children, spanking them for transgressions. But is that abuse? The judge in the case quickly found that there was no evidence of anything that legally qualified as abuse and ordered the children returned to their homes. A fuller account of the Island Pond raid, and others experienced by the Twelve Tribes, is provided in chapter 7.

Since that traumatic time the movement has continued to grow. By century's end it had spread beyond the United States, and in the early

2000s had grown to several thousands of members in communities in England, France, Spain, Germany, Brazil, Australia, and Argentina, as well as Canada and the United States. Its businesses were flourishing—restaurants, furniture-making shops, bakeries, specialty stores, and organic farms. It was a brand-new culture, as the movement proclaimed, that would, once the Twelve Tribes' membership reached 144,000, usher in the returned Christ. By the end of the century no American commune from the 1960s era had prospered more than the Twelve Tribes.[11]

The Jesus Movement and Jesus People USA

The 1960s era was a time of questioning and often rejecting prevailing values. One stream of the new consciousness, however, was a curious mix of the old and the new. What came to be known as the Jesus Movement was populated by hippie Christians who accepted traditional, biblical Christianity (usually Protestant, but occasionally Catholic or Orthodox) but rejected its outward manifestations in the twentieth century—its churches, its dress code, its music, its stodginess.

Once they had gone through a born-again experience many of the new Christians did try to attend conventional churches, but by and large they were rejected. They still wore their outlandish hippie clothing, for God's sake, and had long hair and seemed like they might be a bit dirty. That is, in style they were still hippies. Most respectable churches weren't interested in taking them in.

But a few pastors and their churches were exceptions; the most notable were Chuck Smith and his Calvary Chapel in the Los Angeles area. The Jesus Freaks, as they were usually known, were welcome there. And Smith went beyond acceptance of Jesus Movement style; communes were the order of the day, and some of the new Christians wanted to live out their newfound faith communally. After all, Christian communalism had clear biblical sanction in the Book of Acts. Smith helped it all happen, locating housing for the young seekers. Eventually the largest group of hip communal Christians, known as the Shiloh Youth Revival Centers, settled near Eugene, Oregon, a base from which they developed a network of more than 175 communal homes.[12]

Shiloh was far from the only organized and communal group of Jesus Freaks. One of them, the Jesus People Army, spawned several offshoots, one of which settled in Chicago as Jesus People USA. The members initially expected only a brief evangelizing visit to the city, but they settled in and began to organize communal businesses. Before long they had purchased a place to live—a large older hotel. And there they remain, several hundred strong. The businesses of JPUSA, as the group is known, include a large roofing supply company, a cabinet shop, a recording studio, a print shop, and a retail store, among others. The spirit of JPUSA has remained defiantly countercultural; members, with their piercings and tattoos and the like, would not be mistaken for your average church member. Meanwhile, the outreach programs remain central: JPUSA feeds the hungry, houses the homeless, and provides lodging for low-income elderly people on the hotel's upper floors. The economy remains shared; meals are taken in common. Worship continues to have a countercultural flair. Members live squeezed into modest hotel rooms. All in all, not much has changed since JPUSA arrived in Chicago at the end of 1972.[13]

Twin Oaks and East Wind

Among the secular communities, few have survived as steadfastly as Twin Oaks. The initial inspiration for that community, founded in 1967, was B. F. Skinner's utopian novel *Walden Two*, which the founders, the most prominent of whom was Kathleen "Kat" Kinkade, sought to enact in real life.[14] Over time many of Skinner's strictures have fallen by the wayside; in the book, people are given unequal work credit, the compensation varying with the desirability of the job at hand (it would take many hours of flower gardening, for example, to be counted equivalent to an hour of toilet cleaning), but that seemingly attractive plan was dropped early on. Now all hours count the same, and everyone has to do some less-than-desirable labor.

That said, many early precepts remain essentially in place. Twin Oaks makes a solid effort to be egalitarian, with all members doing equal work and receiving equal benefits. Individuals do not have private cars; the community has a small fleet that members can use. Everyone gets a small (and equal) monthly cash allowance for little luxuries (such as tobacco or travel) not provided by the group. A clothing storehouse ("commie clothes") is open to all—take what you need, and deposit what you don't. Traditional gender roles are spurned; women do most of the auto repair, and men do plenty of cooking and dishwashing. The economies of communal living have led to a comfortable—but not extravagant—standard of living. One of the mainstay industries has been the manufacture of woven rope hammocks, which for years were sold primarily through Pier One stores. That outlet is now gone, but hammocks are still sold elsewhere, and several other businesses, such as tofu-making and the indexing of books, have also helped take up the slack.

Twin Oaks spawned a daughter community, East Wind in Missouri, just a few years after it was founded, and East Wind is doing fine as well, anchored by its own signature business: grinding and selling peanut, cashew, almond, and other nut butters. East Wind subscribes to most of the core principles of Twin Oaks, especially egalitarianism.

The Twin Oaks and East Wind communities still solidly reflect their countercultural origins. Men sometimes wear dresses, and men and women alike are free to wear nothing at all, if they like (bathing suits are rarely seen at the swimming holes of either community). Both communities are heavily focused on environmentally sensitive living, and the members' carbon footprints, in both cases, are undoubtedly among the lowest in the country. At century's end Twin Oaks had about one hundred members, and East Wind about seventy-five.[15]

Lama

The roots of the Lama Foundation lie in the purchase, by Steve and Barbara Durkee, of an old Methodist church in Garnerville, New

York, where Steve worked as an artist. The Durkees were soon joined by members of a New York art collective called USCO, for "company of us," which specialized in the light shows that often illuminated 1960s-era concerts. Seeking a more spiritually ordered community, the Durkees began looking for a home for the community they initially called Solux. The search led them to New Mexico, where the community they founded was called Lama Foundation—not, as one might presume, after a Tibetan dharma teacher, but a local place name.

There, in 1967, they founded Lama, at a site north of Taos. From the beginning it was a spiritual community, although no one path predominated. Elements of Tibetan, Sufi, Essene, Hindu, Buddhist, Quaker, and many other spiritualities mixed together in meditation sessions and rituals. American Indian traditions were important; the Lama pioneers were befriended by some of the Indians at nearby Taos Pueblo. And, as in many other spiritual communities, hard work was part of the regime. In the early years community members spent long hours making adobe bricks and erecting buildings. Discipline was also the order of the day. Three rules were imposed from the beginning: daily meditation, fidelity in marriage, and no drugs, including tobacco and alcohol. In those carefree countercultural days, that eliminated a lot of potential members (and eventually the rules broke down anyway).

Two prominent countercultural figures were crucial to Lama in its early years. One was the spiritual teacher Ram Dass, who first came to public notice as an associate of Timothy Leary in their early experiments with LSD and other psychedelics. Known then as Richard Alpert, he went to India as a spiritual seeker and encountered Neem Karoli Baba, a Hindu teacher, and was given the name Baba Ram Dass. Returning to the United States, he reconnected with his friends the Durkees and came to see them at Lama. He and Steve Durkee soon conceived a book project that became *Be Here Now*, a countercultural spiritual classic, which has sold well over half a million copies and remains in print today. The income from the book was the financial underpinning of Lama for many years.[16]

The other notable figure, who arrived at Lama at about the same time as Ram Dass, was Samuel Lewis, popularly known as Sufi Sam.

He had attracted a following in the San Francisco Bay area for his wide-ranging spiritual explorations, and especially for Sufi praxis that involved, among other things, meditation and what came to be called Dances of Universal Peace. He was at Lama for a week in 1969 and another in 1970, and at his death in 1971 he asked to be buried there. His gravesite remains a sacred place in the community. Other spiritual leaders followed him—the Sufi Pir Vilayat Khan, Rabbi Zalman Schachter, and the Trappist monk Thomas Keating, to name only three.

Two major challenges confronted Lama after 1975. The first came in 1977, when founder Steve Durkee, who had left in 1971, returned as a convert to Islam now known as Nooruddeen. He tried to get the whole community make such a conversion—if not to Islam, then to Judaism or Christianity. The open-ended spirituality of Lama was thus at stake, but eventually Nooruddeen departed and the eclectic spirituality of the community continued. Then a major physical challenge came in 1996, when a devastating fire swept through the area, destroying hundreds of acres of forest and many homes but somehow sparing the dome that has long been Lama's central gathering place. Gradually members and outside supporters have rebuilt the community, and it continues to offer a diverse range of spiritual workshops and retreats.[17]

As I noted earlier, these are just sample stories. Hundreds of communes from the 1960s era survived through the end of the century, and numerous others from earlier times. For years it appeared that many of the thousands of communities founded in those halcyon days would vanish from the record, the memories of them dying with those who lived in or knew them. Happily, that prospect, while still looming, is not quite as inevitable as it once seemed. In the 1990s my colleague Deborah Altus, several of our students, and other volunteers gathered and archived the memories in a collection we called the 60s Communes Project, now housed at the University of Kansas and destined for permanent preservation at an academic library, probably at Hamilton College. Additionally, over the last few years some dozens—at least—of 1960s-era communitarians began to publish memoirs. Those published so far all preserve a great deal of history and convey the optimistic energy that pushed the communes of those days forward. A few are listed in the bibliography at the end of this volume.

One other option was beginning to appear as the century ended: retirement communes. Although many of the 1960s communal veterans had gone on to live individually, many, if not most, held onto some of their early collective vision and as the years passed began to contemplate the possibility of communal retirement living. The available options—assisted living, nursing homes—didn't seem very attractive. Residents of such places did not own or control them, and even though they paid exorbitant prices to live with some level of physical support, they were not in control of the care they were paying for. Moreover, for the many aging persons who could no longer drive in car-crazy America, those facilities were usually located away from urban centers, cutting their residents off from easy, casual contact with the rest of the world. Faced with the prospect of being warehoused on the outskirts of town and paying rent for accommodations they might as well own, community-minded people began to create cooperative alternatives. One of the earliest, and most countercultural, of such projects was Rocinante, founded in the early 1990s by Stephen Gaskin of the Farm community in Tennessee and named for Don Quixote's horse. It was characterized briefly in the previous volume of this series, but, to recapitulate, Rocinante would have handicapped-accessible buildings, a medical clinic, and other support facilities for an aging population. Rocinante's s progress was slow, but it pointed the way to keeping the communal flame burning late in life, and has inspired other retirement communal plans that continued to emerge as the twenty-first century unfolded. Many of them took the form of cohousing, as discussed in a subsequent chapter.

For over three centuries the United States has not been without intentional communities. Rumors of the demise of the commune are greatly exaggerated.

2

Cohousing Comes to America

After 1975 communities continued to be founded at a fairly steady pace, and some of them are profiled in the chapters that follow. However, two new strains came into the communitarian world during the last part of the century. Neither was entirely new, actually, but each added new twists to the existing story. Cohousing was a response to alienation and a perceived need to balance cooperation and private life; the ecovillages were responses to the environmental challenges that became daunting in the latter years of the twentieth century. Both saw human community as integral to addressing the issues of the day, and the aims and interests of the two innovative types of communities converged sufficiently that in several cases new communities were founded specifically to combine the two thrusts. This chapter and the following one will examine these new versions of the communal quest.

The form of intentional communitarianism that has received the most attention since the 1980s has been cohousing, whose goal is to establish something like an old-fashioned neighborhood or village where all residents know each other and cooperate in various ways in daily life but retain private premises and are not compelled to participate in any specific common activities. American cohousing developments typically occupy several acres of land and consist of an average of two dozen units, plus, normally, a shared building known as the common house.[1] Car parking is routinely assigned to the periphery of the development, and a pedestrian-only common space, often with playground facilities for children, is on the interior. Some communities leave a portion of their land, often wooded, deliberately undeveloped.

Although living situations resembling cohousing have been in existence for many years, the specific pattern that adopted that name first appeared in Denmark in the mid-1960s. As Kathryn McCamant and Charles Durrett have recounted, the movement began in 1964 when the Danish architect Jan Gudmand-Høyer began a series of discussions with friends about housing; he and his wife were disaffected with city living, and with the lack of community most contemporary housing (single-family houses, apartment buildings) offered. Over time the group began to look at ways to establish what amounted to a rural village, but one that had access to urban facilities and attractions, including jobs.[2]

By the end of the year they had a plan only somewhat similar to what cohousing eventually became: a group of a dozen houses designed for limited cooperative encounter. He and his associates purchased a tract of land not far from Copenhagen, only to be confronted by hostile neighbors who wanted nothing to do with such an unconventional project. The cohousers spent a year trying to overcome their neighbors' objections, and ultimately failed; they finally gave up and sold the land. Disillusioned, most of the group walked away from the whole concept.

But not everyone despaired. A few of the original aspirants, along with others who had become attracted to the idea of cohousing, persevered, and in 1968 two groups, working in tandem, purchased sites that this time did not attract local opposition. But the bids for the construction were much higher than expected, so the plan had to be shaved back considerably. (An interesting omen—one problem cohousing has typically had is insufficient affordability.) However, despite forced changes in plans, and problems with financing, in 1972 one of the groups moved into its new premises, and the other group followed the next year. Cohousing had moved from concept to actuality.

Other projects followed. The third Danish cohousing development opened in 1976, and by 1980 the number of communities stood at twelve. New communities kept coming, spurred in part by the Cooperative Housing Association Law, which made financing for cohousing easier to come by.[3] The movement has continued ever since, with new projects built every year. Cohousing is solidly established in its birthplace, Denmark, which continues to lead the world in cooperative housing.

The success of cohousing in Denmark did not go unnoticed elsewhere. Before long it was under way in several other European countries, most notably in the Netherlands, where the first project was completed in 1977. The Dutch cohousers modified the Danish model somewhat; their housing units tended to be small and to incorporate more sharing, as in kitchens that served more than one residence. Some Dutch projects also were designed for flexibility, placing a bedroom, for example, between two units in such a way that it could be assigned to one unit or the other as family size or other needs changed.

Before long Americans started to notice what was going on in Europe, and cohousing developments began to appear in the United States as well. Much of the credit for getting an American cohousing movement off the ground goes to the aforementioned Kathryn McCamant and Charles Durrett, a wife-and-husband team of architects who after immersing themselves in the Danish projects began to hold workshops in the United States in the 1980s. Over a few years dozens of groups coalesced to explore the possibility of opening cohousing communities, and by the early 1990s had progressed to the point of selecting sites and beginning to build. The first of the American cohousing projects was Muir Commons in Davis, California, completed in 1991, and by the end of the decade many other cohousing clusters were finished and even more in development. At this writing I can identify nearly two hundred of them, and many more in planning or building stages.[4]

Cohousing is not an out-of-the-box product. Communities take years to plan and build. Typically, the process begins quite informally, with people talking about possibilities, reading common texts, identifying potential members of the group, and batting around ideas. Newsletters, email lists, and Facebook pages often help focus the discussion. It may be easy to find people who like the concept, but the devil, as always, is in the details. Where should a cohousing community be located? What should it look like? How will it be financed?

Who will manage construction or renovation? What kind of environmental objectives (solar energy, low carbon emissions) should it try to meet? Just how much cooperation should be expected—daily or weekly meals, work days, and child care, for example? Should subsidies be provided for low-income participants? New cohousing projects rarely answer questions like those without a *lot* of discussion, often over years.

Site selection is not simply a matter of finding a suitable piece of affordable land. Cohousing, like other forms of intentional community, often stirs fear in its neighbors, who are wary of the consequences of a new and unfamiliar housing development. Moreover, zoning codes often stand in the way of cohousing, which typically does not fit any normal categories. How many housing developments, that is, have a common house? How many actively discourage cars? Convincing a zoning board to allow a project to proceed can be an arduous process. Some groups spend months or even years attempting to persuade both neighbors and zoning authorities that cohousing will actually improve the neighborhood. Once completed, cohousing developments, like other intentional communities, usually become accepted by their neighbors fairly quickly, and the education they have provided to city planners may help ease the way for the next cohousing group.

Those discussions often occur with outside help. Although the early, informal meetings may take place simply among the persons who have somehow found each other and are kicking around ideas, when things get more serious the prospective members often find themselves in need of outside expertise. Over the two or three decades in which cohousing has developed, consultants have emerged. They sometimes have a sobering effect on the enthusiastic backers, laying out the likely expense (often high), potential pitfalls, and many steps that need to be taken for the project to go forward. At that point those in the discussion are paying dues to support the expenses that are beginning to be incurred.

One seemingly universal feature of cohousing communities is the common house, a structure, usually centrally located, that serves a variety of purposes for the member households. Generally cohousing involves some common dining (dinners two or three days a week would be typical, although some communities have as many as five), so the common house would have a large kitchen and dining area. Many communities have some kind of shared child care, so a day-care facility might well be placed in the common house. Any number of recreational amenities would work there—a pool table, storage for basketballs and the like for outdoor sports, a ping-pong table. Cohousing members often share laundry facilities, so they could logically be in the common house as well. A shared guest room might be placed there. Other amenities are often nearby—a garden, a hot tub, a swimming pool.

Most cohousing communities have involved new construction, but some, especially those in urban areas, have retrofitted existing buildings. One notable example of a retrofit community is the twelve-unit Doyle Street Cohousing of Emeryville, California, near Oakland. It occupies a former warehouse that has been remodeled into nine housing units on two levels, plus the community's common house, a newly constructed adjacent building that holds three additional homes. As is often the case, getting approval from the authorities for the project was difficult; initially, the local planning commission voted not to allow Doyle Street to proceed, citing concerns that the project would cause an undesirable increase in neighborhood density and increased traffic. But the determined cohousers appealed the decision to the city council, meeting in the interim with neighbors and generating solid local support for the project. More problems awaited—some members of the group withdrew, the original developer left the project, and financing proved tricky, with lending agencies skeptical about this new way of housing people—but eventually all of the obstacles were surmounted, and the project was completed just two years after the first planning meetings. The project has proved quite popular, with full occupancy, offering, as it does, a comfortable place to live in the congested East Bay and easy access to San Francisco via the Bay Bridge, whose eastern terminus is just a few blocks away.[5]

Another retrofitted community is in nearby Oakland. Swan's Market, a large commercial building, was built in the early twentieth century in vibrant downtown Oakland. However, as the inner city declined, so did the building, which eventually sat vacant for some fifteen years until it was redeveloped with mixed uses, including stores, arts spaces, and housing, including a twenty-unit cohousing project. It was met with predictable problems at the development stage—people hesitant to move to a potentially dangerous downtown area, and lenders skeptical of making a large investment there—but over two years later was finished and has been quite successful ever since, playing a major role in the revitalization of its neighborhood.[6]

Doyle Street and Swan's Market (and several other projects) notwithstanding, many, probably most, cohousing communities do undertake new construction. The process of founding and building can be arduous and drawn out, partly because cohousing communities rarely have strong leaders and instead come to decisions only after long discussions. Site selection is an early step in the process that can be formidable. Given the difficulties of finding land in urban centers, most are established on the fringes of cities and towns where the needed acreage is affordable. And then all kinds of tradeoffs have to be evaluated—how expensive a site can people afford? How close should it be to urban amenities, including public transportation? Quite a few cohousing communities try to use alternative energy sources, so solar access may become a siting issue. Finding and buying the land can easily take a year or two. One study found that cohousing averaged four years from initial discussions to completion.[7]

Financing the project is an ordeal of its own, since financial institutions generally are skeptical of housing projects that are even slightly unconventional. Over time co-op–friendly sources of financing may emerge, but they are by no means easy to find.

Then there are matters of design, which can lend themselves to extended discussion. The size and design of the individual housing units is a matter that will receive a good deal of attention. Cohousing homes are relatively small, reflecting the fact that quite a few functions of typical homes are shared and do not need to be duplicated in every unit. A cohouser would not need a guest room, typically, because a shared guest room or two could serve many homes. Workshops can be joint, not individual, spaces. Children's playrooms can sometimes be shared as well.

Generally a developer is hired to oversee the building process, given the lack of expertise in such matters on the part of most cohousers. Finally, usually several years after the process has begun, people move in.

The financial and managerial structure of a cohousing community is usually that of a condominium development, with more extensive shared features than the typical condominium includes. In many ways cohousing resembles land trusts, although housing units are purchased, not leased, as they often are in a land-trust community. As in other condominia, the resident purchasing a unit has to find financing for it (sometimes a cohousing project itself helps make financing available) and then has to pay dues or fees—typically, fixed monthly dues for ongoing expenses, plus special assessments when major needs (such as a new roof or addition of a new amenity like a swimming pool) arise. The general rule is that units are bought and sold on the open real estate market. In theory, anyone can buy an available unit, although obviously any buyer knows that the project is cooperative in nature and will therefore want to participate in the many shared activities of the community.

Cohousing communities have been overwhelmingly secular in basis, but occasionally efforts have been made to establish them on specific ideologies or spiritual principles. The only cases in which such precepts have worked out well have been those that combined cohousing structures with environmental ideals, especially in ecovillage communities. That hybrid version of cohousing will be discussed in a few pages. Religiously based cohousing communities have been rare and generally have not worked very well. One notable case is that of the Bartimaeus Community at Meadow Wood in Bremerton, Washington. Founded in 2002, it was originally conceived as an evangelical Christian community of "biblically orthodox" members guided by the Holy Spirit. Few joined on such a basis, however, and eventually the religious test for membership was loosened considerably. Meadow

Wood would be the secular cohousing community; within it, some members would participate in Bartimaeus. As things progressed, however, the founders clung to their vision, and new members reportedly found themselves pressured to participate in prayer groups and other spiritual activities. Several individuals and couples who joined subsequently left amid considerable hard feelings.[8] In the larger world of intentional communities, a common religious commitment often seems to act as a communal binder and contributes to its longevity. Not so, apparently, in cohousing.

Are people happy with their cohousing homes? The evidence is somewhat limited and often anecdotal, but the answer, by and large, seems to be yes. One study of a senior cohousing community found that 91 percent of residents were somewhat (28 percent) or very (63 percent) satisfied with their living situation, and that 97 percent of them would recommend cohousing to other seniors.[9] Another examined turnover in cohousing occupancy, concluding that it averaged just under 4 percent a year—remarkably low for highly mobile America. It seems unlikely that unsatisfied residents would move away so rarely.

Lydia Ferrante-Roseberry, of Swan's Market Cohousing in downtown Oakland, California, has written, "Quite simply, my housing now reflects my values more than at any other time in my life," and has gone on to list several cohousing benefits that would be echoed by many of her fellow cohousers:

- One of my spiritual practices is to "Tread Softly" on the earth. Cohousing models an alternative to the consumerism and isolation of the "American dream." Since many of our amenities are shared, as a group we consume less than if we lived independently. Among other things, we share three washers and two dryers, a gas grill, a large, well-equipped children's play room, exercise equipment, power tools and crafts materials, and (hopefully soon) a hot tub. In addition, our shared guestroom means that every unit can be built to fit the needs of the family, not the family plus the occasional guest. Most of the things we share are items that people use intermittently. As my husband simply puts it: Everyone doesn't need their own hammer.

- I value living within my financial means. My husband and I have each made career choices based more on our hearts than our pocketbooks. . . . Because of the shared amenities in cohousing, we are able to have a higher quality of life than if we were living "independently."
- I value living in a diverse community. Having grown up in an immigrant family in an upper-middle class bedroom community, I understood at an early age what my mother sarcastically called the "beautiful isolation." Our houses were far enough apart to limit visibility of any sort of street life and to discourage drop-in visitors. Our tremendous town pride promoted an elitist status quo rather than an attitude that welcomed diversity.
- While much more diverse than the suburbs of my youth, my previous urban residences in Washington, DC and San Francisco were equally as isolating. Because I now actually know my neighbors, I feel like I live in a real community. I am continually broadening my understanding of a variety of lifestyles and life experiences. From my neighbor in a wheelchair I learn about the day-to-day challenges of living with disability. From my Hawaiian-born neighbor, I learn about hula and native Hawaiian ritual. From my school teacher neighbor, I learn about the challenges facing our public schools.
- I value sharing. We live as neighbors used to live. Today, one of my neighbors was making the rounds looking for chutney. I just dropped off some fava bean hummus at another neighbor's home. One of my neighbors recently made curtains for my infant daughter's bedroom. . . . This informal give and take promotes a sense of generosity and trust that is sorely missing from our public life.
- I value choice and balance between my public and private life. . . . Cohousing affords me the magic of impromptu visits, and privacy whenever my family wants or needs it. In my previous housing situations, any knock on the front door was more likely to be [someone else] than a neighbor wanting to know if I'd like to go to the ball game next week.[10]

This is not to say that cohousing for Ferrante-Roseberry, or anyone else, is invariably a bed of roses. Dorit Fromm asked residents to name drawbacks with cohousing and got a long list—difficulty in making decisions (most cohousing uses consensus, which can lead to long, protracted discussions, as well as frustrations when a small minority blocks a proposal), less privacy, time required for maintenance of common facilities, less freedom to modify one's home, and many others. On the other hand, her respondents unanimously agreed that there were advantages to cohousing as well, naming such things as community support, a good social life, a reduced impact on the environment, working with others, and personal support when needed. A strong majority said that, if they moved, they would try another cohousing community.[11]

Reduced impact on the environment is an important item here. The architect Graham Meltzer, whose research has long focused on cohousing, notes that about half of cohousing communities have formal mission statements, and all of them refer to caring for the environment.[12] Many members are thus drawn to cohousing because of its promise of being less environmentally destructive than conventional American ways of living, and by and large cohousing delivers on that promise. With smaller housing units, fewer cars, shared tools and facilities, recycling programs, and in some cases alternative energy production and relatively benign waste disposal, cohousing can hardly help but shrink one's environmental footprint. Many communities, and many owners of individual homes in cohousing, use water-saving plumbing devices and have solar panels on the roof.

Environmental protection, it turns out, is hardly free. One might think that collective housing would be relatively inexpensive, especially given that living units tend to be relatively small. In fact cohousing generally costs no less than other housing, and sometimes more in initial cost. The savings of cohousing come after purchase, and often indirectly. The units tend to be constructed with an eye toward efficient energy use, so utility costs are often lower than average. All of the shared facilities help reduce the cost of living, because individual families no longer need to own every tool or space. Over time, cohousing is usually reasonably priced, even though at first glance sticker shock often trumps long-term economies. Recent surveys have found that people living in cohousing drive 30 percent less, have 50 percent lower utility bills, and use 40 percent less water than the average American.[13] But the initial cost can be so high that would-be cohousers turn away. At Songaia, which was developed in suburban Seattle, Washington, in the 1990s, many prospective members spent several years getting ready to build, but suddenly departed when the construction bids came in. As Graham Meltzer has recounted Songaia's story,

> The outcome of the tender process was devastating. The cost per household was way too high for most participants to bear. Within a short time, all but five families had departed. Morale hit rock bottom for a period that became known as the "dark night of the soul." "The hardest part," recalls one member, "was that so many good and committed people left for financial reasons. We attracted people who were living their dreams—a massage therapist, a woodworker, a yoga instructor—people not earning enough money to buy in."[14]

One seemingly promising direction for cohousing as the twenty-first century progresses is new projects for seniors. The much-discussed aging of the baby boomers is already in progress, and many of them are unlikely to settle for the existing support systems for old age any more than they accepted an unpopular war or a culture they found it necessary to challenge on many fronts. No one should reasonably expect that a generation that came of age challenging established wisdom and institutions would go quietly into outmoded old-age care.

Huge changes have affected retirement options over the last two generations or so. For one thing, people are living much longer than they once did and need to plan on maintaining active, vital lives for decades rather than just months or years. For another, families are not as sedentary as they used to be; where older people once typically lived with their children or other relatives, families scattered across the country and beyond cannot always easily take in the elderly.

It remains the case that some older citizens, especially those capable of maintaining some independence in life, are going to need support beyond what their families or conventional institutions such as nursing homes can offer. Thus there has been a great boom in assisted-living institutions, many of them set up to address life cycle needs (independent living, assisted living, and nursing care). But those institutions do not fully meet the needs of all of those now reaching retirement age. For one thing, they tend to infringe on one's independence. There are some institutions, for example, that will not allow residents to administer their own medications, even when they are fully capable of handling that task. There are others that will not permit residents to keep so much as a bottle of wine in their rooms. Fully capable adults are, more often than one would think, treated like children.

Moreover, many of today's "retirement communities" are for-profit businesses whose bottom-line concern lies with the balance sheet. And even the ones that are operated on a nonprofit basis are still businesses controlled by employees, not the residents.

So how does a retired person get around that kind of treatment? Cohousing offers an attractive alternative to just about anything else in the retirement marketplace. Senior cohousing, like other cohousing, is developed with member input and is always controlled and managed by its members. Resident members, not business administrators, are the owners and operators of the enterprise. They can hire help if they need it, but the help works for them and does not have the control that comes in a typical institutional setting.

Senior cohousing would logically work best in an urban setting, where members who can't drive can walk to many of the stores and services they need. But even when the venue is not conducive to walking, cohousing normally embraces members who have a range of abilities, and in practice the ones who can still drive often take their neighbors with them on errands.[15]

Senior cohousing, like other cohousing, is usually traced to Denmark, where the first projects began to appear in the 1980s and were immediately popular. The United States soon followed. One of the first, if not the first, senior cohousing community was ElderSpirit, located in Abingdon, Virginia. It initially emerged from another intentional community, the Federation of Communities in Service. That community had in turn emerged from a Catholic religious order, the Glenmary Sisters, some of whose members, in the wake of the Second Vatican Council, reformed their community outside the church in 1967. Eventually they opened membership to men and to persons who were not Catholic. As time went by, some members began looking toward retirement, and in the 1990s they began the process of starting what became ElderSpirit. Twenty-nine homes were built. ElderSpirit continues to identify itself as a spiritual community, but no one faith or path is followed by all members. A particular emphasis of ElderSpirit is support to members who are ill or dying; even those who must eventually move to institutional care remain in close contact with the community.[16]

In the wake of ElderSpirit other senior cohousing communities have been built, including Silver Sage Village in Boulder, Colorado, Wolf Creek Lodge in Grass Valley, California, and Glacier Circle Community in Davis, California. Others are in planning stages. It is a reasonable conjecture that, as the population ages, senior cohousing will continue to expand.

Cohousing is not paradise; its members are, after all, people, and cohousing has to work its way through issues faced in other organizations and neighborhoods: How do we deal with destructive pets—or children, for that matter? How do we deal with people who are not carrying their share of the load? What do we do when someone runs short of money and has trouble making a scheduled payment? How do we make major financial decisions that affect us all? How do we respond as a unified group to an outside threat, such as drifting agricultural chemicals that are making some (but not all) of us sick? Life is never entirely easy, in cohousing or anywhere else.

A Note on Housing Cooperatives

For over a century various types of cooperatives have supplied residents with stable, low-cost housing. In New York City, especially, housing co-ops have become a major provider of shelter at all price levels. Thousands of co-ops are widely thought to have produced hundreds of thousands of units, generally apartments, over many decades.[17] A note on co-ops is in order in this chapter, because they resemble cohousing more than they do any other category of intentional community discussed in this volume. However, they represent something of a borderline case in the communal world. My definition of intentional community, as presented in the preface, above, sees intentional communities as not simply group living situations, but group living situations centered on specific causes and visions that set them apart from mainstream society. Housing co-ops most frequently have the provision of affordable housing, often for residents of limited income, as a prime goal, and whether that is regarded as a cause or a vision of the sort that defines an intentional community is a judgment call. Common elements in housing do not inherently constitute a vision, but helping people of limited means, or providing environmentally benign housing—a goal at which some, but not all, housing co-ops aim—could be construed as the kind of applied idealism that is a communal hallmark. Some co-ops are rooted in a specific denomination or religious tradition, and a special dedication to that religious movement might reach the level of making a purpose-driven housing project. However, a housing development intended for Quakers, or Unitarians, or Jews might really be mainly about housing, not the religious tradition in question. It would seem that some co-ops qualify for consideration here, while others do not. Judgment calls can be difficult.

With that, a few words on the genre. Modern housing cooperatives are usually regarded as having begun as part of the cooperative endeavors of the Rochdale movement that began in 1844 in England. That movement's housing component came to the United States in 1916, with the organization of the Finnish Home Building Association in Brooklyn, New York, which built two cooperative apartment buildings that were recently reported as still in operation. In the 1920s the move for affordable cooperative housing was taken up by labor unions, notably the Amalgamated Clothing Workers Union, which had many socialists among its members.[18] Later, federal and state governments promoted housing co-ops, and over the course of the twentieth century a great many of them were built; many endure, although a significant number of them have moved to private, noncooperative ownership. It is difficult to identify precise figures for numbers of co-ops founded in the last quarter of the twentieth century, which is the focus of this volume, but it must be several dozen, at least. One example is the Marathon Low-Income Co-op, founded in 1988 and situated in an abandoned freeway corridor in Los Angeles. Its land base, eleven blocks long and one block wide, has several dozens of buildings. Marathon, which is ethnically and racially diverse, describes its members as "of all ages, religious persuasions, and political beliefs." Its self-identification as an intentional community is confirmed by its appearance in several editions of the *Communities Directory*.[19]

One type of housing cooperative does fit my definition of intentional community more consistently than housing co-ops as a whole do: the student housing co-ops found on or near dozens, if not hundreds, of college campuses. In many, if not most, cases they embody aspirations that qualify as defining visions, usually related to environmental activism and progressive social change. Lothlorien Cooperative House, founded in 1975 near the campus of the University of Wisconsin–Madison, promotes egalitarianism and locally sourced food; its thirty-three members share vegetarian meals. The White House, which has served students at the University of Michigan, Ann Arbor, since 1979, has many members who are involved in progressive political and environmental activities. The Black Elk Co-op, also in Ann Arbor, was founded in 1986, is gay-friendly, and has members who are strongly interested in environmental issues. Hundreds of other student co-ops have similar profiles.[20]

3

The Ecovillage Revolution

Cohousing, although it has plenty of indebtedness to earlier forms of intentional community, is generally regarded as having had a clear beginning in Denmark in the 1960s and 1970s, and in the United States in the 1980s. The true origins of ecovillages, however, are not nearly as easy to date. Fundamentally, their aim is to promote community living with the least adverse environmental impact possible. As Karen Svensson has articulated the vision,

> Ecovillages are communities of people who strive to lead a sustainable lifestyle in harmony with each other, other living beings and the earth. Their purpose is to combine a supportive social-cultural environment with a low-impact lifestyle. As a new societal structure, the ecovillage goes beyond today's dichotomy of urban versus rural settlements: it represents a widely applicable model for the planning and reorganization of human settlements in the 21st Century.[1]

Just when the term "ecovillage" emerged is not clear, but it was in use by the early 1990s. Diane Gilman and her husband Robert Gilman published what would become a seminal text for the ecovillage movement, *Eco-Villages and Sustainable Communities* in 1991.[2] Workshops and seminars began to appear in the ensuing years, and by the latter half of the decade several ecovillages had been founded and many more envisioned. In addition, some existing intentional communities rode the new wave and began to identify as ecovillages, in most cases not changing their practices very substantially, because they were already doing what the ecovillage activists were advocating.

One could argue, however, that such cooperative enclaves have been around forever. The people of premodern societies lived sustainably, or nearly so, and typically in small villages or family groups. Today's ecovillage pioneers seek a return to sustainable living, but with the advantages of new technology and new ideas. Most of them, for example, would be loath to live without electricity but use (or are working toward) sustainable sources of electricity—solar and wind, especially, and also, occasionally, hydropower.

What is a contemporary ecovillage? Several features may be regarded as typical for the genre. First, it emerges in response to a perceived social environmental crisis and is optimistic in that it sees a possible way to a positive future. A key theme in ecovillage life is preparation for a future time without the cheap oil and gas that so fundamentally drive contemporary society. Ecovillagers observe that fossil fuels are finite by their nature and that human beings are going to have to make radical lifestyle shifts if they are to survive the coming post-petroleum age. One such shift is a transition to other sources of energy than oil and to dramatically more efficient ways to use the oil that remains.

Second, it is an experiment, or set of experiments. Ecovillagers have reacted to the unsustainable ways of modern urban culture, but they do not have any single model of a perfect ecological future. The villages are all works in progress, improving steadily and following many twists and turns and dead ends to locate the sustainable culture that is the final goal. The spirit of experimentation covers social relations as well as the more physical side of things—construction, agriculture, alternative technology. But experimentation does not mean that the ecovillage is a transient phenomenon; on the contrary, creating a long-lasting community is part of the vision.

Third, ecovillages are by nature fairly small. One might try to imagine an ecocity with thousands of people living in harmony with nature and each other (and indeed such cities have been envisioned), but cities by their nature are hardly sustainable. "Village" is an important part of the concept; ecovillages aim to be human-scale endeavors, small enough that members are acquainted with one another and that each member can influence the course of the whole project. Most of them have under one hundred members, and it would be hard to identify one with more than a few hundred. If the ecovillage concept grows in popularity, an eco-answer to rising demand would be to found new ecovillages, not expand existing ones indefinitely. A good model here is that of the Hutterites, who have grown a hundredfold since arriving in the United States in 1874 with fewer than 450 members in three original colonies. Hutterites have historically had high birth rates; that, together with retention of a strong majority of their young people, has meant rapid growth. Once a colony reaches around 150 members, it "branches out," as Hutterites like to say, and a new colony is founded. Once it is built the members of the existing colony decide, by lot, who will stay and who will go to the new colony. Thus is human scale maintained.

Fourth, an ecovillage strives to meet the basic necessities of life. It is not a summer camp, or a weekend retreat; it is a place where people live and work and play. Some ecovillagers may need to work outside the community in order to earn the money that is inescapably necessary for modern life, but the goal is to develop on-site ways to meet as many needs as possible. Ideally, ecovillagers grow their own food, build their own buildings, have their own industries (to help generate the money they need), and support their own distribution systems (stores and the like). They often school their own children, although some use the local public school system. A perfect ecovillage would include a clinic with a resident medical doctor.

Fifth, ecovillages seek to mesh human beings and their constructed environment with the natural world. After they have provided space for housing, food production, and other basics, they usually leave large tracts as nature preserves. They typically forbid hunting, although they often allow, even encourage, the gathering of edible plants. Finally, ecovillages frequently embrace sustainable practices that have come to be known, collectively, as permaculture, a term coined by David Holmgren and his professor Bill Mollison. Describing the long-term destructiveness of much modern agriculture, they sought to develop a permanent (that is, sustainable) agriculture, a term they abbreviated as permaculture. Permaculture maintains that sustainability needs to come through a set of integrated agricultural, architectural, and cultural systems. Each element of a local environment must be considered in relation to other elements; the idea is to get a functioning whole life system, not just one or two pieces of it. Ultimately, permaculture is pro-people—not because it enables people to exert mastery over nature, but because they function as part of it. Jan Martin Bang has described permaculture thus:

> Permaculture is about designing sustainable human settlements. It is a philosophical and practical approach to land-use integrating microclimate, functional plants, animals, soils, water management and human needs into intricately connected, highly productive systems. It presents an approach to designing environments that have diversity, stability and resilience of natural ecosystems. It seeks to regenerate damaged land and preserves environments which are still intact.[3]

But, as I noted above, ecovillages are not really new at all. The dream of going back to the land, of living in harmony with nature, must be as old as urban, industrial civilization itself. Jonathan Dawson, a sustainability educator and ecovillage activist, first traced the genre to Sólheimar, an Icelandic community founded in 1931; then, expanding his frontiers, he decided that the early Celtic monasteries of nearly 1500 years ago were first; and, finally, he credited the communal historian Bill Metcalf with pushing the timeline another millennium farther back.[4] Metcalf, a tireless collector of information on all things communal, identifies the vegetarian community of Pythagoras at Crotona, in the sixth century BCE, as "the first intentional community which we would recognize today, and about which we have much information."[5]

One early American example of what today would be called an ecovillage came nearly two hundred years ago, with the Fruitlands experiment in Massachusetts. In 1843, during the heyday of Transcendentalism, two stalwart idealists set out to create a haven of simple living in which (as the name implied) fruit would be the principal food. A. Bronson Alcott is remembered as the leader of the community; its land, with a house and barn, was purchased by Charles Lane. Although property ownership was a necessary formality, in principle the community would not have property, trade, money, hired labor, or use of animals. Members wore simple linen tunics, eschewing cotton (which came from slave labor) and wool (an animal product). Alcott's daughter Louisa May described her father's thinking in these words:

> The greater part of man's duty consists in leaving alone much that he now does. Shall I stimulate with tea, coffee, or wine? No. Shall I consume flesh? Not if I value health. Shall I subjugate cattle? Shall I claim property in any created thing? Shall I trade? Shall I adopt a form of religion? Shall I interest myself in politics? To how many of these questions—could we ask deeply enough and could they be heard as having relation to our eternal welfare—would the response be "Abstain."[6]

Ralph Waldo Emerson visited Fruitlands and commented, dryly, "They look well in July. We will see them in December."[7] The words were prophetic; as fall approached, little food had been stored, and Alcott and Lane, especially, continued to devote their time to philosophizing rather than planning for a New England winter. By winter it all came to a halt. As a practical experiment Fruitlands did not do well, but its ideas were visionary. Later ecovillages, a bit more effectively planned and operated, would fare better.

The ecovillage vision, as we would now call it, survived the demise of Fruitlands. More than a century later another project embodying the ecovillage vision on a grand scale was inaugurated in the Arizona desert. Paolo Soleri, who had gone to Arizona to study with Frank Lloyd Wright, began building Arcosanti in 1970 as a sustainable city that would be home to thousands. Its progress has been slow, but a dedicated corps of participants continues to enact the vision after Soleri's death. Arcosanti was featured in the previous volume in this series.[8] Another large-scale project, also discussed in my earlier volume, was

Cerro Gordo, near Cottage Grove, Oregon, which was begun in 1973 but, like Arcosanti, has experienced slow enactment.[9]

The noted Russian anarchist Peter Kropotkin gave the concept a major boost several decades after Fruitlands with his analysis of farming practices in *Fields, Factories, and Workshops.*[10] He argued that people were integral to a productive environment, and that the biggest agricultural problem lies in the concentration of land ownership in large parcels. Small landholdings, networked into cooperatives, would be far more productive than corporate estates, he maintained. He also believed that agriculture should be integrated with small-scale industry as well as with education. Small units of production, the uniting of farm and factory: although "anarchist" has become a term of derision, and Kropotkin is rarely invoked by name, his ideas influenced the Garden City movement, which sought to decentralize cities, and many agricultural reformers. When Kirkpatrick Sale and bioregionalism came along, Kropotkin loomed in the background. The communes of the 1960s era embodied a good deal of what we now would call ecovillage philosophy; what was still missing was the term itself: ecovillage.

The ecovillage movement got a major boost with the arrival in its midst of Ross Jackson, who had developed an interest in sustainable development and had had his outlook influenced by a dramatic religious experience in India in the 1980s. Jackson had developed a currency-trading system that was consistently profitable, and, unlike a typical capitalist, dedicated most of its proceeds to Gaia Trust, an organization that supports projects in sustainability worldwide. In 1991 he received a copy of the Gilmans' pioneering report and became enamored of the potential of ecovillages for countering the world's ongoing environmental degradation. What emerged from his new focus was the Global Ecovillage Network, a coordinating group for regional ecovillage networks and their constituent settlements. The World Wide Web was just beginning to appear at the same time, and it proved an ideal vehicle for coordinating activities of widely dispersed groups. The GEN website and other activities, all with substantial financial support from Jackson and his wife Hildur Jackson, also an ecovillage activist, elevated the profile of the movement and directed seekers to ecovillages around the world.

And so ecovillages began to crop up in the United States, as well as in Europe and elsewhere. One important, relatively early, example was Earthaven, founded in 1995 on a 329-acre tract of land near Black Mountain, North Carolina. The founders were some of the early permaculture practitioners and teachers. The site they chose was in second-growth forest in the Appalachian Mountains, and integrating the village with nature has been a driving force in Earthaven. Within the property are several clustered housing sites, with houses built from used materials as well as strawbale and cob—or, typically, a combination of such things. One of the housing sites is a cohousing community within the larger ecovillage. The entire community is off the grid; various hydro and solar systems provide electricity that members use sparingly. Almost all buildings are of passive solar design. Earthaven is not economically communal; each member has to make a living, and members practice such professions as writing and consensus training and operate such businesses as construction of environmentally attuned buildings, farming, and landscape design. Recently the community has had around sixty members, including a few nonresident ones; it aims for an eventual population of about 150. Earthaven sees itself as frankly experimental, and it hopes to broadcast its findings to an environmentally challenged world.

A couple of years later, in 1997, an ambitious ecovillage project, Dancing Rabbit, was founded near Rutledge, Missouri. A 1960s-era commune, Sandhill Farm, was nearby and already operating more or less in ecovillage fashion, with an economic base of specialized organic agriculture (specializing in sorghum) and a commitment to living as lightly on the earth as possible. Sandhill's locality, Scotland County, was also a draw, because it had no zoning laws. One might think that zoning would lead to rational land use, but conventional zoning tends to be rigid and not to allow innovative building practices, among other things, and the Rabbits wanted the freedom to experiment with their structures. Much of the 280-acre land base of the community has been left for wildlife, and more is being restored to its presettlement condition. The community's buildings usually use alternative building techniques; there are structures of cob and of straw bale, and many with used lumber (something often prohibited by zoning ordinances), and even one building fashioned from a grain bin. Solar electric panels are everywhere. Dancing Rabbit aims to grow to at least 500 residents—a true small town without many cars (and none within the residential parts of the community) or much outside utility service, and with its own internal money system, to keep dollars circulating within the community rather than flowing outward. The community has specific covenants and guidelines enshrining its vision of sustainable living; it welcomes visitors, and it actively tries to spread its environmentally based ideas abroad.[11]

One ecovillage of the 1990s was the offspring of a venerable 1960s-era commune. Discussed in an earlier volume in this series, Twin Oaks was established in 1967 in Virginia as a project to put the visionary ideas of B. F. Skinner in his novel *Walden Two* into practice. Although it came to discard several of Skinner's precepts, it retained others and has had a long history of growth and economic stability. Its members share their incomes, grow much of their own food, and are thoroughgoingly egalitarian. And while a good many intentional communities struggle to find enough members to keep the venture afloat, Twin Oaks, with a membership of around one hundred, had a lengthy waiting list by the 1990s. After a good deal of discussion, the Oakers decided to help launch another community nearby, after the model of the Hutterites, who split their ranks and start a new colony when their numbers reach 150 or so.[12] They found a farm of some seventy-two acres with an old farmhouse and quickly began building additional housing and business space. Declaring the new community, Acorn, an ecovillage, the members built environment-friendly businesses. One innovative endeavor is the Southern Exposure Seed Exchange, which seeks to preserve heirloom plant species and to save rare and endangered plants. It sells its seeds by mail nationwide.[13] Like its parent community Twin Oaks, Acorn is an egalitarian, income-sharing community that has continued to be home to around twenty to thirty adult members plus, usually, some children and guests.

Most ecovillages are set in rural locations, but several have been planted squarely in cities. Probably the most prominent of the urban ones is the Los Angeles Eco-Village, founded in 1994 by Lois Arkin on two city blocks in the Koreatown area of Los Angeles. The founding goal was to reduce residents' environmental impact while raising their quality of life. The low- to lower-middle-income area was already populated, of course, so the task at the outset was to develop paths to low-environmental-impact living in a neighborhood where not all residents were interested in participating in the project. Activities consist of retrofitting buildings to make them more environment-friendly, holding potluck meals and other social gatherings, and conducting workshops and seminars on making urban life more sustainable. The population of the two-block area is about five hundred, and of those perhaps seventy-five participate in some of the ecovillage activities. Some participants have moved there specifically to take part in the experiment. One goal is to reduce use of automobiles in car-intensive Los Angeles, and about half of the participating residents do not own them. The project itself owns two buildings with forty-eight housing units; car-free residents receive reduced rent. LAEV is about as ambitious an ecovillage project as one could imagine, and its members are determined to make it work.[14]

A somewhat similar ecovillage project, albeit one in a less intensely populated urban area, is the Enright Ridge Urban Ecovillage in Cincinnati. Atop a ridge in the city's deteriorating Price Hill neighborhood was Enright Avenue, a dead-end street surrounded by woods. There, in 1971, Eileen and Jim Schenk founded Imago, an environmental organization dedicated to sustainable living. For several years Imago ran conferences and workshops and developed a program that enabled urban children to visit nature. Then, in 1993, a group of Price Hill residents decided to undertake an urban ecovillage project. Much of the early effort went to home improvement—insulation, energy-efficient windows and appliances, low-energy light bulbs, and other such things. Residents were encouraged to recycle and to use the nearby city bus lines for transportation whenever possible. Other community-building efforts followed—a walking path through the surrounding woods, monthly neighborhood meals, and a newsletter. And so it has endured. Imago continues to do extensive environmental programming, and neighborhood environmental and energy-efficiency programs continue as well.[15]

Yet another project in a similar vein is Maitreya, located on the near west side of Eugene, Oregon. Occupying much of a city block, it was founded in the mid-1990s by Rob Bolman and others who wanted to live as sustainably as possible while remaining in the city. Moving to Eugene in 1991, he and his mother purchased what became the Maitreya property and Bolman plunged into the world of green building. The ecovillage now contains a range of environmentally sensible buildings, including ones made of straw bale and cob. Its largest building is of frame construction and is relatively "normal" in appearance, but it is built of recycled and otherwise sustainable materials. Its ground floor is literally that: earth. Also on the property are several small domes, each eight feet in diameter and built from recycled materials. At a cost of around fifty dollars each, the domes provide some of the lowest-cost housing around.

Bolman has formed his own definition of sustainability based on these five rules:

1. Renewable resources shall not be used faster than they can regenerate.
2. Nonrenewable resources shall not be used faster than renewable substitutes (to be used sustainably) can be found & developed.
3. Pollution and waste shall not be put into the environment faster than the environment can absorb and render it harmless.
4. The human population shall be kept low enough that the above three conditions can be met.
5. The above four conditions shall be met under conditions that are democratic and equitable enough that the people of the world will stand for it.[16]

Thus does Maitreya pursue the ecovillage vision in the heart of an American city.

It may seem like a stretch to call the Biosphere 2 project an ecovillage, but one could argue that it is the *ultimate* ecovillage—one whose goal was true and complete self-sufficiency. The concept was incubated at Synergia Ranch, a 1960s-era commune in New Mexico whose members were environmentalists as well as creators of theatrical productions and spiritual seekers. Gradually they began to envision a completely controlled environment, one that would, among other things, provide information that could be useful to long-term space travel. The Biosphere itself was designed as a miniature replica of the earth in a hermetically sealed environment, complete with an ocean, cropland, and forest under glass in the Sonoran desert of Arizona. It was called Biosphere 2 because it was the second whole-earth environment, the first being the earth itself. The $150 million project was financed by Texas oilman Ed Bass. The plan was for a team of four men and four women to stay in the Biosphere for two years, growing their own food, recycling their own waste, and otherwise surviving without any outside inputs except sunlight and electricity (solar electricity was somehow deemed too expensive). And so the experiment commenced in 1991. As it happened, some supportive outside intervention became necessary, and a second attempt in 1994 had problems that led to some public derision of the project, but it did provide some lessons in human needs and survival. The structure remains in place, and some experiments continue to be conducted there, although no extended residential project seems likely in the future.[17]

Once the ecovillage movement was off and running in earnest, some of the established intentional communities that embodied ecovillage principles embraced the new nomenclature, some of them joining Ecovillage Network of the Americas, the regional affiliate of the Global Ecovillage Network. One of them, Alpha Farm, located in the Coast Range west of Eugene, Oregon, was founded in 1972 by a Quaker-oriented group from Philadelphia. Low-impact living was a priority at Alpha from the beginning; so was close interaction with the larger community in the area, to which end the Alpha members began operating the local rural mail route and opened Alpha-Bit, a restaurant and store in Mapleton, the biggest town in the area. As in other ecovillages, the Alpha farmers have extensive organic gardens and build their buildings from sustainable materials and design and equip them to be as environmentally benign as possible. Alpha keeps one part of the 280 acres it occupies forever wild, and no human sets foot there. As ecovillages go Alpha Farm is relatively small, often with a dozen or so members. Its gentle presence has made it a well-respected part of the larger western Oregon community.[18]

Another existing community that embodied ecovillage principles before the movement had taken on that identity was the Farm, the classic 1960s-era commune near Summertown, Tennessee. It was founded by back-to-the-land hippies who traveled the country in a caravan of buses and other vehicles, finally settling in rural Tennessee, where they set out to build a self-sufficient community. It was a spiritual community of a distinctive sort: all members had to accept Stephen Gaskin as their spiritual teacher. Stephen, as he was always called, blended teachings from a wide variety of the world's religions, as well as from psychedelia, into a gentle spiritual system that stressed meditation and right livelihood. In the early years the Farm was entirely communal; there was no private property or private money, and all members shared work that ranged from farming to building construction to vegan cooking. It really was an ecovillage from the start, and, once that term emerged, the farm was part of the movement. Today it is not only an ecovillage but an incubator of ecovillages. On its land is the Ecovillage Training Center, a hands-on school for those who would learn the basics of permaculture and ecovillage construction. Those enrolling in ETC programs, typically young adults, learn such skills as straw-bale building, cob building, and natural wastewater treatment. The ETC has attracted students from all over the world who proceed to develop new ecovillages and spread the gospel of permaculture far and wide.[19]

In some cases the turning of an existing settlement into an ecovillage has come in response to disaster. The small town of Soldiers Grove, Wisconsin, which grew up on the site of a sawmill on the Kickapoo River, experienced six major floods in sixty years. The US Army Corps of Engineers proposed protecting the town with a dam-and-levee project, but the citizens argued for relocation. Federal and state funding for such a move was finally secured, in large part because the town pledged itself to use solar energy extensively, so much so that it continues to bill itself as "America's First Solar Village." With relocation in progress, a zoning ordinance for the new town mandated energy conservation and solar access. New buildings had to be far more energy-efficient than state law required. Most public buildings, including several private businesses, were built to be heated by the sun, and many new structures were built with rooftop solar collectors. Soldiers Grove is hardly an intentional community, but it continues to be studied as an example of environmentally sound planning, and is sometimes counted in the ranks of the ecovillages.[20]

The Soldiers Grove model proved attractive as the twenty-first century unfolded. Greensburg, Kansas, devastated by a tornado in 2007, recast itself as a GreenTown, and started rebuilding to high standards of energy efficiency and sustainability. Moreover, as the twentieth century gave way to the twenty-first, other similar projects began to take shape. What has become known as the Transition Towns movement, influenced by permaculture and the burgeoning ecovillage projects, seeks to bring sustainable systems to existing cities and towns and became widely visible in the early twenty-first century. The influence of the ecovillages could ultimately prove to be much larger than the ecovillages themselves. Their story would seem to be more in the future than in the past.

Ecovillages of the Spirit

Most of the ecovillages surveyed so far have been essentially secular in structure and outlook, even if they harbor among their members people with a variety of religious and spiritual commitments and quests. Other ecovillages, however, were founded on principles that had major religious components. In some cases religious convictions were major drivers of the environmental concern that all ecovillages share; in others religion was less central, and members might pursue a wide variety of spiritual paths, but it was still a tangible component of community life.

One example of the community-turned-ecovillage type is provided by many of the Camphill villages, which number over one hundred worldwide. Philosophically based in Rudolf Steiner's anthroposophy, which blends Christian and other spiritual teachings, the Camphill villages embody a communitarian approach to the care and development of persons with various disabilities, including intellectual and developmental ones. Camphill began in Scotland in 1939, and it arrived in the United States with the establishment of an American community at Copake, New York, by Carlo Pietzner in 1961. At Camphill the caregivers and patients, known as coworkers and villagers, respectively, live in community together. They have long pursued practices that qualify them as ecovillages; for example, they have extensive biodynamic (a form of organic) gardens and farms and construct their energy-efficient buildings from natural materials. In several cases they have devised natural methods of sewage treatment that keeps the waste material from being flushed into waterways. Kimberton Hills Camphill, in Pennsylvania, is known for its energy-saving use of light tubes for interior daytime light and for its community-supported agricultural endeavor. But it differs only in specifics from the other Camphill villages, all of which were working to develop ecovillage features before the term had been invented.[21]

Sirius, another spiritually driven ecovillage, was founded in 1978, a few years before the term "ecovillage" had come into vogue, and was thus a bit ahead of its time in its institutionalization of environmental commitments. The founders, prominent among them Corinne McLaughlin and Gordon Davidson, who were soon joined by Gordon's brother Bruce Davidson and Bruce's wife Linda Reimer, had spent time at Findhorn, the Scottish flagship of New Age spiritual communities and a community whose ecological work has been unstinting. Findhorn was founded in 1962 and has focused on harmony with nature, and with nature spirits it calls devas, from the beginning. Its first burst of international publicity came with reports of the cultivation of gigantic vegetables and flowers in the community garden—forty-two-pound cabbages, sixty-pound broccoli plants, and eight-foot delphiniums all growing in poor, sandy soil and a cold climate. Peter Caddy, one of the three founders of Findhorn, attributed the community's horticultural success, reported visitor Paul Hawken, to "Devic presences, Nature Spirits, fairies, elves, and the legendary deity named Pan."[22] The big vegetables were hardly the central feature of Findhorn; rather, the community was deeply spiritual in a way that would soon be characterized as New Age—a spirituality that forsook conventional religious institutions but sought inner enlightenment and anticipated a great transformation that would usher in a renewed world. And, beyond all of that, Findhorn became a pioneering ecovillage. With its use of wind energy, advanced natural treatment of sewage, and creation of houses from used whiskey barrels, Findhorn became a model for ecovillage activists, many of whom flocked to Scotland for some of the community's environmentally focused seminars.

After immersing themselves in the spiritual community at Findhorn, McLaughlin and Gordon Davidson, with Bruce Davidson and Reimer, returned to the United States and founded Sirius in 1978, situating it on an eighty-six-acre tract of land near Amherst, Massachusetts. Community members have built substantial facilities and host an array of conferences and workshops, much as the parent community, Findhorn, does. Sirius describes its purpose as fourfold: spiritual, ecological, communitarian, and educational. On the spiritual front, the community posits "a Divine Presence underlying all things."[23] Several of the community buildings, including an assembly hall and a retreat house, are used for spiritual pursuits, and work projects and other activities begin with "attunement"—pausing in silence to focus one's energies on the present.

Sirius describes itself in this way: "Its foundation is spiritual, but in a non-sectarian manner that allows for each person to find their own way to the heart of all beingness and reality. The shared expression reflects reverence for all Life and willingness to live in accord with this intention as much as possible. We thus employ ecologically sustainable methods of living and a consensus-style governance process, striving to honor all that is."[24] Thus the community's spirituality is complemented by environmental concern and an educational mission to the larger community. The ecological commitment is reflected in such pursuits as alternative energy generation, organic gardening, sustainable building construction, and composting toilets. The communitarian commitment is central, as it would be in any intentional community, and the sense of common cause permeates all of the community's life. Finally, education is a central set of community activities and a source of some of the community's income. Workshops in permaculture and alternative energy are among Sirius's educational offerings. Sirius remains a relatively small community, reporting thirty-one members and five nonmember residents (with more associates living in the area) in 2008.[25] It combines communal and private economics and attracts a steady stream of visitors.[26]

In 1974 a group of participants in Transcendental Meditation, the form of meditative practice promulgated by the Maharishi Mahesh Yogi, descended upon Fairfield, a town of some ten thousand in southeast Iowa, where they purchased the closed Parsons College campus and there founded Maharishi International University, later called the Maharishi University of Management. Eventually two intentional communities arose among the TM participants: Maharishi Vedic City, which was begun in the early 1990s, and Abundance Ecovillage, which opened in 2000. The latter was thoroughly dedicated to sustainability and environmentally benign living, with off-grid electricity (from sun and wind), water from the rain, a farm and greenhouse for food, and a "living machine" that purifies wastewater for reuse. Abundance occupies fifteen acres of land; members take lifetime (and longer) leases on building lots, constructing homes to the community's exacting environmental standards and to the Vedic architectural principles that TM embraces. The community's plan calls for the eventual development of about thirty homes.[27]

Ecovillages, like other intentional communities, can come and go, and identifying them all is a daunting task. Nature's Spirit, a spiritual ecovillage located on 210 acres of land near Salem, South Carolina, has been described as having gardens and a greenhouse for its organic foods business, as well as ecologically sound homes, but tracking its more recent course seems elusive.[28] The Potash Hill Community, in Cummington, Massachusetts, was reported to be in active operation in the late 1990s, with a combination of private homesites and community land, a community building and dining facility, and other common amenities, but more recently it has lowered its profile, if indeed it still exists.[29] The website of the Fellowship for Intentional Community at any given moment lists hundreds of ecovillages, but many of them appear to be concepts waiting for realization. What can be said with certainty is that a great many ecovillagers are working hard to show the world a more sustainable and less environmentally damaging way to live, even if their work is not exactly front-page news in mainstream America.

Combining the Forms: Ecovillage Cohousing

A fair amount of overlap exists between cohousing and ecovillages, which is not surprising, given that living more economically and efficiently, and with a lowered impact on the planet, is a theme in just about all intentional communities. Among the ecovillage and cohousing communities, most are happy with one self-definition or the other, but a few specifically combine the two, using a cohousing arrangement for property ownership and management along with advanced environmental projects typically found in ecovillages.

One pioneer of ecovillage cohousing is the EcoVillage at Ithaca, New York, which combines cohousing clusters with alternative energy projects, organic gardening and farming, energy-efficient structures, and preservation of land in its natural state. Early on its mission statement laid out an ambitious plan:

> The ultimate goal of EcoVillage at Ithaca is nothing less than to redesign the human habitat. We are creating a model community of some five hundred residents that will exemplify sustainable systems of living—systems that are not only practical in themselves but replicable by others. The completed project will demonstrate the

> feasibility of a design that meets basic human needs such as shelter, food production, energy, social interaction, work, and recreation while preserving natural ecosystems.[30]

The initial vision for the project was articulated by Liz Walker and Joan Bokaer, who began the long project of turning it into reality in 1991. By that fall they had raised the support to buy a 176-acre tract of land near Ithaca, and by the time the deal closed the next year the long process of planning was under way. Construction began in 1995, and despite several financial crises (and interventions from financial angels), interest grew and the initial housing cluster soon became two. As financial and construction pressures eased, new initiatives were undertaken—an organic farm, resource-conservation projects, and an array of environmental education programs. Walker's rather autobiographical book on the village, published in 2005, amplified what was already substantial outside interest in the project by demonstrating that cohousing and ecovillage features could be successfully woven together.

Several other communities have followed that path in recent years. The thirty-four-unit CoHo Ecovillage in Corvallis, Oregon, which opened in 2007, has made ecological considerations central to its existence. Its members have preserved much of the natural environment of their site, worked to minimize use of energy, and otherwise made the community as sustainable as reasonably possible.[31] Belfast Cohousing and Ecovillage in Maine began construction in 2011 and embodies typical ecovillage goals—clustered housing, preservation of much of the land in a natural state, and programs aimed at creating a sustainable community.[32] The features of these two distinct types of intentional communities do seem to mesh well.

By Any Other Name . . .

The name "ecovillage" has wide currency in the world of sustainable communities, but a fair number of communities with similar outlooks avoid that name for reasons that vary case by case, sometimes because a community has a distinctive outlook or distinctive programs that its members see as setting the community apart from the larger genre. Nevertheless, the goals of sustainable living and showing the world a better way to live are always central. One example of such a community is the Narrow Ridge Earth Literacy Center near Washburn, Tennessee, which was originally founded in 1972 by Bill Nickle, but refounded by Nickle and others on a more permanent footing in the 1990s. The community's name is meant to convey its mission not just of environmentally sensible living but of education, of spreading sustainable ideas to a wide public. Narrow Ridge does that in a variety of ways, especially through workshops and courses that can carry academic credit through cooperative arrangements with colleges in the area. The community has grown to encompass over five hundred acres with a scattering of members' solar-powered and straw-bale homes plus visitor facilities that include housing, a library, and more. Low technology is the order of the day at Narrow Ridge; a distinctive kind of washing machine, for example, is powered not by electricity but by a person who patiently agitates the laundry by hand. One of the notable initiatives at Narrow Ridge is a "green" burial ground, in which bodies, preferably unembalmed, are laid to rest in unmarked graves on a quiet hilltop. The community is so committed to its burial program that its natural graveyard is open to all at no charge. The community's name comes from the writings of the philosopher Martin Buber, who described his own standpoint as "on a narrow rocky ridge between the gulfs where there is no sureness of expressible knowledge but certainty of meeting what remains undisclosed." And just what is earth literacy? In the community's understanding, "it goes beyond the usual academic criteria for critical thinking and good communication skills. To be Earth literate is to understand the basic languages 'spoken' by Earth. It is to be knowledgeable about Earth's expertise as economist, educator, healer, lawgiver and storyteller. Earth Literacy requires more than intellectual understanding. You become aware at the deepest level of your consciousness that Earth's story is your story."[33]

Many ecovillages have a sense of urgency about them. A conviction that underlies most ecovillage work is that the planet desperately needs healing, but some go a step farther and maintain that the world is in such deep trouble that it is probably beyond redemption through well-intended human work. Thus ecovillage work can become mingled with other passions and concerns. Ponderosa Village, near Goldendale, Washington, maintained a prevailing conviction that ruin was on our collective doorstep, that the edifice of modern society was immensely fragile and could collapse disastrously with only a small push, such as a disruption of our transportation system or a war that spins out of control. In 1980 the founders, Larry and Meg Letterman, purchased a tract of more than one thousand acres of rural land and invited like-minded persons to purchase small lots and build their own homes in ways that would help them survive disaster. Residents constructed energy-efficient buildings that often incorporated reused materials; one early house was made of rammed earth, and sometimes water barrels served as solar collectors. The community as a whole owned equipment, shop facilities, a library, and a meditation chapel, and participated in group activities that included a group buying club. By the mid-1990s Ponderosa Village had reached a reported membership of about sixty.[34]

Many communities—most, perhaps—had the characteristics of ecovillages by the latter years of the twentieth century. The members of Far Valley Farm, near Amesville, Ohio, which operated from the late 1970s onward, tried to live simply and harmoniously with the earth and with each other. The Quaker-influenced Oak Grove, also founded in the late 1970s, had a primary mission of providing services to residents in its neighborhood in the Virginia Appalachians, but also pursued low-impact, environmentally sensitive living. The Sundance Extended Community of Tennessee, yet another product of the late 1970s, had alternative energy and sustainable living as central precepts. Environmental living was on the map.[35]

The Ark and the Lighthouse

In the previous volume in this series I mused that most American communes see themselves as either arks or lighthouses.[36] In the former case, communitarians band together to protect themselves from the outside world—from environmental collapse, millennial tribulation, or other threats of disaster or catastrophic change. In the latter, persons equally despairing, perhaps, but nevertheless hopeful of finding a way out of the morass, build communities as shining examples of just how wonderful the world could be if we would live in better ways than most of the world now does. At the time I saw those two types as mutually exclusive. But now the ecovillages seem to embody both types. They see environmental disaster on our very doorstep, but at the same time their members are earnestly trying to work out ways for the human race to survive its own excesses, and they want the world to see what they are doing. Arks or lighthouses, they are beacons of hope.

4

The Spiritual Search I

Christian and Jewish Communities

Communities founded on spiritual impulses and principles have long been the most numerous of all intentional communities, and in the last quarter of the twentieth century this venerable tradition continued. In a country dominated by Christianity in its various forms, the largest numbers of communities were, predictably, Christian in basis, but the widespread and growing interest in Asian religions during that period had its communal manifestations as well.

Christian Communities: The Catholic and Orthodox Examples

One of the largest groupings of intentional communities in the world (possibly *the* largest, although the Buddhist Sangha, considered as a whole, would compete for that honor) is that of the monasteries and convents of the Roman Catholic and Eastern Orthodox churches (as well as a small number of Protestant churches), which have been in existence since the early centuries of Christianity and were given systematic order by Benedict of Nursia some 1,500 years ago. They have been in what is now the United States at least since 1727, and perhaps much earlier, depending on how one defines a monastic presence.[1]

Catholic Communities

Within American Christianity, the Roman Catholic Church has by far the most substantial tradition of operating intentional communities, most of them single-sex monasteries and convents that follow traditional patterns of committed life under the authority of the Congregation for Institutes of Consecrated Life and Societies of Apostolic Life in Rome (although a few communities that identify as Catholic operate on different models and are not embraced as canonical, or officially recognized, orders by the Church). In the twentieth century their membership probably outnumbered that of all other religious communities combined.

Catholic communities have been in serious decline for the last half-century or thereabouts, and many of the hundreds of them face possible closure, or at least radical alterations, such as taking in associate members who do not make the usual full monastic or apostolic commitment, or operating short-term volunteer programs. Nevertheless, some new communities do continue to appear, including several in the last quarter of the twentieth century. Some are offshoots of existing communities; others are entirely new. The *Bulletin* of the Alliance InterMonastères, based in France, lists several new American communities of women:

- The Monastery of the Immaculate Heart of Mary, founded in 1981 in Westfield, Vermont, an "enclosed" community of women who maintain minimal contact with the outside world as they pursue lives of prayer and contemplation as well as work;
- The St. Scholastica Priory, founded in 1980 in Petersham, Massachusetts, a community of contemplative Benedictine sisters;
- The small Transfiguration Monastery in Windsor, New York, also a contemplative community, founded in 1979;
- The Missionary Benedictine Sisters of Tutzing, a Korean community with two American houses—one in Los Angeles, founded in 1985, and the other in New Jersey, founded in 1997;
- The Monastery of Our Lady of the Desert, founded in 1990 as an adjunct to the (male) Monastery of Christ in the Desert and now located in Gobernador, New Mexico.

All, or at least most, of the communities of women founded in the late twentieth century are more traditional than the many communities that liberalized their practices after the Second Vatican Council in the 1960s; their members still wear traditional nuns' habits, lead a traditional lifestyle, including an extensive prayer life, and maintain some degree of separation from the outside world.[2]

Similar communities of men have emerged—again, typically branches from established institutions. St. Mary's Monastery in Petersham, Massachusetts, was founded in 1985 and follows traditional Benedictine practices, including Latin masses and Gregorian Chant. Our Lady of Clear Creek was founded near Tulsa, Oklahoma, in 1999, by monks from a French abbey. It too has Latin masses and uses Gregorian chant.[3]

Some new Catholic communities have challenged the Church's traditional separation of men and women in religious orders, and that challenge has pushed them toward, and sometimes over, the limit of what the Church will accept. Our Lady of Guadalupe Monastery in Pecos, New Mexico, began admitting women in the 1970s, when it became part of the burgeoning charismatic movement in the Catholic Church, which it saw as welcoming women as well as emphasizing speaking in tongues and pursuing other charismatic practices. The Pecos monastery spawned two satellite communities between 1975 and 2000: the Monastery of the Risen Christ near San Luis Obispo, California, founded in 1987, and Mary, Spouse of the Holy Spirit Monastery in Waialua, Hawai'i. All three of the Pecos-related monasteries are quite traditional in dress and discipline, but their practice of not separating men and women nearly as completely as Rome normally requires has led them into conflict with Church authorities.[4]

Some new communities that identify as Catholic go farther, not only mixing men and women but also welcoming married couples as members. John Michael Talbot, a Christian musician of note, founded the Brothers and Sisters of Charity and established the Little Portion Hermitage near Eureka Springs, Arkansas, in 1979. With its mix of married and celibate members, the monastery had attracted over forty members by the early 1990s, and the larger Brothers and Sisters of Charity movement had hundreds of noncommunal members as well. The daily life of the monastery is traditional, with a mixture of work, worship, and service, and it has been recognized as officially Catholic, if not a canonical order; it is identified as an Association of the Faithful by the Diocese of Little Rock.[5]

A bit less monastic than the Little Portion Hermitage but still solidly Catholic in commitment, the Agape Community of Ware, Massachusetts—which was organized in 1982 and moved to central Massachusetts in 1987—combines a spiritual focus with commitment to progressive social action and service. Members join in daily prayer and, occasionally, when a priest is present, in a Catholic mass. They also embody many of the commitments of a typical ecovillage, embracing what has often been called ecospirituality with organic gardening, energy-efficient housing, alternative energy, and a general commitment to sustainability and simple living. Social justice is another theme in Agape's life; members engage in peace and antiwar actions and are sometimes willing to commit civil disobedience. Its programs are subsidized, in part, by donations from Catholic dioceses and religious orders.[6]

Yet another noncanonical Catholic enclave is the Assisi Community of Washington, DC. In 1985 a group of people who had formerly lived in communities of various sorts began to gather to discuss their experiences, and the following year they created their own community. Its members are both religious (meaning members of canonical Catholic orders) and laypersons, men and women, married and single. They have daily spiritual meetings and engage in social action, especially concerning Central America, refugees from which they sometimes shelter. Assisi is housed in two adjacent houses in Washington.[7]

Although we are now reaching beyond the Catholic Church, one other community fits here as well as anywhere. The Community of Celebration considers itself a monastic order within the Episcopal Church, living under a modified version of the Rule of Benedict, but like the Little Portion Hermitage it defines its membership rather unconventionally: "We're different from traditional orders. We don't wear habits, for instance, and our membership includes men and women, married and single, adults and children, clergy and laity."[8] The community has its origins in the Church of the Redeemer of Houston, Texas, which in a period of dramatic revitalization in the mid-1960s organized many communal households among its members. Eventually some members ended up in England and became known as the Community of Celebration, or Fisherfolk. The American branch of that community has been located in Aliquippa, Pennsylvania, where its members live lives of worship and public service.[9]

Eastern Orthodox Communities

Just as new Catholic communities were emerging in the last quarter of the twentieth century, so were new Eastern Orthodox monasteries. The Protecting Veil of the Theotokos Orthodox Community in Anchorage, Alaska, for example, was founded in 1996 under the authority of the Russian-based Orthodox Church in America, and St. Anthony's Orthodox Monastery was founded in Florence, Arizona, in 1995 by monks sent from the great Mt. Athos monastic domain in Greece; it operates under the authority of the Greek Orthodox Archdiocese of America. Orthodoxy in America, once a set of churches populated primarily by immigrants from traditionally Orthodox countries and their descendants, has enjoyed a steady stream of converts—mainly from evangelical Protestant churches—since the 1970s, and with that influx has expanded its monastic presence. Some new monastic and communal centers were founded outside the jurisdiction of the traditional Orthodox churches: for example, the Campus Crusade for Christ chapter at the University of California, Santa Barbara, which had already moved in a communal direction, had a group conversion, and reorganized itself as the Evangelical Orthodox Church (and later St. Athanasius Church).[10]

Another variant, and communal, version of Eastern Orthodoxy came with a change in direction of the Holy Order of MANS in the 1980s. That movement (MANS was an acronym with a secret meaning) was founded in the cultural upheaval of mid-1960s San Francisco by Earl Blighton, whose background included involvement in several esoteric and countercultural religious movements such as Rosicrucianism, Spiritualism, Freemasonry, and Theosophy. To a following that emerged from the local hippies, Blighton promulgated what he called "esoteric Christianity," an eclectic blend of ideas and practices that included a belief that the world was moving toward greater spiritual illumination, and the Holy Order of MANS would be the vehicle leading the change. Members lived in community under monastic conditions, engaging in prayer and fasting as well as taking vows of poverty and obedience. The group differed from historic Western forms of monasticism, however, in its admission of both men and women, and especially in its ordination of women as priests. After Blighton's death in 1974 he was succeeded by Andrew Rossi, a longtime member, who experienced a conversion to Orthodoxy and came under the influence of Father Hermann Podmoshensky, abbot of the St. Herman of Alaska Brotherhood, a monastic group with irregular status in the Orthodox tradition. In 1988 the remaining members of the Holy Order of MANS underwent conversion and baptism into a small, independent Orthodox group, and continued under the direction of Father Podmoshensky and his associate, Metropolitan Pangratios.[11] Orthodoxy does not permit women to be priests, so, for the many ordained women in the movement, that status was revoked. Some disaffected members tried to continue more or less in Blighton's footsteps; one such group, the Order of Christ/Sophia, has a number of members living communally and somewhat monastically, although not necessarily celibately. It once again ordains women.[12]

Others have taken unconventional paths into Orthodoxy but have finally landed under the aegis of historic Orthodox churches. Such was the case of a group of Franciscan monks who founded a Catholic monastery known as New Skete in Cambridge, New York, in 1966, and later converted to Orthodoxy and were received into the Russian-originated Orthodox Church in America in 1979. In 1983 another communal group, the Companions of New Skete, emerged alongside the monks; its members were married couples. They continue as Orthodox parishioners.[13]

Protestant Christian Communities

Although traditional Catholic and Orthodox monasticism represents by far the largest type of American communal living in both numbers of members and numbers of communities, other Christians have felt moved to emulate their example. Some of them have taken the communal passages in chapters 2 and 4 of the Book of Acts as guidance:

> All who believed were together and had all things in common; they would sell their possessions and goods and distribute the proceeds to all, as any had need. Day by day, as they spent much time together in the temple, they broke bread at home and ate their food with glad and generous hearts, praising God and having the goodwill of all the people.[14]

> Now the whole group of those who believed were of one heart and soul, and no one claimed private ownership of any possessions, but everything they owned was held in common. With great power the apostles gave their testimony to the resurrection of the Lord Jesus, and great grace was upon them all. There was not a needy person among them, for as many as owned lands or houses sold them and brought the proceeds of what was sold. They laid it at the apostles' feet, and it was distributed to each as any had need. There was a Levite, a native of Cyprus, Joseph, to whom the apostles gave the name Barnabas (which means 'son of encouragement'). He sold a field that belonged to him, then brought the money, and laid it at the apostles' feet.[15]

And they can find other biblical support for their communitarianism as well. Quite a few passages call for radical dedication and discipleship. When Jesus is portrayed as saying, "So therefore, none of you can become my disciple if you do not give up all your possessions," he seems to be making a straightforward call for community among his followers.[16]

Others have taken the biblical model less literally, but nevertheless have found communal living useful, if not divinely commanded.

Some unite in pursuit of common goals, such as missionary activity, publishing, or social activism and service. Some simply prefer to live in the close company of the faithful. And some have decided to circle the wagons, to build a community in defense of the corrupting influence of the outside world, perhaps in anticipation of a coming apocalypse.

Protestant Christian communities have been common throughout American history; the ones I have been able to identify within the time period in question are included in the list of communities at the end of this volume. Telling the stories of each would be prohibitively onerous, so here will be featured a few representative samples, including the more prominent and substantial of them.

Two of the notable Anabaptist-oriented communities founded before 1975, Reba Place in Evanston, Illinois, and Plow Creek Fellowship in Tiskilwa, Illinois, eventually formed an umbrella group for like-minded communities, and in due course others joined the new organization, Shalom Mission Communities. One of them was the Church of the Sojourners (not to be confused with the Sojourners Community, a Christian community dedicated to social justice that was discussed in volume 2 in this series), founded in 1988 in the Mission District of San Francisco. Much of the church's activity has focused on service to its neighborhood, whose residents are largely Central American. Although visitors regularly worship with the core community, the church remains fairly small, usually with around ten members who live together and share their finances.[17] Hope Fellowship, founded as Hope Community in 1993 in Waco, Texas, is another of the Shalom Mission Communities. Two Waco families felt called to live in community, and together they moved into a common home. The following year the local church the members had been attending closed, and they decided to fill the gap by becoming a church as well as a community. The church has not required everyone to live communally and share their incomes to belong, but communal arrangements still existed among some of the several dozen members of Hope by the end of the decade.[18]

The Church of the Sojourners also belonged to another Christian communal network for a time. That umbrella organization, the

West Coast Communities, brought together four small communal churches, including, in addition to the Sojourners, the Church of the Servant King, the Wesleyan Community, and the Church on West Street. The Church of the Servant King was founded in Gardena, California, in 1979. Members sought to emulate the biblical early church and to that end took on a commitment of strong spiritual discipline, engaging in daily prayer, Bible reading, and meditation. The church grew, and in 1987 it established branch churches in Eugene and Portland, Oregon. The Eugene church has come to occupy several houses; worship services are held in one of the living rooms. Families maintain independent finances, but many work for the church's businesses—among them a café, a bookstore, and a publishing company.[19]

The Wesleyan Community had its origins in a large Methodist church in Ingleside, Illinois, that had an extensive counseling program in the 1970s. Some of those involved envisioned an intentional community that would provide a place of retreat for clients, and to that end purchased fifty-eight acres of mostly wooded land on Vashon Island, Washington, and began to build a community centered in their church. It has continued since; members keep separate finances but contribute to common needs.[20]

The other member of the West Coast Communities is the Church on West Street of Garden Grove, California, which, in 1996, thirteen years after its founding, had twelve adult members and five children. Although it is organizationally independent, its life and beliefs have been influenced by Seventh-day Adventism. Thus church members observe a Saturday Sabbath, a time of rest and sharing. Unlike some similar communal churches, the Church on West Street has a political outlook that is solidly conservative, and where its fellow believers in West Coast Communities churches might be activists against war or racism, this church's political work is against abortion and homosexual practice. But, like the other churches, the members of West Street are devoted to living out the gospel as they understand it.[21]

In the 1960s the Charismatic Movement, a revamped and reconceived wave of the Pentecostalism that had been a part of American religious life for over half a century, burst forth from the old-line

Pentecostal churches and found a niche in many, even most, other Christian denominations, both Protestant and Catholic. At the same time the Jesus Movement, made up largely of hippies who had turned to conservative Protestantism, was challenging the entrenched evangelical establishment with its flamboyant style and insistence on deep religious commitment in the daily lives of believers. The dynamic new fervor of the time penetrated several well-established congregations, sometimes leading to congregational renewal and sometimes to conflict and division. One church thus impacted was a Lutheran congregation in La Jolla, California, that ended up splitting into several smaller groups, one of which moved to an eighty-acre tract of land near Fulton, Missouri. There they built the disciplined Shepherdsfield Community that reached about one hundred members, supporting themselves with several businesses (among them a bakery and a window-washing service), and living from a common purse. With an intense common spiritual life, many shared meals, and its own publishing house, Shepherdsfield became widely admired among Protestant communities and cultivated close ties with several of them. In the early years of the twenty-first century the community encountered setbacks, but as the year 2000 approached it was thriving as one of the largest common-purse communities in the country.[22]

Simple living was a notable theme of many twentieth-century intentional communities, but the concept is hardly original. The Amish, to name one eminent example, have lived in a remarkably simple fashion for over three hundred years, so it should not be surprising that some communitarians have emulated them. One such group was the Community at Cookeville, whose membership included persons with both Amish and Mennonite backgrounds. The backstory is that many farmers who have resisted the use of modern machinery have found it difficult to compete with highly mechanized farming in the marketplace and have been looking for new ways to make a living without compromising their principles of simple living. In the early 1990s this group came together under the leadership of Elmo Stoll, an Amish minister, and purchased some 200 acres of land in Tennessee. By 1995 they numbered sixteen families and were speaking English in their daily lives rather than the standard Amish dialect of German. Like many "regular" Amish they focused on specialty crops that are labor-intensive and that do not require large acreages. Thus they grew truck crops and vegetables, along with such crops as sorghum that is cooked into molasses. The community was successful enough that it spawned branch communities in Tennessee and Kentucky, as well as one in Canada. However, it closed after Stoll's death in 1998.[23]

Like the Community at Cookeville, the Brazos de Dios Community near Waco, Texas, emulates the Anabaptists, although it is not formally of Anabaptist heritage. It emerged from a storefront church founded by Blair and Regina Adams in New York City in the 1970s. Eventually the congregation decided to move to a rural location, and purchased land north of Waco, Texas, in 1990. There the members began farming with horses; the goal was to live simply, but as the community grew it developed several businesses as well. Soon it created a sort of living museum; a crafts village operated as a tourist destination called Homestead Heritage. Different buildings in the village include a furniture-making shop, a water-powered flour mill, a blacksmith shop, a pottery, and other such reconstructions of nineteenth-century frontier village ways. By the early twenty-first century the community had more than forty resident families, and the community church had hundreds of noncommunal members from the surrounding area. A steady stream of visitors patronized the old-fashioned village, and thousands attended the community's crafts fair each fall.[24]

One rather unusual community of the late twentieth century was founded in opposition to North America's largest and one of its most respected networks of communities, the Hutterites. The Hutterites well deserve their reputation as peaceful and practical people, but like any human institution they have spawned some dissenters, members who have become disaffected for a variety of reasons. One community made up largely of such ex-members was the Ark of the New Covenant, located in Tabor, South Dakota, near the site of the oldest surviving Hutterite colony, Bon Homme. In 1988 more than twenty dissatisfied members withdrew from Bon Homme, claiming that Hutterism had become formal and cold, without much fire in the spiritual belly. They organized as an independent Christian community, attracting some members from other colonies and a leader, James Wainscoat, whose background was not Hutterite. Within a year they had thirty-two members and had endured a series of confrontations with the Bon Homme colony. But soon thereafter the group moved to California, and members began to drift away, many back to South Dakota. By 1997 only Wainscoat's family remained, and the Ark community disbanded.[25]

One last Protestant denomination deserves mention for its long history of communitarianism: the Society of Friends, or Quakers. Dozens of communities founded by Quakers on the principles of their faith have dotted the American past, and a few were founded in the last quarter of the twentieth century. One was the Friends Community of North Easton, Massachusetts, founded in 1979, whose members built solar condominium homes and dedicated themselves to cooperative living.[26] Another was Oak Grove, founded in the late 1970s near Round Hill, Virginia, as a base from which to provide services to the many low-income residents in the area.[27] In 1980 a group of Quakers built a meetinghouse near Kerrville, Texas, and after a few years decided to plant an intentional community on the land as well; known as Quakerland, it closed in the early 2000s, however, amid financial problems.[28] The Ashland Vineyard Community, founded in 1986 near Ashland, Virginia, was yet another Quaker project, one with individual homes but a good deal of close communal sharing.[29] In the 1990s another group of Friends began to explore the possibility of forming a cooperative and over the next few years built the Quaker Intentional Village-Canaan in East Chatham, New York, erecting housing on a small part of their 135-acre tract of land and leaving the rest undeveloped.[30] Several other small communities, usually affiliated with local Quaker meetings, were founded in cities as well. When those are added to the many communities founded by Friends before 1975, the Quaker contribution to communal living can be considered quite substantial.

The list could go on. The Sword of the Spirit communities, a network founded earlier but still active after 1975, continued to add new communities to its network of dozens.[31] New independent communities were founded as well, as in the case of Holyland, a controversial community of African Americans in Alabama said by its supporters to be working for the uplift of its largely poor members but later accused by others of abusing some of those members at the same time.[32] The Wooden Bridge Community, near Monroe, Wisconsin, is not itself a church (its members attend different churches in the area), but members live and work closely together and join in social-justice and other activist projects.[33] The ARC Ecumenical Retreat Center was begun through the work of Ruth I. Halvorson and her husband Loren Halvorson, who purchased a tract of rural land that eventually encompassed ninety acres north of Minneapolis, Minnesota, and on it created a Christian-based but inclusive spiritual retreat center. ARC stands for Action, Reflection, Celebration; the center's communal staff serves a broad constituency of spiritual seekers.[34] As is traditional, the committed members of the communities sought to work out their spiritual visions—whether focused on social service, prayer, self-sufficiency, millennialism, or any number of other primary concerns. In many cases the commitment went forward past the end of the century, and often is still being worked out at this writing years later.

Latter Day Saint–Related Communities

The various branches of the Latter Day Saint tradition have a long history of forming intentional communities. As early as 1831, just a year after the founding of the Church of Christ, as it was originally known, Joseph Smith Jr., the founder, promulgated the Law of Consecration and Stewardship, which called for cooperative arrangements among the faithful. In that year the church moved its headquarters, and most of its membership, to Kirtland, Ohio, and there an attempt was made to organize the church along communitarian lines. That effort was short-lived, however, and a second endeavor at the church's next gathering place, Independence, Missouri, was also of limited duration and extent.

In 1844 Smith, whose church was now headquartered in Nauvoo, Illinois, was killed by a lynch mob, and in the chaotic aftermath of that traumatic event several men rose up to claim leadership of the church. Ultimately Brigham Young commanded the largest faction, which soon left for Utah, but several others moved splinter groups to other locations where they often took up communal living. James Strang in Wisconsin and then Michigan; Alpheus Cutler in Iowa (and his followers, after his death, in Minnesota); Lyman Wight in Texas; and several others were all leaders of factions that practiced communal living in the mid-nineteenth century.[35] Still others emerged after the founding of the Reorganized Church of Jesus Christ of Latter Day Saints (now known as the Community of Christ) by Joseph Smith III, the son of the original founder, in 1860. In the 1870s, after the main body of the Mormons had become well established in Utah, Brigham Young called for the development of what by then was known within his church as the United Order of Enoch, and the believers responded by forming various cooperative endeavors in many Mormon locales. Those projects ranged from loose sharing to the establishment of cooperative stores and industries to fully communal villages, as at Orderville, Utah, where for several years all church members lived in full community of property.

After Young's death in 1877 the church deemphasized the cooperative projects, and the most ambitious of them soon came to an end, although some remained in place for years thereafter. But another wave of LDS communitarianism lay just ahead. In the early 1880s a federal government campaign against polygamy among the Mormons was launched, and through the decade raids against the "cohabs" (cohabitators) sent hundreds of them to prison. Others fled to Mexico, where they established several communal settlements beyond the reach of the US authorities. After nearly a decade of intense conflict, in 1890 the church officially gave up polygamy (although the actual end of the practice was at least two decades later in coming), and with that some polygamist stalwarts broke away to start their own churches. They claimed that they had been ordered by the third president of the church, John Taylor, never to give up "the Principle" of polygamy. Partly in self-defense, these new churches, which came to be generally known as "Fundamentalist," often undertook communal living.

Most of the Fundamentalist/polygamist LDS churches were formed before the time frame of this volume, although many of them have continued since 1975, living in various communal arrangements and practicing plural marriage. However, several new communal churches, most of them small and local, have been founded as well. In 1975 John W. Bryant, who had been a member of the Apostolic United Brethren, a polygamy-practicing LDS church based in Salt Lake City, withdrew from that church and founded his own, the Church of Christ (Patriarchal), later known as the Evangelical Church of Christ. That church developed several communal locations in Utah and Nevada, with a headquarters in Mesquite, Nevada. In 1981 the headquarters was moved to Oregon, where Bryant reportedly had a born-again experience that led him to disavow his earlier commitment to polygamy and patriarchal rule. At some point he dissolved the Evangelical Church of Christ, and those who remained loyal to him reorganized as the Church of the New Covenant in Christ. At last report Bryant had retained his six wives but resolved not to take any new ones.[36] Another branch of his movement had taken shape in the meantime; Gilbert Clark split from Bryant in 1981 and started his own group whose name changed from time to time. It was variously known as Sons Ahman Israel and Yesai Israel. Clark's followers formed a small commune near Fredonia, Arizona. Like many other LDS groups they had their own revealed scriptures and combined Mormon theology with New Age and Pagan ideas and practices. Just how long it endured is unclear.[37]

1978 saw the founding of two new communal LDS groups. Eugene O. Walton was for a time a member of the Reorganized Church of Jesus Christ of Latter Day Saints (now the Community of Christ) and later of the LDS church generally known as Cutlerite. Finally he started his own church, the Restored Church of Jesus Christ, in Independence, Missouri. The small communal church is probably best known for its educational institution, the School of the Prophets.[38] At about the same time, Gerald W. Peterson, a member of the polygamy-practicing Apostolic United Brethren, split from that group and founded Christ's Church, Inc., better known as the Righteous Branch of the Church of

Jesus Christ of Latter Day Saints. As other similar groups have done, the group moved to a remote rural location, in this case west of Cedar City, Utah. Peterson died in 1981, but the church and community have continued under his son, Gerald W. Peterson Jr.[39]

One accusation frequently leveled against polygamy-practicing LDS groups is that they force underage girls into marriages and thus are guilty of sexual abuse. One group for which that allegation was adjudged true was the Zion Society, founded by Arvin Shreeve, an excommunicated Mormon, in the early 1980s. Shreeve lived with ten wives in an enclave of houses in Ogden, Utah. The police raided the Zion Society in 1991 and charged Shreeve with several counts of child sexual abuse, to which he pleaded guilty. He died in prison in 2009, his church and wives long scattered.

The largest of the communal LDS-based groups, the Fundamentalist LDS Church of Colorado City, Arizona, experienced the withdrawal of some of its members into yet another communal group in 1984. In this case the motivation for the split was political and apparently unrelated to the practice of polygamy; the members simply rejected the increasingly authoritarian leadership of the FLDS prophet, Rulon Jeffs, and his predecessor, LeRoy Johnson, instead advocating government by a council of elders. A group numbering as many as 1,500 purchased some 1,000 acres of land just across the road from Colorado City and began to develop Centennial Park, so named in 1986 because of the Fundamentalist belief that LDS Church president John Taylor received a revelation in 1886 commanding Mormons to stand fast in continuing the practice of polygamy. The Centennial Park polygamists, with their independent Fundamentalist LDS church, appear to inhabit the second-largest polygamous community in the LDS world, smaller only than the original FLDS center in Colorado City.[40]

The story of LDS-derived communitarianism in the twentieth century ends with two rather unusual stories, one seemingly benign, and one decidedly not. Both had their roots in the Reorganized branch of Mormonism, emerging in Lamoni, Iowa, the home of the

RLDS's Graceland College. In the first case, in the late 1970s a group of members of the Reorganized Church of Jesus Christ of Latter Day Saints (now renamed the Community of Christ) began to pull away from that church under the leadership of Ron Livingston, who for a time abandoned any conventional name and became known simply as "Grandpa." They began purchasing land in 1987 and soon built two small villages. In 1990 they quit their outside jobs and devoted themselves to achieving self-sufficiency. Like the Amish they avoid motor vehicles and do not use electricity; in their early years they did not use animals for farming, although eventually they decided that they would use draft horses as a practical necessity. Like several other Latter Day Saint–derived groups, they claim to have, through revelation, special scriptures that have been translated miraculously.[41] But they have distinctive beliefs and practices as well, such as an interest in the ancient Essenes and a six-day weekly calendar. At its peak the community, which adopted the name "Brotherhood of Christ," had between fifty and one hundred members, although their numbers have more recently declined somewhat. With at least five hundred acres of land, the community has followed its own distinctive path—without benefit of motors or electricity.[42]

The other late-twentieth-century group, however, was decidedly more tragic than the Brotherhood of Christ. Jeffrey Lundgren was an active RLDS Church member in the denomination's historic former home of Kirtland, Ohio, who grew increasingly critical of the church and left it in 1987, in the meantime having declared himself a prophet. He and some two dozen followers lived on a rented farm and shared a common purse. Two members, however, a married couple, eventually began criticizing Lundgren's leadership, and he ordered that they and their three daughters be executed. The killings occurred in 1989; the rest of the community then moved to West Virginia to await the Second Coming of Christ. They later moved to Independence, Missouri, where word of the murders eventually reached the authorities. Lundgren was tried and sentenced to death, but reportedly still had followers believing that he was a prophet after his execution in 2006. The Lundgren story will be recounted in greater detail in chapter 7.[43]

Jewish Communities

The heyday of American Jewish colonization was in the 1880s, when refugees from the pogroms of Eastern Europe came streaming into the United States and were assisted in settling in rural agricultural cooperative colonies by the Jews who were already here. A few specifically Jewish communities were established in the twentieth century, most notably several inspired by the Havurah movement, which sought to inject joy and close community into a Judaism these mostly young dissenters believed had become overly formal and cold.

A few more came later in the century, however. One was the Kabbalah Centre, with headquarters in Los Angeles and branches in several countries around the world. In the late twentieth century it became widely known that some Hollywood celebrities, such as the singer Madonna, were studying at the Kabbalah Centre. The Centre had a boom in popularity, attracting hundreds of students and at the same time expanding its staff. A core group of staff took up collective living in Centre-owned buildings near the headquarters. Conflict eventually ensued, as some former staff members and outsiders accused the Centre leader, Philip Berg, of exploiting his associates. The Centre, however, including its communal component, survived that conflict as well as Berg's death in 2013.[44]

Jewish-identified student housing cooperatives have been around for many years, and at least one new one was founded in the latter years of the twentieth century. Ofek Shalom, in Madison, Wisconsin, founded in 1986, has promoted observant Jewish living, despite the fact that not all of its dozen or so members are Jewish. The group has weekly Sabbath services and other observances such as Seder meals during Passover and traditional rituals for other holidays. Kosher food is always available, and separation of milk and meat dishes and utensils is observed. Jewish community remains alive and well in a large house in Madison.[45]

Beyond such examples of Jewish communal living, other groups rather informally identified as Jewish, even though their focus was elsewhere. The Center for Well-Being of Creswell, Oregon, for example, occupied a thirteen-acre tract of common land with several buildings in the 1980s, but its focus was not so much the Judaism of its members as a holistic healing program. In that regard it resembled such predecessors as the Sunrise community of Alicia, Michigan, that in the 1930s was heavily Jewish in membership but never intended to be a "Jewish community."[46]

It is worth noting that defining "Jewish" is an imprecise art. Beginning in the late nineteenth century several groups of African Americans began to identify themselves as Jewish and to observe many of the traditions of Jewish life, and some of them incorporated communal living into their lifestyles. Mainstream Judaism has generally not found these groups to be truly Jewish, since Jewish tradition holds that to be a Jew one must be born to a Jewish mother or undergo a rabbinically supervised conversion, neither of which the Black Jews, as they are typically called, have done. At least one such group emerged in the post-1975 period, the Nation of Yahweh, headed by Hulon Mitchell Jr., who took the name Yahweh ben Yahweh. Some members lived independently, but others lived communally at the group's headquarters in Miami, Florida. Together they developed several businesses and various African American self-help programs. It all began to unravel, however, in 1990, when the authorities arrested Yahweh and twelve of his followers on charges of racketeering, extortion, arson, and murder. Yahweh himself was sentenced to eighteen years in prison.[47]

Thus was the stage set for a revival of Jewish communalism in the early twenty-first century with such groups as the three-house Ravenna Kibbutz in Seattle and the Moishe Houses, which numbered more than two dozen after their founding in 2006.[48] In the new century some new interest in farm colonies also emerged, often related to the passion some Jews had to produce kosher (and often organic) food using traditional Jewish farming methods, which involve such practices as leaving small portions of fields unharvested so that people in need can glean from them, and allowing the land to go fallow every seventh year. Thus, for example, was the Eretz HaChaim farming community founded in 2002 near Amherst, Massachusetts, by several Lubavitcher Hasidic families under the leadership of Rabbi Chaim Adleman.[49] Most Jews do not live communally, as this book defines the term, but, as an ancient minority tradition within the larger Jewish population, intentional communities continue to have a presence.

5

The Spiritual Search II

Other Religious Communities

Beginning in the 1960s the United States saw a great surge in immigration from Asia and other parts of the world, abetted in large part by an expansion of immigration laws that had discriminated against Asians. Among the many who arrived on American shores were spiritual teachers of all sorts, and more than few of them attracted American followings. Thus we saw a great spate of the opening of ashrams, temples, meditation centers, and other communitarian places where believers could gather to nourish their spiritual souls. In this chapter we will survey communities that emerged between 1975 and 2000, rooted in the major world religions of Islam, Hinduism, and Buddhism, as well as in Native American traditions, the new Paganism, and Western esotericism.

Muslim Communities

Islam enjoyed considerable growth in the United States in the latter decades of the twentieth century, largely from immigration from traditionally Muslim countries and from converts, mostly African American, who found what many consider the most egalitarian of the world's religions attractive. Islam in America has tended to be communal in the larger sense—people living in neighborhoods in which their coreligionists have a strong presence and sharing an identity—but not rife with intentional communities. Nevertheless, some have cropped up here and there.

Some of the earliest American Muslim intentional communities were established in the 1960s and 1970s by Elijah Muhammad—then the leader of the Nation of Islam—typically as farming communities that could provide ritually proper food for members and their grocery stores and restaurants. Some traditional Muslims would argue with the idea that they were really Muslim, since the NoI was not regarded as an orthodox version of the religion. However, under the leadership of Elijah Muhammad's son and successor, Warith Deen Muhammad, most of the NoI later moved toward conventional Islam, and several of the communities, some of which still exist, came to be accepted as truly Islamic. Later, other Muslims, again predominantly African American converts to the faith, founded new traditional communal enclaves.

One of the newer communities, New Medinah, has its roots in the desire of Muslims, mainly African Americans, to build a retreat center, an effort that was launched with the purchase of land near Sumrall, Mississippi, in 1983. The project was successful, attracting new participants who wanted to build a mosque and then a residential community. The community grew steadily, and by the early twenty-first century reported over two hundred resident members. Some of them farmed; others worked in nearby towns. The community has become a supplier of halal meats and fresh vegetables to the surrounding area, and has operated its own school as well as the mosque that, after some setbacks, was finally opened in the 1990s. Today the community continues to expand and its members continue to study the beliefs and engage in the practices of Islam.[1]

Not every community that has identified as Muslim has enacted a version of the faith that others would accept as legitimate, and some have changed over time, moving from one religious identity to another. Perhaps the most notable example of such an evolving and eclectic community was begun in the late 1960s in New York City by Dwight York, who first called his new movement Ansaar Pure Sufi and then, after a few other changes of nomenclature, the Ansaaru Allah Community. His form of Islam, rooted in the American black nationalism of Marcus Garvey, Elijah Muhammad, and other seminal visionaries, was hardly orthodox; he denounced some Muslim teachings right along with those of Christianity and Judaism.

In the early 1990s York abandoned Islam and announced that his followers were Hebrews, and soon thereafter that they constituted the United Nuwaubian Nation of Moors. He eventually began to teach that he and his followers were descended from the ancient kingdom of Nubia in Sudan and were to be called Nuwaubians. By 1993 they had become the Yamassee Native American Moors of the Creek Nation. About that time York moved his headquarters to Eatonton, Georgia, where his followers built a fantastic collection of shrines and buildings they called Tama Re, which served not only as their communal home but as a tourist attraction, an Egyptian-themed enclave with a large pyramid, sphinxes, and other idiosyncratic structures, that was finished by about 2000. The project quickly became the focus of building and zoning code disputes with the local authorities. By the late 1990s allegations that York was sexually abusing children began to emerge, and in 2002 he was arrested. After dozens of legal procedures marked by the courtroom theatrics of York and his supporters, he was convicted of over one hundred sexual offenses as well as racketeering and sentenced to 135 years in prison. The government seized Tama Re, bulldozed the property, and sold it. The Nuwaubian Nation dispersed.[2]

One other Muslim community has received far less publicity than York's Nuwaubians but has hardly been less controversial. Muslims of America members live in several rural intentional communities scattered around the United States. The movement describes itself as an African American Muslim educational and charitable organization, but its opponents call it a front for South Asian–based terrorism. Members of the organization living at a commune near Red House, Virginia, and another in California have been accused of violent felonies, although details are elusive. The headquarters of the movement, which has been said to have as many as perhaps ten communal enclaves, is a community known as Islamberg near Hancock, New York.[3]

American Sufis often do not identify as Muslims, but Sufism was founded within Islam and in most of the world continues that identification today, so mention of their communities is warranted here.

American Sufis have built several intentional communities, most of them founded in 1975 or later. The Abode of the Message, discussed in the previous volume in this series, opened in that year, and several others followed. It is also the case that many communities for which Sufism is not central to their identities have been influenced by Sufism—perhaps more of them than the ones that consider Sufism their principal spiritual center.

Prominent among the Sufi communes founded during the last quarter of the twentieth century are these:

- The Bawa Muhaiyaddeen Fellowship in Philadelphia was opened by M. R. Bawa Muhaiyaddeen, a Sufi mystic who came from Sri Lanka (then known as Ceylon) in 1971 and soon acquired an American following. In the 1980s, members of the movement purchased one hundred acres of rural land in Coatesville, Pennsylvania, and established the Bawa Muhaiyaddeen Fellowship Farm, where some of them farmed and lived communally. On the property they built Bawa's mazar, or mausoleum. The farm has continued since Bawa's death in 1986.[4]
- Light of the Mountains Retreat Center, which is affiliated with the International Sufi Healing Order, was begun in 1978 by followers of the teachings of Hazrat Inayat Khan, one of the first teachers to take Sufism to the West. Located on 105 acres of land near Leicester, North Carolina, Light of the Mountains was founded as a communal center of the Sufi Order International, and then became a farm and retreat center in 1988. It continues to offer individualized spiritual retreats.[5]
- Sami Mahal, a community located in San Rafael, California, and associated with the Sufi Ruhaniat International, was housed in a building leased in 1976 by the Sufi teacher Shahabuddin Less (and purchased by the group in 1983). A resident community averaging around a dozen members helped support a larger community participating in Sami Mahal activities.[6]
- The Southwest Sufi Community has a residential community known as Khankah Noor Inayat as well as a retreat center and

a nature preserve. It was established in 1995 on 1,900 acres of land near Silver City, New Mexico. Like many other Sufi centers, it is open to persons on a variety of spiritual paths, not Sufism exclusively.[7]

Asians in America: Indian and Hindu Communities

Hindu Communities

Indian spiritual teachers were among the beneficiaries of the relaxation of immigration laws in 1965, and by 1975 were busily establishing ashrams and other spiritual communities throughout the United States. They were too many of them to cover in any detail here, but these brief sketches of some of the more substantial and publicized ones serve to capture the spirit of the time.

In a few cases the new Hindu communities were offshoots of earlier ones. Some of the offshoots had their roots in the International Society for Krishna Consciousness (ISKCON), an organization which became troubled in the late 1970s. Several problems plagued ISKCON after the death of its founder, A. C. Bhaktivedanta Swami (known to his followers by the honorific Prabhupada): it had organizational issues, interpersonal rivalries, and leadership failures that threatened its very existence. Bhaktivedanta had left a dual structure, with spiritual leaders (gurus) empowered to initiate new members, alongside geographically based regional leaders without that key spiritual power. The ambiguity that resulted from that structure caused deep divisions that nearly destroyed the organization. Worse, perhaps, were the failings of a few of the new leaders, and soon ISKCON was riven with sex scandals (including sexual abuse of children), weapons violations, and criminal conduct on community property. The most publicized of those sets of problems took place at New Vrindaban, the movement's rural community in West Virginia, where transgressions included murder and its founding leader Kirtanananda (Keith Ham) ended up in prison.

Although level heads eventually prevailed, and ISKCON survived and even prospered, several groups of members bailed out, unhappy with the organization but not at all unhappy with its version of Hindu spiritual practice. ISKCON had long emphasized rural life, recalling village life in India, and several of the offshoots took the form of farm projects. One example is Audarya, a small ashram located near Philo, California. Its leader, Swami B. V. Tripurari, originally known as Tom Beaudry, joined ISKCON during the lifetime of Swami Bhaktivedanta, but left it during its period of turmoil thereafter. He was finally able to open a residential center in Eugene, Oregon, in 1992, and soon a dozen devotees (from a much larger nonresidential congregation) were living there. That apparently came to an end around the turn of the century; by the early 2000s Tripurari was resident at a new ashram near Philo, California. There a community of monks continues to lead an ISKCON-like life, with cows, gardens, and daily worship and meditation. Other ISKCON offshoot communities follow similar patterns.[8]

ISKCON was not the only Indian-based movement to suffer division. Another prominent one was Siddha Yoga Dham, whose communal property in the Catskills of New York State was purchased in 1979. Siddha Yoga was the movement headed by Swami Muktananda Paramahamsa, who had begun teaching in the United States earlier in that decade. The division came after Muktananda's death in 1982; he had appointed a brother-sister team to succeed him, but they fell into conflict and the sister, known as Swami Chidvilasananda (and Gurumayi to her followers), emerged as the sole leader of the Catskills community, known as the Shree Muktananda Ashram. Her brother, Swami Nityananda, went on to found his own organization, Shanti Mandir, which opened its own ashram in Walden, New York. Thus does Muktananda's bifurcated spiritual lineage continue.[9]

One of the most flamboyant and controversial of Indian spiritual teachers to appear in America was Bhagwan Shree Rajneesh, who had developed an international following as a spiritual teacher based in Pune, India. Born into a Jain household as Chandra Mohan Jain in 1931, he began teaching in the 1950s, attracting notoriety for his controversial views. He criticized organized religion and found fault with Mahatma Gandhi, and he scandalized traditional Indians with his liberal (to say the least) attitude toward sex. From 1974 to 1981 his ashram at Pune attracted a largely Western following, due to its high-energy lifestyle that featured dynamic meditation (sometimes called "chaotic meditation") and group therapy sessions that were sometimes marked by violence and by open sexual encounters. As the ashram grew its unpopularity among Indians grew as well, and by the late 1970s Rajneesh sought to move. In 1981 his disciples purchased a sixty-four-thousand-acre cattle ranch in central Oregon and a new intentional community, Rajneeshpuram, began to take shape.

Rajneeshpuram grew rapidly, eventually reaching a population of perhaps five thousand, making it probably the largest (or second-largest, after Colorado City) single-site intentional community in American history. It also quickly became one of the most controversial communities the country has ever seen. Rajneesh had quite a few monied and professional people among his devotees, so building went quickly. One noted extravagance was the fleet of nearly one hundred Rolls-Royces the believers gave their master. But the conflict between believers and outsiders never abated, and was exacerbated by malevolent acts by some Rajneeshees, including the poisoning of food in several public restaurants in a nearby city and the importing of hundreds of homeless persons in an attempt to control a local election. Repeated disputes over Oregon's land-use laws also inflamed relations. The commune began to decline, and it all culminated in Rajneesh's arrest in 1985 on charges of immigration fraud. A plea bargain let him return to India, and Rajneeshpuram was finished. The small city in the middle of the high desert stood nearly empty.[10] (The story of the downfall of Rajneesh and his community will be recounted in more detail later.) Some of the Rajneeshees regrouped, however, and a few smaller communes were started in various locations. One was the Rachana Community, also known as the Osho Rachana Longhouse (Osho being the name Rajneesh used after he left Oregon). It was founded near Redmond, Washington, in 1996, and seems to have operated for the next few years, although it apparently disbanded sometime after 2000.[11]

Another Indian adept who founded an intentional community, albeit also with some controversy late in his life, was Swami Rama, who had studied in Europe and had become interested in combining Western science with the many and diverse Asian spiritual paths. He arrived in the United States in 1969 and soon subjected his alleged yogic powers to scientific investigation at the Menninger Clinic in Topeka, Kansas. There he demonstrated, to the satisfaction of the investigators, such extraordinary powers as the ability to stop and start his heart at will and to control his brain waves. He soon gathered an American following and in 1971 founded the Himalayan Institute, which in 1977 purchased a four-hundred-acre ashram property near Honesdale, Pennsylvania. Some later cast doubt on Swami Rama's unusual yogic powers, showing, for example, that there are nonyogic ways to simulate heart-stopping, and then a series of allegations of sexual transgressions clouded the swami's image.[12] However, the community continues, having survived Swami Rama's death in 1996, and, under the leadership of Pandit Rajmani Tigunait, offers the kinds of workshops and retreats that similar Asian-oriented communal centers do.[13]

One of the most recognizable of the Indian spiritual teachers of the 1960s era was Swami Satchidananda, whose moment of greatest glory came when he addressed the massive crowd from the stage at the Woodstock Festival in 1969. The moment was captured in the hit movie about the festival, and his image thus became familiar around the world. Satchidananda committed himself to the spiritual path in India in the 1940s, and a few years later his spiritual master sent him forth to teach people in other lands. He taught what he called Integral Yoga, meaning that the whole person—body, mind, and soul—should be involved in the spiritual quest. First in Sri Lanka and then in many other lands he undertook teaching tours, finally arriving in the United States in 1966. In due course he founded the Integral Yoga Institute, and by 1979 he had managed to raise the funds to purchase a 750-acre tract of land in Virginia where he opened a substantial intentional community known as Yogaville. There his followers built the LOTUS, the Light of Truth Universal Shrine, an unusual domed building in the shape of a lotus flower that embodied Satchidananda's inclusive outlook, providing niches for many religions and showing them as united by an upward flow of light. Satchidananda was the master of the Yogaville ashram until his death in 2002 at age eighty-seven. Since then his followers have continued the work of Integral Yoga, spreading Satchidananda's teachings through workshops and seminars at the ashram, as well as welcoming the many visitors who visit, especially to see the remarkable LOTUS.[14]

Another teacher whose career in some ways paralleled Satchidananda's was the Maharishi Mahesh Yogi, whose public visibility rivaled Satchidananda's not because of a Woodstock appearance, but because he became the guru of many persons prominent in American and European popular culture, most prominently the Beatles, who made a much-photographed pilgrimage to India to sit at his feet. For a time his meditation movement took the country by storm, with hundreds of thousands, or even millions, of Americans emptying their minds in meditation for twenty minutes twice a day. It was inevitable, perhaps, that such a movement would spawn an intentional community, and in the early 1970s the Maharishi's organization purchased the campus of the defunct Parsons College in Fairfield, Iowa, turning it into the Maharishi International University (later the Maharishi University of Management). The campus was not exactly an intentional community, but the meditators soon had a strong presence in the quintessential midwestern small town. The two intentional communities that arose among the meditators were discussed above, in chapter 3.[15]

One of the most flamboyant of the Indian-oriented spiritual teachers of the last quarter of the century was Ma Jaya Bhagavati, who founded Kashi Ashram in Florida in 1976. Joyce Green DiFiore was a Jewish housewife in New York City who began having visionary spiritual experiences in the early 1970s. An early visionary encounter with Jesus opened her to new spiritual paths and led her to India, seeking a guru and enlightenment. Once she returned to the United States she began teaching and fairly soon attracted some hundreds of students. In due course they purchased eighty acres of land near Sebastian, Florida, and began to develop a spiritual community. Kashi Ashram has always been open to all spiritual paths, and in the center of the community Ma's followers built shrines dedicated to Christianity, Hinduism, Buddhism, Judaism, Sikhism, and other religions.

Hindu themes dominate Kashi because, as Ma has said, it is more open and tolerant of diverse spiritual paths than most major religions are. But the real spiritual center of Kashi was (until her death in 2012) Ma herself, a boisterous, glamorous, witty woman whose high-energy darshans (teaching meetings) embodied what some have called "crazy wisdom." Kashi has a school, several businesses, and so far has continued its programs without Ma's dynamic presence.[16]

Mata Amritanandamayi has perhaps the most unusual way of relating to her followers of any Indian spiritual teacher: she hugs them. Often called simply "the hugging saint," Amma, as she is known, first developed a following in her home state of Kerala, India, and later became a world traveler as her far-flung following grew. Known for her humanitarian programs, she has, through her followers, provided services ranging from disaster relief to hospital work to antipoverty activities. In 1989 her followers built an ashram in San Ramon, California, known as the M.A. Center, that serves as her American headquarters; the group now also has a few small satellite ashrams in other parts of the country, as well as noncommunal centers in dozens of cities. The ashram residents, who are celibate, serve a much larger public that gathers weekly for service projects and other programs. Amma's work is not without controversy; she has not always kept to Indian norms. In fact her very status as a revered teacher is untraditional in a land in which that position is almost always reserved for males. She is devoted to gender equality and has ordained women as priests. Her following, which is predominantly female, is said to be in the millions, and those she has hugged in the tens of millions.[17]

After the well-known jazz saxophonist John Coltrane died in 1967, some of his devotees formed a church based on his music and canonized him: St. John Coltrane of the St. John Coltrane African Orthodox Church. That church has been active ever since in San Francisco. His widow, Alice Coltrane, however, took a different spiritual direction; she said she was receiving messages from God and meeting with spiritual persons of the past ranging from the Virgin Mary to Ramakrishna to the Buddha, as well as several living spiritual adepts, including Swami Satchidananda. She eventually took the name Swamini

Turiyasangitananda and founded the Shanti Anantam Ashram (now known as the Sai Anantam Ashram) near Los Angeles in 1983. She called her religion Vedic and described its practice as bhakti, the yoga of devotion. Nevertheless, she professed respect for all religions and elements from beyond the Hindu tradition were present in her teachings. Following her death in 2007 a group of followers continued to live at the ashram and at least for several years welcomed visitors to Sunday services.[18]

The ancient Indian religion of Jainism has an American communal presence as well. In 1983 the Jain monk Sushil Kumar, following a lengthy American tour, founded Siddhachalam near Blairstown, New Jersey. As the first major American Jain center, it attracted many members of the far-flung American Jain population, as well as converts to the faith. Jainism is known for its devotion to ahimsa, or noninjury, and the precept is followed carefully at the ashram. Siddhachalam has several temples as well as a meeting hall and regularly hosts visiting monks and nuns. It also functions as a nature preserve and in the spirit of ahimsa protects animals on the property. Members also have tree-planting days in the spring and fall.[19]

And Many More . . .

Ashrams based in Indian spiritual traditions are abundant in the West. Beyond those discussed above, several more were established between 1975 and 2000. The Arsha Vidya Gurukulam was founded in 1986 in Saylorsville, Pennsylvania, as a communal center for the Vedanta movement, which has had a communal presence in America since 1900 in the wake of Swami Vivekananda's triumphant appearance at the World's Parliament of Religions in 1893. In 1987 followers of the Indian ascetic Ramana Maharshi opened Arunachala Ashram in Queens, New York. The Rajarajeshwari Peetham, a community largely composed of persons of Indian descent but led by Caucasian American women, has been operating in New York State since 1978. Another female-led Hindu community is the Shree Maa Ashram, whose Indian teacher, Shree Maa, came to the United States and established an ashram in 1984. The Sanatana Dharma Foundation has been operating a spiritual community at St. Helena, California, since 1977. The American-born Maharishi Sadashiva Isham created an original blend of teachings from various religions, but especially Hinduism, and founded the Society for Ascension near Asheville, North Carolina, in 1995.[20] And, as always, there have been many more.

Buddhist Communities

Quite a few Buddhist communities were founded before 1975, and although that stream has slowed somewhat, several new meditation communities appeared in the latter years of the century. Probably the most prolific of the post-1975 founders was the Chinese master Hsuan Hua, founder of the Sino-American Buddhist Association (now the Dharma Realm Buddhist Association), who came to the United States in 1962 and began opening American teaching and meditation centers. In 1976 Hua acquired the extensive premises of a California state hospital for the criminally insane at Talmage, near Ukiah, which had dozens of buildings on its nearly five hundred acres of land. Called the Sagely City of Ten Thousand Buddhas, the monastery has both male and female residents and houses schools and other projects. Hua went on to found several other communal centers as well:

- the Gold Wheel Sagely Monastery, founded in Los Angeles in 1976
- the Snow Mountain Monastery, founded in Washington in 1983
- the Gold Summit Sagely Monastery, founded in Seattle in 1984
- the Avatamsaka Vihara, founded in Bethesda, Maryland, in 1990
- the Long Beach Monastery, founded in Long Beach, California, in 1990.
- the City of the Dharma Realm, founded in West Sacramento, California, in 1993
- the Berkeley Buddhist Monastery, founded in Berkeley, California, in 1994

- the Blessings, Prosperity, and Longevity Monastery, founded in Long Beach, California, in 1994
- the Gold Sage Monastery, founded in San Jose, California, in 1995[21]

The Sagely City of 10,000 Buddhas was evidently prosperous enough that it could help another fledgling monastery as well, one in a different Buddhist tradition. The Abhayagiri Buddhist Monastery describes itself as situated in the Thai Forest tradition, a branch of Theravada Buddhism that is quite different from the Mahayana of Master Hua. The communal monastery was envisioned in the 1980s after visits to the United States by the Thai monk Ajahn Sumedho, and finally created in 1995 following the donation of 120 acres of land (later expanded to 250 acres) along the Russian River north of Redwood Valley, California, some fifteen miles from the Sagely City. It was initially quite small, consisting of one modest house and a meditation and teaching hall in a converted garage, but its industrious residents have expanded the facilities, erecting several other buildings, including a large reception hall and kitchen. Guests are accommodated within the monastery's tight limits, but public teaching is generally done in San Francisco. In 2014 Abhayagiri reported twenty residents, eighteen of them male, and work was under way on further construction projects. A 2006 film, "Fearless Mountain" (the English translation of the monastery's Pali name), provides a detailed look at the monastery and its monks.[22] A California wildfire gravely threatened the monastery in 2017, but was stopped just short of the buildings.

In 1967 Denis Lingwood, who had taken the spiritual name Urgyen Sangharakshita, with other English Buddhists founded the Friends of the Western Buddhist Order. Sangharakshita had studied Buddhism extensively for twenty years, associating with several teachers from different branches of Buddhism—Theravada, Mahayana, and Vajrayana. FWBO reflected the diversity of Sangharakshita's background; from the beginning it did not situate itself in a single Buddhist lineage or school, but sought to teach and live what might be called Buddhist basics that transcend any single path—meditation, ethical living, ritual practice, study of the tradition, creative arts, and a sangha, or spiritual order. It also deemphasized external trappings, such as special robes or other clothing for Buddhist practice, trying to craft a Buddhism that worked in the Western world while remaining faithful to traditional Buddhism. In 2010 the name of the FWBO was changed to the Triratna Buddhist Community; by then the organization had expanded considerably beyond its English base, and in 1985 the American branch founded a residential community known as Aryaloka Buddhist Retreat Center near Newmarket, New Hampshire. Members purchased a small acreage with two joined geodesic domes that had served the previous owner of the property as a house. Aryaloka now houses members of the sangha and serves a larger public with weekly meditation gatherings and other programs.[23]

Many Zen communities had been established in America by 1975, but at least one more emerged during the last quarter of the century. D. T. Suzuki was a well-educated Japanese intellectual who became a Zen practitioner and an early teacher of the Zen tradition in the United States and Europe. In the late nineteenth and early twentieth centuries he lived for several years in Illinois doing editorial and translation work. His major impact, however, came in the 1950s; after initially traveling to the United States for a lecture tour, he went on to teach at Columbia University and wrote several books that helped propel American interest in Zen. Although Suzuki died at age ninety-five in 1966, his influence continued through the Zen centers and other organizations founded by him and his students, notably through the Zen Studies Society, which had been established in 1956 to promulgate Suzuki's work. Revitalized under a younger teacher from Japan, Eido Tai Shimano-roshi, in 1965, the ZSS opened a meditation center, the New York Zendo, in 1968, and then in 1976 founded a rural retreat center called the Dai Bosatsu Zendo on 1,400 acres of land in the Catskill Mountains in New York State. There residents (including laypersons as well as ordained monks and nuns) live as a sangha in traditional Rinzai Zen monastic fashion, engaging in work and meditation under the direction of a resident abbot.

Soon another monastic center opened, again in the Catskills.[24] Known as the Zen Mountain Monastery, it was founded in 1980 by John Daido Loori, one of the several well-known students of Taizan Maezumi Rōshi, who was probably best known as the founder of the Zen Center of Los Angeles. After studying Zen for several years in New York and Los Angeles, Loori became an ordained monk in 1977 and soon thereafter founded the Mountains and Rivers Order of Zen. In 1980 he purchased a 230-acre tract of land with a large house that remains a center of the community's activities. Although nominally rooted in the Soto school of Zen, Loori, like his spiritual master Maezumi, drew on Rinzai as well as Soto teachings and practices. Extensive facilities have been added since the community's founding, including residential buildings, hermitages, and gardens. The community's life has continued since Loori's death in 2009; short-term and long-term residents, lay and monastic, follow rigorous disciplines of work and Zen practice.[25]

The Dai Bosatsu Zendo and the Zen Mountain Monastery were outposts of Japanese Zen, but by the time they arrived Korean Zen had an American presence as well. The Korean Master Seung Sahn had gathered a following in the early 1970s, but only toward the end of that decade did his Providence (Rhode Island) Zen Center establish a communal headquarters, the Diamond Hill Zen Monastery. It was less cloistered than some of the other residential Zen centers, with members often holding outside jobs to support the community.[26] Meanwhile, at about the same time, another Korean Zen Master, Chang Sik Kim, opened the American Buddhist Shim Gum Do Association in Brighton, Massachusetts, where a monastery soon was established as well. Known as Shim Gwang Sa, the Mind Light Temple, it has housed as many as several dozen monks who help serve a larger noncommunal constituency. Shim Gum Do is said to be a complete system that combines traditional silent meditation with active meditation, the latter including various kinds of martial arts.[27]

Tibetan Buddhism has had a strong appeal since the arrival in America of spiritual teachers who fled their country as the Chinese swept over it in 1959. Two of the earliest arrived before 1975: Chögyam Trungpa moved to the United States from the United Kingdom in 1970 and established several retreat centers and monasteries, some of them communal; Tarthang Tulku settled in Berkeley, California, in 1972 and similarly opened several communal centers. Both of those early teachers and their institutions were discussed in the previous volume in this series.

More communal development of Tibetan Buddhism came after 1975, usually with the arrival of new Tibetan teachers or, sometimes, with the rise of Americans who had studied and meditated with Tibetan masters. At least a dozen new monasteries and other teaching centers appeared across the United States.

One of the first was the Vajrapani Institute. In 1977 the students of Lama Thubten Yeshe and Lama Thubten Zopa were given thirty acres of land in the Santa Cruz Mountains in California. Over the next several years they constructed a building to house a prayer hall, library, offices, and a kitchen and dining room. The institute is affiliated with the Foundation for the Preservation of the Mahayana Tradition, and as such is related to an extensive international network of monasteries and teaching centers. Another communal center, the Milarepa Center of Barnet, Vermont, founded in 1981, is also a part of the FPMT.

Some of the more prominent of the other communal Tibetan Buddhist centers opened over the next two decades were these:

- Karma Triyana Dharmachakra, begun near Woodstock, New York, in 1980
- Namgyal Monastery—a branch of the Namgyal Monastery in Dharamsala, India—founded in 1992 in Ithaca, New York
- Rigdzin Ling, founded in 1993 in Junction City, California, by H. E. Chagdud Tulku
- Tara Mandala at Pagosa Springs, Colorado, founded in 1993 by the American-born Lama Tsultrim Allione
- Tashi Chöling, built in the 1980s near Ashland, Oregon, under the leadership of the Venerable Gyatrul

Buddhism grew substantially in the latter years of the twentieth century, and at the same time millions of gay and lesbian Americans were emerging from closets and forming a new civil rights movement that has been one of the most influential social movements of the age. Perhaps it was inevitable that the two new and influential movements would merge. Gay Buddhists joined several of the newly founded communal retreat centers (often as monks pledged to celibacy), and at the same time some new, explicitly gay-focused centers were created. One prominent example was the Hartford Street Zen Center in San Francisco, which was founded by gay members of the San Francisco Zen Center, the leading Buddhist institution in the city, with a constituency that was primarily non-Asian. The center began as an interest group, the Gay Buddhist Club (founded in 1980 and later known as Maitri), and eventually turned the house in which some of its members lived into a communal Zen institution. The resident members of the Hartford Street Center are fairly few in number, but they serve a larger group of gay Buddhists who gather for meditation and teaching.[28]

As with Hindu communities, these brief sketches of Buddhist communities and monasteries are hardly exhaustive; Buddhism has found a substantial following among non–Asian Americans, as well as Asian Americans, and the drive to channel commitment and practice into communal venues has been strong. No doubt we have not seen the last of such enterprises.

East Meets West

Some communities with substantial grounding in Asian religions draw from other traditions as well. One of them is Heartlight Center of Sturgis, Michigan, which shows its inclusion of Asian themes with such self-enunciated goals as "to break free from the bondage of our ego world" and "to finally move out of illusion into reality." On the other hand, the life and writings of St. Francis of Assisi are the most important of all of the sacred texts and other inspirational works of East and West used by the community. One of Heartlight's projects is the distribution of hand-painted angel figures to nursing homes, disaster areas, and other places with people (and even animals) in distress, conveying a message of hope in hard times. The small community is solidly grounded in the spiritual quest, but no one path dominates to the exclusion of others.[29]

Another community combining similarly diverse traditions and pursuing a spiritual foundation that incorporates Tibetan Buddhism, certain Native American traditions, and some New Age precepts has taken shape under the leadership of the Cherokee teacher Dhyani Ywahoo. She established the Sunray Peace Village in Lincoln, Vermont, in the early 1980s, and has attracted a following consisting largely of nonnative people. Ywahoo's practice seeks peace for the individual as well as for the world, and has a strong environmental element, a dedication to respect for and preservation of the planet. Although Sunray has been designated a teaching center (and Ywahoo a teacher) for certain schools of Tibetan Buddhism, the teachers of its workshops and courses come from a wide variety of spiritual backgrounds, all of which are welcome and respected. Sunray Peace Village has resident members, and small communal living situations exist elsewhere as well among Ywahoo's followers.[30]

A variation on the theme of combining Eastern and Western spiritualities has arisen in the San Luis valley of Colorado just outside the town of Crestone on land known as the Baca Grande. The Baca had been a huge Spanish land grant that was being sold in pieces for homesites. In 1978 Hanne and Maurice Strong arrived in the area and began purchasing some two hundred thousand acres of the grant land. They established a charitable trust, the Manitou Foundation, and then began parceling the land out to a variety of religious and educational groups for retreat centers and ashrams. Quite a few groups accepted the offer of free land in the remote, high, and semiarid spiritual center, and by century's end communities representing a good range of the world's religions were present. Over time the spiritual communities that landed at the Baca included the Crestone Mountain Zen Center, the Haidakhandi Universal Ashram (Hindu), the Sri Aurobindo Learning Center (Hindu/Interfaith), the Karma Thegsum Tashi

Gomang Stupa and Retreat Center (Tibetan Buddhist), Sanctuary House (interfaith, with a replica of the labyrinth of Chartres Cathedral), and the Nada Hermitage (a Carmelite Catholic monastery). The Baca also has noncommunal religious sites and monuments, most notably, probably, a ziggurat that recreates the pyramidal religious structures found in several places in the ancient Middle East.

Beyond the Major World Religions: Other Religious and Spiritual Communities

American Indian-focused Communities

In the 1960s era a wave of fascination of and admiration for American Indians swept the country, and several new communities sought to perpetuate traditional Indian ways. In a sense the real communities of Indians were the reservations, but my definition of intentional communities excludes them. In my understanding, one of the elements of an intentional community is separation from the mainstream society; as I have put it in an earlier work, "somehow the group must have a sense of being withdrawn or set apart from conventional society and operating in pursuit of a goal that transcends simply living together."[31] That understanding excludes Indian tribes, which were not withdrawn from a larger society, but *were* the dominant societies in their own environments, especially before the arrival of Euro-Americans.

What did occur in the 1960s, however, were several attempts by non-Indians to recreate traditional Indian culture, or at least to emulate Indian ways, attempts that were often led by Indian spiritual teachers who wanted to spread their teachings to a larger public. Thus came about such communities as Meta Tantay and the Bear Tribe, both mentioned briefly in the predecessor to this volume.[32] Few such Indian-led intentional communities appear to have been founded after 1975, but at least one did emerge: Kanatsiohareke, or Ga Na Jo Ha Le Ke, was founded in 1993 as one expression of what has been a revival of traditional ways among the Mohawk of New York State. One group of Mohawks left their reservation for a new location near Fonda, New

York, in the original homeland of the tribe in the Mohawk River Valley. On some 372 acres of land the community members are working to preserve the language and culture of their ancestors, farming and raising livestock but also conducting workshops (making traditional baskets and drums and learning traditional dances, for example) and holding festivals that perpetuate traditional rituals. By the end of the century Kanatsiohareke had about a dozen resident members.[33]

Beyond such communitarian projects of native peoples themselves, the emulation of Indian traditions continued in many new communities. To cite just one example, a community called Coldfoot Creek was founded in the late 1970s on 520 acres of land near Pembine in northern Wisconsin. The community did not appear to have had ethnic Indians among its members, but it made its sentiments clear in its statement to the public:

> In the land where the Hermit Thrush sings with the rippling Tannin Waters dwells a tiny band of gentle forest people who seek their place with the Earth, sky and water. We dance, sing, work for change, hunt and gather that which Earth Mother bounteously provides. We search the ways of our native predecessors, that we may grow in balance with our woodland king and in peace with our fellow humans.[34]

There can be no doubt that American Indian spirituality has resonated and continues to resonate with large numbers of Americans, including some who have lived in intentional communities.

Pagan Communities

Modern Paganism claims to be reviving religions that have roots a thousand years and more in the past, but its revival (some would say creation) of the old ways has come only in the last few decades. In the 1960s and 1970s several Pagan organizations appeared on the scene, and with them intentional communities of Pagans arose as well. One of the earliest American Pagan groups was the Church of All Worlds, founded in the 1960s; it was not wholly communal, but some local chapters had members living in communal "nests." A more substantial Church of All Worlds communal enterprise came into being in 1982, when the church received, as a bequest, a fifty-five acre tract of land on the sprawling Greenfield Ranch outside Ukiah, California. A small group known as Annwfn lives cooperatively on the land, which serves as ceremonial center for a much larger Pagan population.[35] In a similar vein, in 1987 Pagans in the Bloomington, Indiana, area established an intentional community based on a 109-acre tract of land they called the Lothlorien Nature Sanctuary. The community itself has never been large (it reported seventeen resident adults and children in 2010), but Lothlorien is also an events center, and hundreds travel to the land for festivals and private nature retreats.[36]

Several other small Pagan intentional communities exist as well, although they often try to keep low profiles due to popular prejudice against those who take the name Pagan. There are also dozens of communities, not expressly Pagan in orientation, that nevertheless incorporate elements of Paganism into their lives—celebrations held on Pagan holidays, for example.

Spiritual but Not (Necessarily or Conventionally) Religious

One of the fastest-growing categories of American religiosity in recent decades is populated by those who consider themselves "spiritual but not religious." Inevitably, that means different things to different people, but it often identifies a person with a sense of spirit, of reality beyond that of the material world, who does not find fulfillment in any single organized religion. Many of them could be called New Age believers, but many more simply deny fitting any category at all. Dozens of communities that could be thus characterized were founded in the last quarter of the twentieth century; a few will serve as examples of that genre.

Of the communities that identify as part of the New Age movement, none has been more prominent than Findhorn, the Scottish community founded in 1962 by a married couple and one friend who were guided by a "still small voice within" and empathy with nature.

Findhorn was described in an earlier chapter that does not need recapitulation here, but suffice it to say that many of the thousands of spiritual seekers who have visited that pioneering New Age community went home determined to found new communities along similar lines. In the United States the most visible of them has been Sirius, founded in 1978 near Amherst, Massachusetts; it too has been discussed earlier.

However, New Age communities do not end with Sirius. Several other American communities have similarly espoused eclectic and inclusive spiritual paths and principles. Sparrow Hawk Village, for example, has its foundation in the Light of Christ Community Church, an inclusive New Age organization. Founder Carol W. Parrish had a near-death experience in 1959 that propelled her on a spiritual quest, and in 1974, with her husband Charles Harra, she founded a community called Villa Serena in Florida. A sense of spiritual direction led them to relocate to land near Tahlequah in northeastern Oklahoma in 1981, and there they founded the Sancta Sophia Seminary, which trained ministers in esoteric and metaphysical wisdom traditions, as well as a residential community, called Sparrow Hawk Village after the nearby Sparrow Hawk Mountain. However, declining enrollments and resulting financial problems caused the seminary to close in 2012 and list its property for sale. Sparrow Hawk Village continues, nevertheless, no longer with the strong communal ties and sense of the spiritual quest that characterized its early years. At least a dozen other communities founded between 1975 and 2000 shared the inclusive spiritual outlook of Sirius and Sparrow Hawk.[37]

Venerable resorts, especially hot springs resorts, have hosted quite a few communities over the last century or more. Existing lodging can house community members as well as guests, and a well-run hot spring can be a magnet for paying visitors, thus giving the community a viable business. One communal enterprise of that sort was Healing Waters, which in 1977 opened in a resort previously known as Indian Hot Springs, located near Eden, Arizona. The communal group that occupied the site numbered about thirty; the members operated a spiritual growth and holistic healing center, offering a steady stream of workshops and seminars. Anastasia Machacek, who spent time there as a child with her mother, wrote in her memoir,

> During the night, the sky grew really dark and as big as any I had ever seen before, since there were no trees or buildings to block the view. The nights were peaceful and a bit chilly. We went to the communal kitchen to eat all of our meals and were served in accordance to the strictest of diets.
>
> Visitors came to Healing Waters primarily to cleanse. The center offered a variety of all-natural, organic, vegetarian foods, including an assortment of completely raw foods. They offered every type of freshly squeezed juice, along with an array of sprouts—not just alfalfa sprouts. Mung bean sprouts, sunflower sprouts, lentil sprouts, sprouted soybeans, sprouted wheatgrass—you name it, they sprouted it. Every morning they served freshly-squeezed orange and grapefruit juices, as well as cleansing drinks made from oranges, grapefruits and lemons mixed with [cayenne], garlic, and seaweed powder.
>
> Most of the kids got tired of all the healthy food. We rebelled by getting someone to take us into town for pizza or Mexican food.[38]

Other communities with similar goals for spiritual and physical development managed to operate without hot springs. Personal growth and holistic health were the core of programs offered by the Joy Lake Community in the Sierra Nevada near Reno, Nevada. The Spring Hill Community in Ashby, Massachusetts, offered similar New Age programs, with an emphasis on music and dance. Some such communities did not endure; the Alcyone Light Center, a community with similar goals and programs located near Hornbrook, California, never attracted very many members and finally lost its land to foreclosure in 1995. And some simply evolved into other forms. The Reevis Mountain School of Self-Reliance near Globe, Arizona, started with a focus on New Age spirituality, but over time became a business, a secular organic farm and nature retreat with classes as well as a mail-order business in herbal medicines. The spirit leads in many directions.

Most of the communities based in the various branches of the Theosophical movement were founded in the late nineteenth and early twentieth centuries, but a few have come along later. One was the group that eventually took the name Church Universal and Triumphant and made a big media splash in the 1980s, when the apocalyptic side of the church's belief system became known. Mark Prophet emerged in the 1950s as the leader of the Summit Lighthouse, which was inspired by the theosophically derived I AM movement. In 1966 the movement moved its headquarters to Colorado Springs, Colorado, where its first limited experiments in communal living took place. But Mark Prophet died suddenly in 1973 and leadership passed to his widow, Elizabeth Clare Prophet, who had been Mark's successor-in-training for several years. In 1978 she relocated the headquarters of the movement now known as the Church Universal and Triumphant to Malibu, outside Los Angeles, and three years later it bought a twelve-thousand-acre ranch from the financial publisher Malcolm Forbes. By then the apocalyptic strain was becoming dominant in her teachings, with predictions of war, civil disorder, and natural catastrophes she said she was channeling from spiritual masters. Soon other purchases more than doubled the size of the church's holdings, and local controversy surfaced over the potential environmental destructiveness of the large acreage with many major building projects. Before long it became known that the church was building large underground shelters to protect the members from disasters, including, many of them believed, a nuclear attack by the Soviet Union, and was reportedly amassing a large store of weapons; thus the conflict soared. But then Prophet made a mistake that is classic in the history of millennialism: she set dates in late 1989 and early 1990 for nuclear war. As many as three or four thousand believers had gathered in the vicinity of church property by early 1990, and with the failure of prophecy many of them left, in many cases with financial problems because of their payments to the ranch. The communal population at headquarters was slashed, in stages, by as much as ninety percent from its peak size of seven hundred. Some members left the organization to start their own movements, some of them claiming to be receiving messages from distant masters in the well-established Theosophical tradition. At the end of the decade Prophet was diagnosed with Alzheimer's and relinquished control of the organization. She died in 2009. Although the church and community have continued since, the days of conflict and controversy over what was once one of the largest communities in the United States seem well in the past.[39]

These samples hardly exhaust the list of spiritual communities founded in the last quarter of the twentieth century. Many of them have kept low profiles, but the impulse to pursue the spiritual search in a communal setting was alive and well as the twentieth century moved toward its conclusion.

6 Communities on Purpose

The previous chapter sketched the stories of some communities gathered around specific religious or spiritual precepts. In the late twentieth century, however, a great many communities were organized around principles and concepts that do not exactly qualify as spiritual, but are nevertheless dedicated to missions that usually are centered on human services. Herewith I provide a sampling of a few communities with a wide variety of purpose-driven commitments.

Intentional communities have long been centers of political and social activism, and the period in question has seen plenty of such ventures. Work for world peace, to name only one prominent example, has long been central to any number of communities. The post-1975 period did not see a great many such communities founded; more typically, ones from the past continued their work, as in the case of the Catholic Worker, whose members feed and house the down-and-out of society as well as promote such causes as world peace and economic justice; or the Sojourners Community, whose members are active in peace and justice causes and publish a magazine, *Sojourners*, expounding socially progressive evangelical Protestantism. But a few new ones did emerge nevertheless.

One was the Doreá Peace Community, which was active in the 1980s and possibly thereafter. It began in the late 1970s when two families settled on eighty-nine acres of rural land in Polk County, Wisconsin. The adults of the two families were committed Christians; one husband and wife, Max and Nancy Rice, were both Methodist ministers who had divinity degrees from Garrett Theological Seminary, and members who joined later included a Lutheran minister who served a local Lutheran church, and a former Capuchin monk. All community members were committed to social justice work, with peace a central focus. In those latter days of the cold war a major focus was nuclear disarmament; members organized several direct action events, in some cases getting arrested for their actions. Some were war tax resisters who refused to support a government that maintained a vast military and that invaded other countries. In 1979 the Rices founded the Wisconsin War Tax Resistance Alternative Fund into which they (and others) paid the amount they owed for federal income taxes. Knowing that the federal government sometimes seized property belonging to tax resisters, they put their land into a trust that they did not own. They pursued simple living, keeping their income and expenses minimal, and sought to minimize their impact on the environment by building passive solar, earth-bermed houses. The community seems to have continued through most of the 1980s, after which its public face receded.[1]

Service Communities, Spiritual and Secular

Several communities dedicated to service to society, often spiritual in basis, marked the communitarian scene in the latter years of the century. Those years saw the beginnings of what became an important Christian communal movement that soon became known as the New Monasticism. The movement's origins are difficult to identify definitively; some of its communities go back as far as the 1970s, while most are more recent, with several coming after 2000. The term "New Monasticism" gained currency with Jonathan Wilson's book *Living Faithfully in a Fragmented World*, which was published in 1997.[2] Generally, the New Monastic communities differ from traditional monasticism most visibly in their acceptance of both men and women, including married couples and their children. Beyond that they are committed to communal living and sharing of resources; most of the communities are located in socially marginal areas and attempt to serve the underprivileged in their neighborhoods. They also have disciplined spiritual lives. Although they can be categorized as evangelical Protestants theologically, they differ from the majority of their fellow evangelicals in remaining skeptical of high-level political activism and identification with the American nation-state. Instead, their commitment is to the provision of service to people in immediate need. They seek to live simply and to share whatever they have. Some have compared their local communes to Catholic Worker houses. One New Monastic group is the Potter Street Community, which was founded in the 1990s in Philadelphia and serves its neighbors with a meals program and a community garden. Some of the groups associated with the Shalom Mission Communities, such as the Church of the Servant King and Church of the Sojourners, discussed above, also embody many of the New Monastic principles and identify with the movement.[3]

Social services missions are found in Christian communities far beyond the circles of the New Monasticism, of course. One faith-based community that carries on a vital service program is Jubilee Partners, founded in 1979 at Comer, Georgia. Jubilee's roots lie in the Koinonia Community of Americus, Georgia, which was founded in 1942 by Clarence Jordan and others as a "demonstration plot for the Kingdom of God." Koinonia was interracial, something that was daringly radical in South Georgia in the days when Jim Crow racism was still flourishing, and it sought to lift up its impoverished neighbors. One of its projects was the building of homes for the poor, homes that were sold at bargain prices with interest-free loans; that effort became the seed from which grew Habitat for Humanity, now a worldwide endeavor. From Koinonia's matrix of outreach programs came Jubilee Partners, which took as its own special task the provision of shelter and advocacy for refugees from other countries, many of them fleeing persecution in Latin America. Jubilee provides not only food and housing but English lessons and respite from persecution. Guests and the two dozen or so full-time members work side by side, growing much of their own food on their 258-acre tract of land and sharing most of their resources. They also share in spiritual life, with daily prayer and devotional gatherings. The visiting refugees typically stay for several months, acclimating themselves to their new lives, and then depart for new homes in the United States and beyond.[4]

Many other communities have members just as dedicated to their service work as are the people of Jubilee. One good example is the Open Door, started in 1981 in Atlanta, Georgia, by Ed Loring and his wife, Murphy Davis. The community is housed in an old hotel; in a fashion reminiscent of a Catholic Worker house, the thirty or so members of the Open Door serve their community in the most basic of ways, housing the homeless and feeding the hungry. And like the Catholic Workers the community members are strong workers for social justice, fighting racism, working to create jobs, and demonstrating for peace. The religious element is not neglected; worship and Bible study are regular parts of Open Door life. The service the community provides is widely esteemed in Atlanta.[5]

Many other communities have similarly conducted their outreach work in the cities in which they are located. In Jackson, Mississippi, for example, a community within the Voice of Calvary Church took up communal living in pursuit of the extensive outreach programs of the church. Voice of Calvary had grown out of the civil rights work of John Perkins and was interracial from its beginning in 1973, but in the mid-1980s a group seeking deeper commitment purchased six acres of property with an old farmhouse. Thus, after some renovation work, emerged the Antioch Community, whose members lived a common life for the next twelve years, sharing just about everything—food, money, and living space—while providing basic services to people in their neighborhood and expanding to encompass several other nearby houses. One member later noted that the members were normal, flawed people with the usual weaknesses—a "motley crew" that included a computer programmer, a social worker, a single mother, and a secretary—but "we did not accept 'the way things are' as the way things must be. We dared to imagine a different world, to give ourselves to it through fidelity in sickness and health, and to seek God's help."[6] That communal experiment eventually closed following the death of a key member in 1998, but the Voice of Calvary continues, with strong outreach programs to the larger Jackson community.[7]

Quite a few communities providing public service were focused on health, healing, and general well-being. In a country in which millions of people lack access to good health care, many clinics are run as charities, and quite a few of them have at least some staff members who live communally. In Salinas, California, for example, the Companions of the Way began their work of providing food and health care to the poor in 1982; the members lived communally in a small housing complex called Mercy Center. Many other communities provided similar services; some combined conventional health care with alternative therapies and preventive programs. The Great Oaks School of Health, which operated in Creswell, Oregon, from 1975 to 1982, offered a largely alternative series of health therapies and saw a number of its patients join the intentional community that operated the services. In yet another case a group called the Medical Opera, which had taken shape in San Francisco, moved to Huerfano County, Colorado, in 1975 and opened a simple clinic that served both the many counterculturists, such as those at the Libre community, who had moved into the area and the longer-term resident population, which was largely poor. Maharishi Vedic City, a community of practitioners of Transcendental Meditation near Fairfield, Iowa, that was founded in 1991, provides a range of alternative health-care services as well as a spa in a health center called the Raj.[8]

The counterculture put a heavy focus on the body, so it isn't surprising that several communes were devoted to massage, hot tubs, saunas, yoga, and other practices that were sometimes about health, and sometimes more about simply feeling good. One such community took shape at Breitenbush Hot Springs in 1977. Springs that had been discovered many years earlier were developed into a resort in the 1920s, but it eventually closed. The facility was vacant until 1977, when Alex Beamer purchased it with the aim of making it the home of an intentional community. Thus started what has since become a worker-owned cooperative that operates the modest resort as its collective business. Many visitors simply go to Breitenbush to soak in the waters or heat up in the sauna; others go to organized retreats and other activities.[9]

One of the longest-established networks of service communities is the Camphill movement which, like the Waldorf Schools and other initiatives, derived from the anthroposophy of Rudolf Steiner. The first Camphill community was envisioned by the Austrian pediatrician Karl König in 1939 near Aberdeen, Scotland, where König and his associates were offered the use of a large estate (although König and his male associates were sent to wartime internment camps and the founding of the community was actually effected by the group's women).[10] From that beginning the international network has grown to over one hundred communities, including about a dozen in the United States. The communities are dedicated to helping individuals with developmental disabilities, in keeping with König's belief that all humans have healthy personalities despite their outward limitations. In the Camphill model all community residents, both those with disabilities and those who work with them, live together. Most of the communities are in rural locations and are engaged in farming, although some have other activities and businesses instead of, or in addition to, agriculture.

The communitarian predecessors of the Camphill movement came to the United States with the establishment in 1926 of the Threefold Community in Spring Valley, New York, which offered anthroposophical educational programs and a retirement village, among other things. Other anthroposophically focused communities followed, including Sunny Valley Farm in Copake, New York. Although the Sunny Valley founders, Gladys and Bill Hahn, moved their work to Pennsylvania, Sunny Valley Farm was purchased by another anthroposophist, Toni Roothbert, who made it available for what was really the first American Camphill community, Camphill Village USA, founded in 1961.[11]

Since then the movement has grown steadily, with a good deal of its growth taking place in the last quarter of the twentieth century. That period saw the opening of Plowshare Farm in Greenfield, New Hampshire; Camphill California in Soquel; Camphill Minnesota in Sauk Centre; Triform Camphill in Hudson, New York; and Camphill Soltane in Glenmoore, Pennsylvania. The movement's success and compassion in working with its members in need has been widely noticed and increasingly emulated. Between 1975 and 2000 several other communities with the same ideals and procedures were established outside the formal Camphill network, among them Libertee World in Seattle, Washington; the Lukas Community in Temple, New Hampshire; the Cadmus Life-Sharing Association in Great Barrington, Massachusetts; Community Homestead in Osceola, Wisconsin; and the Four Winds Community in Temple, New Hampshire. Since 2000 still other similar communities have been founded. Many communities have specific missions, and the Camphill and similar communities have outstanding track records in pursuing their compassionate goals.

Colonies for the Arts

Artists have been banding together in collective enclaves for many decades, if not centuries. The nineteenth century saw an outburst of artists' colonies in Europe and then the United States, and later in the century a wave of communal or at least cooperative settlements accompanied the spread of the arts and crafts movement that had been spurred by such creative souls as John Ruskin and William Morris. Just before and after the turn of the twentieth century the United States saw the establishment of the Roycrofters, Byrdcliffe, Rose Valley, and several other art colonies in various American locations. Another wave of such projects came with the communes of the 1960s era. Drop City, which can plausibly be counted as the first hippie commune (1965), was founded by visual artists. Then came such communities as Libre, located not far from Drop City in southern Colorado and populated mainly by visual artists; Packer Corners and Montague Farm in Vermont and Massachusetts, both with healthy populations of writers; and Synergia Ranch, which became widely known for its entertainment programs, and especially for its troupe called the Theater of All Possibilities. All of these arts communities were profiled in the earlier volumes in this series.

Collective pursuit of the arts continued throughout the twentieth century and beyond. Some artists' communities were ambitious, as in the case of the Apex Belltown Co-op in Seattle. It was founded in the early 1980s by a group largely made up of artists who wanted affordable housing where they could do their work; over time the membership base expanded beyond the arts and came to include "cooperative-minded folks, including artists, craftspersons, activists, longshoremen, musicians, poets, plumbers, geeks, and all sorts of other good people."[12] The founding group purchased an old hotel building and after prodigious investments of labor and money had a collective residence for around twenty-five members. Private living spaces are complemented by collective kitchens and bathrooms; members share expenses and upkeep chores, thus enjoying reasonably priced housing in Seattle's downtown.

Sometimes communities that are centered on artistic endeavors also support other interests. The community called Mariposa Grove from the beginning has had two core foci: the arts and social activism. Hank Obermeyer was an activist who envisioned such a two-track community, and in November 1998, he and a group of friends found the property that would be the community's home, three adjacent houses in north Oakland, California. Then the work began, a renovation project that lasted three years, creating apartments and common spaces for community members. Obermeyer owned the property for the first few years but then sold it to a limited-equity land trust. The group adopted a condominium form of ownership that set permanent limits on resale prices, which otherwise were increasing rapidly in their neighborhood. The community has continued since and has followed its original twin focus, with visual artists and musicians as well as others who embrace activism. Members eat some meals together and share common space that includes an art studio, a workshop, and, in the common outdoor yards, gardens and fruit trees.[13]

Sometimes artistic enclaves run into resistance from neighbors, and such has been the experience of Bellyacres, where an intentional community is interwoven with a performing arts center that features circus and juggling classes and performances as well as a local farmers' market. SPACE, the Seaview Performing Arts Center for Education, is nestled into twelve acres of tropical jungle on the Big Island of Hawai'i. The Bellyacres community, an "artistic ecovillage," as its members called it, was begun in 1987, and members set out recovering an old homestead that was being engulfed by the jungle as a first step in building a sustainable community. In the early 2010s, however, local conflicts emerged. The community was accused of building illegal structures and encroaching on public land adjoining its property. Although the community sought changes in state law that would promote sustainability and alternative building practices, it was not successful, and by about 2015 the community had closed and the members dispersed.[14]

Some artists' collectives were, inevitably, fairly short-lived. Compound "i" was located in a warehouse in an industrial part of Oakland, California. The resident artists used the expansive space not only for living but for artistic work, including performances and exhibitions. The vegan collective shared chores and meals; it was founded in 1993 but it seems to have vanished a year or two later.[15] Similarly the Art Colony at Eden Falls, in Berry Creek, California, announced itself to the world in 1993 as "a loose association of artists, retirees, and nature lovers of all ages, races, and religions." But it seems not to have survived a great deal longer.[16]

It is probably an understatement to note that most, if not all, communities have artists among their members, and artistic endeavors—visual arts, architecture, music, writing—can be found just about anywhere a community exists. Intentional communities are creative ventures that look at new ways to build social institutions, and just as monasteries of old were great centers of artistic expression, so today's communities have flourishing arts scenes.

A New Model: Ganas and the Pursuit of Feedback Learning

Most communities can be categorized, but Ganas defies any easy pigeonholing. It might be seen as a community that seeks psychological health and wholeness for its members, but that would overlook the fact that quite a few of its members don't participate in activities promoting those goals. It might be seen as a community out to serve its larger community or neighborhood, with its second-hand stores and other involvements in its local area, but some members work at jobs elsewhere and are not deeply involved with local activities. What Ganas has achieved, in any event, is stability; at this writing it is closing in on forty years of stable existence and slow but steady growth.

The pillar and matriarch of Ganas until her death in 2015 was Mildred Gordon. After studying biofeedback in San Francisco she created her own version of it, calling it Feedback Learning, which involves sessions in which participants identify one person's strengths and weaknesses and suggest ways the person can improve—a process rather reminiscent of "mutual criticism" at the nineteenth-century Oneida Community, or the "Gestalt-O-Rama" of Kerista in San Francisco in the 1970s. Gordon and five others founded a community based on Feedback Learning in 1979 on New York City's Staten Island. Starting with a single house, the community gradually expanded until it owned eight houses for some seventy-five members (as of 2016) and several buildings for the community's retail stores, all resale shops (books, furniture, clothing) known as "Every Thing Goes." The houses are mostly connected by boardwalks and residents share gardens and other amenities. The name Ganas is a Spanish word that the community translates as meaning "motivation sufficient to act."

Membership in Ganas is not all of one kind. A "core group" of about a dozen is fully communal, sharing incomes and assets. Beyond the core, members have varying levels of commitment to the community. A second group has members who generally (but not always) participate in decision-making and Feedback Learning, but do not pool their incomes. The third and largest group consists of people who agree to live by the rules and customs of the community and to communicate interactively with others but are otherwise less involved than the first two groups.

Finances are private, each resident paying a fixed amount (unusually low for New York City) for room and board. Some members work in the communal businesses; others have outside jobs. Ganas has experienced controversy; sexual relations are relatively flexible, and some former members denounce Feedback Learning as too intense, too controlling. In May 2006 one member was shot, allegedly by a former member, and later sued Ganas as well as the alleged assailant. Despite the internal and external conflicts that seem inescapable in any intentional community, Ganas remains one of the most stable and long-lived of American secular communities.[17]

The Communal Gay and Lesbian Life

In 1975 gay men and lesbians were coming out of closets in large numbers, and although quite a few communities that were de facto or de jure gay/lesbian had already appeared by then (the women's community and retreat center called Willow, for example, was begun in Napa Valley, California, in 1973, and Butterworth Farm in Massachusetts was purchased by five gay men the same year; those and several others are listed in the predecessor to this volume), at the time for the most part they kept their profiles low, and documentation of them in many cases is sparse. Later, however, more and more of them appeared and did not hide their identities. I can identify some thirty-five lesbian communities (some of them open to heterosexual women as well) and about half that many gay men's communities founded between 1975 and 2000. To provide a sketch of each would be overkill; here I will provide a few basics on some of the more notable ones and of the Radical Faeries movement, which had more than a little to do with the development of gay men's communities.

Communities of Lesbians

Lesbian communities have outnumbered gay male ones since communities openly identifying as gay/lesbian began to surface in the late 1960s, and there is likely not a single answer for that disparity. It is clear that some women who sought all-female communal living had been abused and needed safe space to live in; others saw all-female surroundings as essential to the empowerment and liberation of women in a patriarchal society. As Ayla Heartsong wrote,

> We still need women-only spaces because those are the only places where women are able to focus movement on themselves and themselves on movement. We still need women-only spaces because those are the only places where women can voice realistic and radical rage. We still need women-only spaces because that is where women will find the energy and tools to dismantle that which oppresses us all.[18]

An article written in 2015 suggested that the women's communes are declining in number and sought to document a few of them before it was too late.[19] Joyce Cheney, writing in 1985, already saw a decline in progress and lamented it (but at the same time saw it as inevitable):

> Why did we form lesbian lands? To pursue vision. And why did many leave? We found out that country life is hard. Where are the jobs, the hot baths, the harmonious song circles, the peaceful afternoons? In addition, we found land payments due, cars stuck in the mud, bugs, cold, endless group meetings, loneliness and isolation, especially if we were not youngish, white and able-bodied.

But at the same time she saw some returning to the land, as well as a younger generation taking up the rural communal torch.[20] The lure of the land is powerful, gender issues aside. As one back-to-the-land feminist wrote in the 1970s,

> Today was like a revelation, walking nowhere, just being there. I am learning to see and smell and feel all over again. I am moved almost to tears by the tiniest details: the hint of purple in the spring green grasses; the curve of a foxglove blossom against an ancient redwood stump, the taste of sun-warmed blackberries. The longer I live here the more my senses keep expanding.[21]

If decline is indeed the case (numbers are difficult to come by here), perhaps it means that the need for lesbians to escape to a private, closed community is receding as American culture generally has come to accept and embrace gay and lesbian people much more in the last few years than it did even just a decade or two ago. In any event, just as communes of all kinds remain very much with us over the centuries, those with specific missions and goals are not likely soon to disappear.

Oregon is a logical place to begin a survey of lesbian communities, since it apparently has the highest concentration of lesbian and feminist communes in the country. Cabbage Lane, founded in 1972, had been a pioneer of the movement for women's communes in the southwest part of the state, and WomanShare, whose early residents published a book about themselves, opened in 1974. Soon others followed.[22] In the 1980s came Golden, which was originally a community of gay men and lesbians in southern Oregon, but the men soon left. The peak population of Golden was reported as thirteen; the women built their own cabins to live in and had such common facilities as a barn and a kitchen. It all went well until a fire put an end to Golden in 1991. One notable achievement at the community was the founding, by Ruth and Jean Mountaingrove, of *WomanSpirit*, one of the first, if not *the* first, magazines focused on feminist spirituality.

WomanSpirit was not destined to stay long at Golden, because soon after its founding the Mountaingroves went on to found, or re-found, Rootworks, another lesbian community, on a seven-acre tract of land near Sunny Valley, Oregon, they purchased. Lesbians had rented the property earlier and given it the name of Rootworks. Life was rugged in the community's early years, with no electricity or running water. Gradually improvements were made, although conditions were never luxurious. The residents lived in two cabins, and built a barn to provide a production space for *WomanSpirit*. Over time the barn came to house a considerable library of feminist books and periodicals. Although the relationship of the Mountaingroves ended and they both, separately, moved away, at last report Rootworks was still functioning as a small lesbian community.[23]

As southern Oregon gathered steam as a home for feminists and lesbians, several of them formed a land trust and began planning a community that would be open to all women, regardless of their economic circumstances. In 1976 they purchased 147 acres near Days Creek, and that year the first new settlers moved onto what they called Oregon Women's Land, or OWL Farm. It eventually reached a population of about thirty. Problems arose, however, that some attributed to the open-land credo and lack of a workable governing structure. Some say that alcohol and drug problems contributed to what they called the chaos that came to engulf OWL Farm. By the 1990s it was closed, despite several attempts to repopulate it.[24]

Three other lesbian communities appeared alongside the others. One of the most stable of the lesbian communities of southern Oregon has been Rainbow's End, which took shape in the 1970s. The forty-seven-acre property was reportedly purchased with the proceeds of marijuana sales in the mid-1970s. The half-dozen or so residents live in separate houses and keep separate finances, with most of them working at outside jobs. An offshoot community, Rainbow's Other End, soon was created nearby on a separate forty-one-acre landholding. And still another, Fly Away Home, opened in 1976 near Myrtle Point, Oregon. It has remained small, recently with just two members, but hosts events for the much larger lesbian population of southwest Oregon. Taken together, these communities constitute the epicenter of American lesbian communitarianism.[25]

Although the strongest nexus of these lesbian lands, as they are often called, is in southern Oregon, several other communities were founded between 1975 and 2000 not only in the Pacific northwest but indeed across the country. Dozens of them are among those listed at the end of this volume. In the meantime, here are a few samples.

Across the continent from Oregon, Sugarloaf Women's Village was founded in 1976 by Barbara Deming and her partner Jane Verlaine. Deming was a prominent peace and justice activist in the mid-twentieth century, one who was arrested many times for her nonviolent participation in direct campaigns for peace and civil rights beginning in the late 1950s and carrying on through the 1960s and into the 1970s, frequently going to jail for her convictions. As the movement for gay/lesbian rights became more powerful she participated in that as well. But by the mid-1970s her health was declining, and she and Verlaine purchased a two-acre residential enclave on Sugarloaf Key, Florida, that had been established in the 1930s—with four houses, two cottages, and a campground. A few women soon began to visit, and eventually ten were living there, some for extended visits, some permanently. But by the 1980s Deming's health was getting worse, and she died of cancer in 1984. Sugarloaf Women's Village continues; its statement of purpose declares that "Barbara Deming's life and work is the spirit and guide" and affirms its resolve to "resist injustice and abuse of power, racial and sexual inequalities and the hegemony of the nuclear and industrial complex."[26]

Somewhat similar in structure to Sugarloaf, but shorter-lived, was Nourishing Space, located in a quiet place in a canyon near Tucson, Arizona. Katharine Parker "Kittu" Riddle had seen a need for a place of refuge for women in distress, and opened Nourishing Space in 1975. Rather like Sugarloaf, it had both a main house and small cabins, although, unlike Sugarloaf, it was open to all women, not only lesbians. Women came to visit, and some stayed on for lengthy residencies, camping when facilities were overcrowded. Other women came out from Tucson to help maintain the property and conduct workshops and spiritual rituals. In the end Riddle's financial resources ran out and the community could not be sustained, so the land was sold late in 1978. Riddle went on to work on human-service projects, especially world hunger relief.[27]

One of many other women's communities of note is the Susan B. Anthony Memorial Unrest Home, more recently known as the Susan B. Anthony Womyn's Land Trust. Its founders purchased 150 acres of land ten miles from the university town of Athens, Ohio, in 1979 and began building small houses for community members. The women have been active in local social activities and in the 1980s began hosting educational events. Events ranging from music festivals to counseling workshops have been held at SuBAMUH, as it is known, and members are active in women's programs at Ohio University. Typically around half a dozen women have been resident on the land.[28]

Lesbian (and other feminist) communities have typically been small, and some have had short lifespans. However, they have touched thousands of women who lived there or visited. Individual communities may come and go, but the larger movement seems destined to survive as long as women need close, supportive communities.

Gay Men's Communities

Gay men, like lesbians, were heavily closeted until the Stonewall riots in 1969, so most gay communal activity has taken place in the 1970s and beyond. Some, such as the Baltic Street Collective in Brooklyn and the 23rd Street Collective in New York, came soon after Stonewall and thus predate the focus of this book. Many more, however, sprang up in the late 1970s and beyond.

Much of the story of gay male community in the latter years of the twentieth century is that of the Radical Faeries. The 1970s were breakout years for gay culture, with many gay men and lesbians agitating for acceptance in the larger society. At the same time, others began to develop a vision of a new gay culture largely separated from mainstream society, one in which gay people could relate to each other honestly and supportively. Harry Hay, probably the most influential of the new activists, coined the term "Radical Faerie," and with others organized a Spiritual Conference for Radical Faeries at the Sri Ram Ashrama, a Hindu center in Arizona, in 1979. Over two hundred self-professed Faeries showed up, overwhelming the ashram's facilities, and the movement was off and running.

From the beginning Hay and his comrades envisioned the establishment of communal centers, apart from the mainstream world, where Radical Faerie culture could develop on its own terms. Eventually around a dozen of the communities were established across the United States, and more emerged in other countries. By the early 1980s efforts to establish such sanctuaries were up and running; one of the first of them was the Bear Mountain Sanctuary in northern California, which was devoted to the exploration of "faggot spirituality."

About the same time, Blue Grass Valley, in the eastern United States, transformed itself from a gender-inclusive countercultural commune to a Faerie Sanctuary.[29]

Meanwhile, another Radical Faerie community was forming in Tennessee. In 1980 a few gay men began living on Short Mountain in the central part of the state, and gradually the Short Mountain Sanctuary began to take shape. Eventually it encompassed two hundred acres of mountainous land, accumulated in small parcels. Other similar communities emerged, one by one, in the surrounding area, and individual sympathizers, mainly gay men who choose not to live communally, also have purchased land and built homes in the area. Residents have largely built their own houses and live simply on the land. Large festivals bring hundreds of visitors to Short Mountain and its environs.[30] Of the other communities that have grown up on the area the largest in landholding, if not population, is apparently IDA, which occupies 243 acres of land and typically has perhaps a dozen residents. It was established in 1993. The name IDA is ambiguous, but was once thought to mean Idle Dandy Acres, or Arts.[31]

Another of the Radical Faerie communes, and one that became well known as a center of gay publishing, was Wolf Creek Sanctuary. In its early years it was known as Magdalen Farm, which opened in 1976 on land that the gay activist Carl Wittman had purchased in 1969 in southwest Oregon. Magdalen's land base was eighty acres, and in 1978 it reported ten residents. In 1979 Magdalen was the site of a horrific homophobic crime, an arson that burned down the communal house. Not surprisingly, Magdalen went into decline, and little communal activity took place on the property for several years. Then in the early 1980s a group of Radical Faeries on the West Coast began to discuss acquiring property on which they could hold gatherings without having to use government or private land. Pursuing that plan, they formed an organization called Nomenus in 1984 and then in 1987 purchased Magdalen Farm, which then became the Wolf Creek Sanctuary. It was to be home to a small community of permanent residents and long- and short-term visitors, all of whom work to host the festivals and other gatherings on the property. Residents have built cabins, cultivated gardens, and maintained altars and other spiritual places. Normally the land is open to all, but occasionally events are restricted to male participants, and once a year there is an event for gay men only.[32]

At least two Radical Faerie communes were established in the 1990s, Zuni Mountain Sanctuary in 1996 and Starland in 1997. Both are open to women as well as men, although they are male dominated. Zuni Mountain is in western New Mexico and occupies over three hundred acres of rural land near the continental divide. The initial plans for the community had ecovillage features, with buildings clustered in a central location and permaculture-based land use. Permanent residents have never been numerous, in part because of the challenge of living in a high-altitude environment. Problems, however, seem to have made havoc with the ambitious plan; reports of financial misdeeds and other missteps have caused other Radical Faeries to break ties with the community. At this writing Zuni Mountain's status is unclear.[33] Starland, however, continues. Located in Yucca Valley, California, it functions as a retreat center that welcomes not only Radical Faeries, but also naturists and other open-minded people. Resident members, who typically number about five, live in modest homes on the land and host those who come for weekend getaways or longer.[34]

Other communities of gay men do not identify with the Radical Faerie movement, and some never quite achieve critical mass. One rather unusual example of another sort of gay community is the one now called the Hermitage, located near Pitman, Pennsylvania. It has been the work of two gay men who met in college and founded their community, originally called the Christiansbrunn Brotherhood, on a sixty-three-acre tract of rural land. The two were inspired by the community building of the Moravians in colonial America and located their community about eighty miles from the historic Moravian communal settlement of Bethlehem, Pennsylvania. They renamed themselves Johannes and Christian Zinzendorf, after the early Moravian leader Count Nicholas Zinzendorf. Working hard, the two erected several buildings and established the foundation of what they hoped would be a substantial community. Many visitors and short-term residents joined them briefly, but they never managed to attract stable, long-term members. Finally, and sadly, they changed their focus to the arts, and renamed their would-be community the Mahantongo Spirit Garden. Later they changed the name again, to the Hermitage. At last report the two Zinzendorfs remained, still without permanent colleagues.[35]

I should reiterate that the above accounts are only samples from a much larger pool of communities. Given that for most of the last quarter of the twentieth century homophobia was rampant in the United States, and that many gay people, especially women, perhaps, felt vulnerable, many communities and their members went out of their way to stay out of the public eye. In the early twenty-first century, with the rapidly evolving acceptance of gay people and gay relationships in American society, that attempt to avoid notice is changing. The Short Mountain Sanctuary, to name a prominent example, is well known as a gay outpost in a part of the country not noted for its inclusive tolerance, and seems likely to endure for years to come. What that means for other gay and lesbian intentional communities is unclear. On the one hand, public acceptance may mean that communities will flourish as never before. On the other, the need for private space where persecuted people can breathe peacefully may be much less than it heretofore has been. At this writing several of the communities are still active decades after their founding, and it seems unlikely that gay and lesbian communitarianism will vanish anytime soon.

Free Love Survives the 1960s

Unconventional sexual practices have been present, if not highly visible, in our midst for the last two hundred years. In the mid-nineteenth century a free love movement developed a devoted, if small, following, challenging the societal norm that the only acceptable sexual expression is heterosexual activity within a monogamous (and typically male-dominated) marriage. Free love often meant nonmonogamy, but it was also tied to advocacy of rights for women (this was the time of the rise of feminism, after all), birth control, and other things that challenged the social status quo.

For a long time, adherents of unpopular points of view have sometimes gathered into intentional communities in self-defense against a hostile outside world as well as to live life in the company of like-minded people. Thus between 1830 and 1860 over a dozen free-love communities were founded in the United States (Berlin Heights, Ohio, was especially notable for its several such households), and more came in the 1960s era, when millions of counterculturists questioned all kinds of social norms, including sexual ones. That second wave of liberated sexuality was waning as 1975 arrived, but it was still the case that several free-love communities were founded in the last quarter of the century (and, of course, some founded earlier were still alive and well). Defining the genre as encompassing group marriage, polyamory, and recreational sex with multiple partners, our time period saw such endeavors as these:

- Crabapple, founded in 1975 near Florence on the Oregon coast. In the 1980s the community moved to Eugene, where its members continued to practice polyfidelity.
- Liberty Cluster, a small polyfidelitous community located in Eugene, Oregon, and active in the 1980s.
- Shady Grove, founded in 1996 in Penngrove, California, by leaders of the Church of All Worlds, one of the country's earliest pagan religious bodies. Members are polyamorous and conduct workshops on earth religions and other topics.
- Shivalila, a polyamorous community of farmers and artists founded in 1994 on the big island of Hawai'i. Members lived from a common purse.
- Network for a New Culture. Not a community itself, the Network for a New Culture is an umbrella organization and

communications tool for persons interested in sexual freedom and other issues such as radical honesty and equality. Inspired by ZEGG, the noted German free-love community, the NFNC disseminates information about movement-related communities and clothing-optional summer camps.

And several others. In addition to these communities, it should be noted that the several polygamy-practicing communities of Latter Day Saints could be included in this category of people with unconventional sexual relationships and practices. They have been discussed above, in chapter 4.

Survivalists and Identity Crusaders

One other category of new communitarianism in the late twentieth century is that of the political and social Far Right. Communities in this category are as diverse as those in any other communal grouping, but they tend to have a few things in common: opposition, sometimes violent, to governments, especially those above the local level; racism and anti-Semitism, in many (but not all) cases; and plans for surviving what is believed to be a coming world disaster, up to and including the collapse of industrial civilization. They are part of a rather loosely defined larger movement of people who often call themselves "patriots" and "sovereign citizens" and typically argue that most established governments are hopelessly corrupt (or should not exist at all) and have no legitimate authority over anyone.

Some such communities (as well as their noncommunal kindred spirits) are religious in basis, in several cases adhering to some form of Christian Identity politics. The Identity movement typically argues that white people in English-speaking countries are the true descendants of ancient Israel, which means that modern Jews are imposters, as well as sinister agents with enormous influence over American financial and media life, not to mention a goal of destroying the white race. In a small minority of cases Identity believers and activists have tried to practice polygamy, and to that end have invoked bits of the

Latter Day Saint tradition. Other parts of this strain of political-religious ultraconservatism have Pagan connections, especially that branch of paganism know as Asatru. Asatru focuses on ancient Norse religion, and is often, but not always, racist in character. Beyond all of those religious inclinations and commitments there are, of course, secular groups, communal and noncommunal, that have similar political agendas.

In the 1970s some groups of Far-Right (and often racist and anti-Semitic) activists began to talk of communal homelands where they could live in all-white seclusion. Richard Butler, pastor of the Church of Jesus Christ Christian, was prominent among them, and in 1980 he announced the founding of an Aryan (white) homeland on his forty-acre landholding near Hayden Lake, Idaho. By that time quite a few Identity believers were already in northern Idaho, so Butler must have found the area culturally attractive. Early on the Aryan Nations enclave flourished as arguably the principal center of white American racist Christianity, and for several years it held an annual conference known as the Aryan World Congress that attracted large numbers of sympathetic attendees. Toward the year 2000 membership began to drop off, however, and then in that year the organization lost a lawsuit that held the Aryan Nations liable for the assaults perpetrated on two individuals by AN security guards. In losing the lawsuit the Aryan Nations had to take bankruptcy and thus lost its land. However, other similar, if less visible, racialist enclaves persisted.[36]

Not long after the Aryan Nations announced the opening of its new headquarters, a Vietnam War veteran, James "Bo" Gritz, became involved in the radical Right and in 1994 he too announced the creation, in Idaho, of a radical-Right "Christian Covenant Community" known as Almost Heaven on 280 remote acres of land near Kamiah. The covenant was an affirmation that residents would be God-fearing Christians and would fight for each other if any member's constitutional rights (presumably as such rights are understood in the far right milieu) were threatened. Lots sold quickly, so much so that he soon bought a second tract, 400 acres this time, for a community to be called Shenandoah. Again many lots were sold, but many of the land purchasers did not build homes there, and soon disputes among the various owners and between the residents and the larger local community swamped the projects. Not surprisingly, some of those who joined the project identified as "sovereign citizens" who belonged to the Idaho State Republic, and filed documents affirming their claims. Others were accused of conspiring to commit acts of violence to settle grievances. Gritz moved away from Almost Heaven in 1997, settling in Nevada, and only a few others remained in their scattered homes on the land.[37]

Several other communal enclaves of white racists and Identity adherents have existed with less public attention than the Aryan Nations and Almost Heaven. James Ellison, who had a history of involvement with the Aryan Nations and other far-Right groups, founded a communal farm that came to be called Cherith Brook near Elijah, Missouri; later the community relocated to another property initially called Mountain Creek, but before long named Zarephath after the biblical place where a poor woman shared her last bit of food with the prophet Elijah.[38] In 1978 they moved to yet another location in Arkansas just across the state line from Pontiac, Missouri, and called it Zarephath-Horeb. There, on 220 acres of land, the community attracted around 100 members, generally survivalists who stockpiled food, arms, and other supplies, and did weapons training, anticipating coming crises and disasters. Members worked together to build their isolated community, constructing homes, cutting timber, and gardening. Later the community's name was changed to the Covenant, the Sword, and the Arm of the Lord, or CSA. Planning for aggressive actions, including mass poisoning, against the group's perceived enemies—Jews, governmental bodies, cities—seemed to be extensive, but before many of them could be carried out various federal, state, and local government agencies mounted a raid against the CSA in 1985. Amazingly, after a three-day standoff the raid was concluded without violence. Law enforcement agents seized explosives and weapons as well as a thirty-gallon barrel of potassium cyanide, which the group was allegedly planning to use to poison the water supplies of American cities. Ellison and two others were convicted of multiple weapons and racketeering charges and sent to prison, whereupon the CSA broke up. After Ellison was released from prison he moved to Elohim City in Oklahoma and married the granddaughter of Robert Millar, the founder and leader of that community.[39]

Elohim City was founded in 1973 and thus would not normally qualify for inclusion in this volume, but it rose to visibility only with the rise of a more widespread and visible Identity movement in the 1980s. Its founder and leader until his death in 2001 was Robert Millar, a Canadian Mennonite who began to speak in tongues and had a series of visionary experiences that led him to formulate beliefs that were similar to those of Identity theoreticians, although he had not yet encountered others with such convictions. Guided by yet another vision he purchased four hundred acres of land near Muldrow, Oklahoma, in the Ozarks. Kerry Noble, a former Identity believer who knew Elohim City well, says that in its early days it was a pacifist community, presumably reflecting Millar's Mennonite roots. In 1982, however, members came into contact with several far-Right groups and began buying weapons and undertaking military training.[40] Much was made by media observers of the alleged ties between the community and Timothy McVeigh, the bomber of the Alfred P. Murrah Federal Building in Oklahoma City in 1995. Never, however, did Elohim City have quite the in-your-face spirit of racism and military resistance to government that characterized the larger Identity movement. A team of academic observers who visited in 1997 concluded that "by mainstream definitions, Elohim City is racist, but compared to the Ku Klux Klan or Aryan Nations, its racism is mild."[41] To Millar, the goal of the community was to be separate from a corrupt larger society, not to cultivate hate. Members live in private homes and keep their own finances, supporting the community through tithes and a lifestyle of common activities, including frequent worship, as well as several businesses. Kinship ties also provide a social bond, with interrelationships among most of the families, a few of which are polygamous. By the 1990s membership at Elohim City approached one hundred. After Millar's death leadership passed to two of his sons, John and David Millar.

The optimistic idealism that was the stock in trade in so many communes founded in the 1960s and early 1970s clearly did not survive in all communal projects founded in the last quarter of the century. The dark and often violent vision of the Identity and other far-Right communes puts a new and ominous stamp on the predominantly uplifting and peaceful communal vision.

7

Communities in the Media Spotlight

Crisis and Controversy

Human organizations, being populated by fallible humans, do not always march in an orderly fashion toward high goals. What movement, what experiment, what group has never had a crisis, either of its own making or of external origin—or perhaps some entangling of the two? Political entities, religious bodies, the world of commerce, educational institutions, eleemosynary organizations, and just about every other conceivable type of human corporate creation are subject to affliction with sex scandals, financial scandals, bitter persecution, and more other types of crises than can easily be enumerated. Moreover, some collectives find themselves at the center of saturation media coverage apart from anything that constitutes an actual crisis.

Inordinate public attention has been given to crisis episodes and, in the process, to the groups involved in them. One might think, as do huge numbers of members of the general public, that most communal groups are disaster-prone, or even pathological. But the groups that have been stricken with adversity are a small handful among the thousands active in the period under consideration here, and these crises sometimes descended upon them unexpectedly and undeservedly.

Often crises in intentional communities can be characterized as internal, as stemming from human misfortune or misbehavior, or of breakdowns in group dynamics and disciplines. Sometimes they stem from poor or even toxic leadership, which can be manifested in a variety of ways. Although few communal leaders are actually wicked, using communal idealism to mask an actual agenda of financial gain, sexual exploitation, or simply a pathological addiction to power, many have weaknesses that can be devastating to the community. Sometimes a leader can have sweeping power, even though his or her real leadership skills do not extend to every part of communal life (a leader capable of inspiring followers, for example, might lack the skills in financial management to make an organization work). That seems to have been the case at the Farm community in Tennessee, where the spiritual leadership of Stephen Gaskin was compelling, even as the huge commune was sliding toward bankruptcy. Conversely, sometimes a leader with a good grip on organizational issues lacks good people skills. And, often, the organizational skills, and sometimes financial means, that get a community established and functioning do not translate into ongoing leadership. These themes play out in all kinds of human situations, and communities are not exempt from them.

Other "internal" problems lead to crisis as well. Financial problems can become disastrous when a community simply cannot pay its obligations; such shortfalls have led to the dissolution of hundreds of American communities, sometimes amid recriminations and lawsuits. Inadequate skills can lead to serious problems—when community members with stellar back-to-the-land commitments simply do not know enough about farming, for example, or finance, or marketing, to make it all work. Moreover, problematic interpersonal relationships can blow up into catastrophes. A sort of Gresham's law—that the bad drives out the good—has worked its wiles in more than a few communities, especially open-land communities that found themselves inundated with people simply unsuited for communal life who took over and essentially forced the more capable members out.

But calamities can also come from outside the community, and I think external matters play an underappreciated role in many communal crises, often contributing to a group's dissolution. Pressure from neighbors has led to the demise of many an intentional community. The well-entrenched fear of the "different" surfaces when a new community emerges in just about any existing neighborhood, urban or rural. These anxieties, fears that are manifested when a community is founded in a given locale, typically subside once the various neighbors get to know each other, but initially relations can be rough. When a community has its own internal dysfunctions, outside pressure can build, and a community may not be able to withstand it.

Zoning laws are prime tools that are often used by opponents of community. Many urban (and sometimes rural) areas have occupancy limits—ceilings on the numbers of persons who may live in one home, usually with an exception for a family unit. In my own town a limit of three unrelated persons prevails in most neighborhoods—if you have four or more living together, you're breaking the law. Intentional communities are, therefore, expressly banned. (Of course laws like these are typically enforced selectively; a Catholic monastery would likely not be forced to disband, but a group of young people trying to build an urban ecovillage might well run into a brick wall.) In rural areas the rule often is dispersion: homes should be built on tracts of land of at least several acres (which is thus usually taken out of agricultural production), not in a cluster that would provide for more efficient use of the land. The Love Israel Family of Arlington, Washington, ran into that problem; it had enough acreage to make its population fit within the zoning law, but its members lived in a central cluster, not sprcad out.

There is a powerful legacy of social fear of cooperation in the United States, a legacy aggravated by the fear of communism that pervaded the nation after the Bolshevik Revolution. The word "communist" became profane, even though it had been freely used by democratic communitarians for many years. America is the land of individualism, is it not? To a remarkable number of people, cooperation was simply subversive. Earlier in the twentieth century that sentiment brought several intentional communities to grief. Commonwealth College, a communally organized educational institution in Arkansas, was the focus of a great deal of harassment in the 1930s, and was put out of business by the state in the following decade. The Red Scare also brought most of the New Deal community farming projects to an end; about one hundred of them had been founded, mostly in the 1930s, when Congress, in a spree of righteous indignation about their cooperative (and therefore subversive) nature, closed almost all of them down. Earlier the Hutterites were attacked for their pacifism and their use of a Germanic dialect, not to mention their communal economy, during the wave of anti-German prejudice that accompanied World War I. They were subjected to economic boycotts and worse; two of their young men were tortured to death for refusing military service. The Hutterites responded by fleeing to Canada, where a majority of them remain today. It is hard for any intentional community to withstand such onslaughts.

Occasionally what would normally be just a problem can turn into a catastrophe. What follows is a synopsis of a few of the largest and most dramatic communal crises of the late twentieth century. To be sure, these stories are not typical of the course of American communal history; they are all, in their various ways, aberrations from an overwhelmingly healthy norm. Nevertheless, they have received saturation media coverage and undoubtedly contribute mightily to the negative image that a great many Americans have of communitarian and other unconventional groups.

Jonestown

The story that ended in the worst communal disaster in American history had its beginnings in Indiana in the 1950s, when Jim Jones, a Protestant minister, began gathering a following in a church called Wings of Deliverance. With a fervor that has been described as nearly Pentecostal he appealed to society's rejects, many of them African Americans. He also became known as a healer, and the occasional debunking of his healing miracles did not deter the followers who believed that cures had actually come their way. Before long he also began to espouse communal living, preaching on the second and fourth chapters of the Book of Acts, in which the first generation of Christians gave all of their assets to the church and received according to their needs—an economic system most Christians would denounce as Marxist, even though it is reported favorably in their own scriptures. He also took his church, however distinctive it might be, into a mainstream denomination, the Disciples of Christ.

In 1964 and 1965 Jim Jones and many members of his congregation, escaping harassment of their racially integrated church in Indianapolis and looking for a safe haven from the nuclear holocaust Jones thought imminent, moved to the Ukiah, California, area. There the congregation, now called the Peoples Temple, grew slowly, but by 1968 it began to expand into the San Francisco area. In 1970 the church purchased a large building in the city and grew steadily, building a racially integrated, black-majority congregation under the leadership of Jones, who was white. But as the Peoples Temple's California presence grew, Jones also began to look at leaving the United States for a place where an interracial movement of radical socialists could flourish free of the institutional racism and structural oppression he found deeply ingrained in American society. By 1974 the church owned property in the South American nation of Guyana, with a crew of church members clearing land, building structures, and farming in anticipation of a large-scale migration to the new "agricultural mission."

In the meantime, pressure on the church was growing in San Francisco. Although Jones had been, and would be again in the future, publicly recognized for his charitable and educational work, a rising tide of hostile press coverage, atrocity tales from defectors, criticism by public officials, and contentious accusations by disenchanted relatives of some members strengthened Jones's determination to move out of the country, even as the church's financial empire was growing through members' generous gifts, such as their homes. In 1977 Jones, amid a huge flood of controversy, left for Guyana, taking many of his most devout members with him.

The drumbeat of criticism, in the form of hostile press coverage and various investigations, continued through the rest of 1977. On several occasions officials from the American embassy in Guyana visited Jonestown to investigate allegations of abuse and denying residents the right to leave, but the visits produced no conclusive evidence of any wrongdoing. A particular conflict centered on the young boy John Victor Stoen; his parents, Timothy Stoen, a Peoples Temple lawyer who had become disaffected with the group, and Timothy's estranged wife Grace Stoen, sought to reclaim custody of their son. The boy had been left at Jonestown when his parents departed, and Jim Jones, who was passionately attached to him (he claimed that the boy was his own biological child from an affair he had had with Grace Stoen), rebuffed all efforts to return him to the Stoens. At the same time, drug use and mental illness led Jones sometimes to behave erratically. The details of all of the events are far too numerous and complex to itemize here, but, according to sources both internal and external, at that time Jonestown was slipping into crisis.

The climax came in November 1978, when California Congressman Leo Ryan, pressured by ex-members and relatives of members, announced that he would go to Guyana to investigate the charges. Attempts by the Peoples Temple to stop him were to no avail, and on November 15 Congressman Ryan, with an entourage of his own staffers, some fourteen concerned relatives, and seven newsmen arrived in Guyana. Two days later they flew to Jonestown, where Jones gave them a manufactured cordial welcome. The next day, November 18, the visitors prepared to leave, taking with them a few Temple members who had asked to depart. When they reached the airport a Temple member who had posed as a defector began shooting, as, at the same moment, several Temple sharpshooters drove up. Congressman Ryan, three reporters, and one defector were shot and killed.

With that, Jones gathered his people at the community's central pavilion and told them they were facing an existential crisis. Medical staffers prepared vats of Fla-Vor-Aid infused with cyanide and tranquilizers while Jones told his people that drinking the poison would be a revolutionary act. Although a few objected, and some managed to escape, most community members lined up and drank the poison. Jones died by gunshot near the end of the fatal assembly.

"Jonestown" is etched into American memory. "Drink the Kool-Aid" has become a national catchphrase. Jim Jones is viewed as a towering symbol of evil, and those of his followers who went to their deaths have been derided as fools at best, and more probably lunatics. In the American mind the Peoples Temple is the very epitome of a "cult," something in urgent need of eradication, and, since its demise, innumerable intentional communities have been suspected to be potential "suicide cults."

But the people who died at Jonestown were real people—victims, perhaps, but not fools. They were high idealists who really believed that a new world could be created: the same belief that fuels intentional communities everywhere. The deaths were tragic, but the meaning of what happened at Jonestown is probably beyond our full understanding, now or ever.[1]

Rajneeshpuram

Indian spiritual teachers have been coming to the United States since the 1890s, if not before, and in larger numbers than previously because of the passage of the Immigration and Nationality Act of 1965, which permitted more Asians to enter the country than had been the case for several decades. Most have taught one or another version of Hinduism in a fairly traditional way, gathering students into classes and sometimes residential ashrams. None of them, however, had quite the meteoric rise and fall of Chandra Mohan Jain, better known as Bhagwan Shree Rajneesh (and later as Osho). A synopsis of his story was provided in an earlier chapter. Herewith I offer a more substantial account, with an emphasis on the crisis that brought his saga to an end.

After college and graduate work Rajneesh taught at the University of Jabalpur, but in the mid-1960s he resigned from his post and became a spiritual teacher whose long discourses drew from a variety of the world's religions and philosophers, and whose message was unconventional, in India, for its criticism of Gandhi and Rajneesh's denial that asceticism was useful to spiritual advancement. In 1974 he opened a headquarters/ashram at Pune that attracted many followers from Europe and North America. He became especially noted for his denial of the value of sexual abstinence for spiritual advancement, which put him at odds with most other Indian spiritual teachers, and was widely known as the "sex guru."

Social pressure on Rajneesh increased steadily in Pune, and in 1981 he moved to the United States. Soon thereafter his followers purchased a 64,000-acre ranch near Antelope, Oregon, which soon became home to Rajneesh and a following numbering in the thousands—so many that Rajneeshpuram, in its heyday, was probably the largest single-site intentional community in American history, with the possible exception of Colorado City, Arizona, and Hildale, Utah. Followers spent large amounts of money on extensive development of Rajneeshpuram. Eventually the ranch became a communitarian city, including a downtown, public transit system, hospital, and an airport.

The rapid development of the property ran afoul of Oregon's strict development laws, and the group frequently clashed with state and local authorities. Frustrated at the state's failure to approve their plans for the spiritual city, some members moved to the tiny hamlet of Antelope, hoping to use its status as an incorporated city to legitimize land use that was permitted only to legal municipalities. The Rajneeshees quickly outnumbered the fewer than one hundred local residents, and with a majority of the electorate changed the name of the town to Rajneesh. Meanwhile, longtime residents feared the social upheaval that seemed to be taking place, due to the arrival of this large red-robed group of believers, which included armed bodyguards for their sex-friendly spiritual teacher, who took daily drives in one of his nearly one hundred Rolls-Royces, all given to him by followers.

The Rajneeshee leaders were not exactly accommodating to their Oregonian critics, and on occasion were given to provocative acts. In 1984, with Wasco County officials denying the community the building permits it needed to proceed with its plans, Rajneeshee leaders began to plot a political takeover of the county. Initially they urged other Rajneesh followers to move to the area and register to vote, but when it became apparent that they would still fall short of political control, they adopted an innovative tactic: they rounded up homeless persons in several cities, bused them to Rajneeshpuram, and registered them to vote. But the county did not buckle easily, and put up new roadblocks to voter registration.

At the same time the Rajneeshee leadership attempted to suppress voter turnout among local residents through mass poisoning. Salmonella was sprinkled on salad bars in ten restaurants in The Dalles, the county seat and largest city in Wasco County; some 750 people were sickened (none died, luckily) in the largest biological attack in American history. But the crime was quickly exposed. Meanwhile, housing, feeding, and simply coping with some three thousand homeless people at Rajneeshpuram was a massive undertaking, and that part of the scheme quickly collapsed. The homeless "guests" were hauled to cities in the area and unceremoniously dumped on the streets.

And thus came the end of Rajneeshpuram. By September 1985 the Rajneeshee leadership stood accused not only of poisoning and voter fraud, but also arson, attempted murder, and other crimes. It became clear that Ma Anand Sheela, Rajneesh's second-in-command, had been the chief perpetrator of it all, and she eventually served more than two years in prison for her role. After denouncing her, Rajneesh tried to flee the country. He was apprehended, however, and worked out a plea bargain that would let him go free in return for agreeing never to come back to the United States. After hunting in several countries for a new headquarters, he returned to Pune and resumed his leadership there. He died in 1990, but his movement has survived, even prospered, since then. After his return to Pune, Rajneesh announced that he would henceforth be known as Osho, and he continued teaching and publishing. Centers devoted to his teachings appeared regularly; they now number in the hundreds in many countries.

Popular opinion in America has it that in situations like that of Rajneeshpuram a maniacal leader has probably led a group of either vicious coconspirators or, more likely, brainwashed followers to a horrific catastrophe. Once again that was not the whole truth, or even a large part of it. Rajneesh claimed that he had never known of the insidious actions taken by Ma Anand Sheela and a small circle of her top associates, and in any event the rank-and-file Rajneeshees were more victims than culprits. So were members of other religious groups during that period, given that one disaster brings all under suspicion. Things in general went terribly wrong.

As for Rajneeshpuram, the city that bloomed in the desert, it has become home to a religious youth camp, and many of its buildings are thus in use. And as for the tiny town on Antelope, it has reverted to its former status as a remote crossroads hamlet in the high plains of north-central Oregon.[2]

The Lundgren LDS Community

The Mormons today are mainly known as an ultranormal group of upstanding citizens who have a few unusual beliefs and rituals, and a somewhat unusual past, but what is less known is that hundreds of splinter groups have appeared throughout Mormon history, some of them involved in various crises and controversies. Jeffrey Lundgren was a member of the Reorganized Church of Jesus Christ of Latter Day Saints, the second-largest of the LDS (Mormon-derived and -related) denominations, which was the church of the family of Joseph Smith Jr., the movement's martyred founder. The RLDS Church, now known as the Community of Christ, was established in Illinois and in 1920 moved its headquarters to Independence, Missouri, which LDS belief holds to be the site of the future Second Coming of Christ. In the fashion so frequently seen in American religious history, the church experienced a number of schisms, some deriving from the longstanding LDS belief that selected members can receive divine revelations, and others embodying dissatisfaction with changes in the church's doctrines and practices, especially the ordination of women to the priesthood, which came about in 1984.

Jeffrey Lundgren was raised in an RLDS family in the church's hometown of Independence. After serving in the US Navy he moved back there with his wife, Alice, and their four children. He was active in his church and in 1984 accepted a job with it, working in the RLDS Temple in Kirtland, Ohio. That edifice had been built by the first generation of Mormons in the 1830s, but had been largely abandoned as the communal Saints moved first to Missouri, then to Illinois, where founder Smith was taken from a county jail and lynched. A leadership controversy in Smith's wake had led to a splintering of the LDS movement, and after various twists and turns the Temple became RLDS property after it and the larger faction, under Brigham Young, had split.

Despite having been given the honor of serving at one of the church's most sacred sites, Lundgren soon ran into problems. He was fired by the church for stealing from Temple funds and for deviating from RLDS doctrine in his teachings as a lay minister, a position from which he was defrocked in 1987. Soon Lundgren was living in a rented house with his wife, their children, and some eight followers, and, by several accounts, amassing an arsenal, allegedly for an attempt to take over the Temple in May 1988 that in the end never took place. Although not residents of the communal household, among the followers were five members of the Avery family: Dennis Avery, his wife Cheryl Avery, and their daughters Trina, Rebecca, and Karen. By 1989 Lundgren seems to have come to believe that Dennis Avery was undermining his authority, and on April 17 the Avery family joined other followers for what was to be a "wilderness trip."

That evening the Averys were led, one by one, to the barn on the property, where other Lundgren followers had dug a large pit in the dirt floor, and shot. Another follower ran a chainsaw during each shooting to hide the noise of gunfire.

Coincidentally, Kirtland police chief Dennis Yarborough, accompanied by other officers and some sixteen FBI agents, arrived at the house the next morning to interview Lundgren and others about the persistent allegations of the amassing of an arsenal on the property. They had no way of knowing what had happened the night before, and the discussion centered on the alleged Temple assault plan that had been concocted a year earlier. With that the Lundgrens and their following believed they had to flee. That evening a caravan of fourteen adults and ten children headed south-southeast, a direction they thought had been inspired by a passage in the Book of Mormon. The group finally arrived at Davis, West Virginia, and camped nearby.

On December 31, 1989, a disgruntled former Lundgren follower, Keith Johnson, told law enforcement officials of the murders. By January 3, police chief Yarborough had search warrants in hand and oversaw the exhumation of the Avery family. Within two days the Lake

County prosecutor, Steve LaTourette, had obtained felony indictments. In another week the suspects had been located and arrested. Some of them made plea bargains and testified against the others; in the end four were convicted of felonies, and Lundgren of murder. He was sentenced to death. After the usual long appeal process, he was executed by lethal injection on October 24, 2006.[3]

Jon Krakauer, in his bestselling *Under the Banner of Heaven*, highlights the historic role of "blood atonement" in the LDS Church, a doctrine of homicidal revenge propounded soon after the death of founder Joseph Smith. Until 1927 believers swore an official Oath of Vengeance as a part of a sacred LDS Temple ritual, an oath that nominally committed them to the shedding of the blood of certain high criminals.[4] Moreover, throughout its history the LDS Church has held that its president is a prophet able to receive messages directly from God, a doctrine that has led to the creation of hundreds of independent LDS-based churches by founders who have claimed that the mantle of prophecy has fallen on them. Those two tenets of the faith may well have guided Jeffrey Lundgren to believe that it was the will of God that the Avery family die, and his duty as God's representative on earth to carry out this divine punishment.

Joseph Smith's family split with Brigham Young and the larger LDS church shortly after Joseph's death and apparently never advocated blood atonement or homicidal vengeance. Nevertheless, the doctrine and the oath are well known through the mosaic of LDS-based churches, and in all probability Lundgren knew of it. Just how much it fueled his barbaric actions remains a mystery.

MOVE

On May 13, 1985, sixty homes burned down in Philadelphia, Pennsylvania, in a horrendous fire ignited when a bomb was dropped on the communal home of MOVE, a radical group that combined black nationalism with a back-to-nature primitivism, advocacy of animal rights, and espousal of a hunter-gatherer lifestyle that included abandonment of modern medicine and technology. The group began to take shape in the early 1970s and was initially known as the Christian Movement for Life. Its founder, Vincent Leaphart, soon changed his name to John Africa and the group's name to MOVE—not an acronym but an evocation of dynamism, a statement of the group's members' commitment to being active. The members, who also took the surname Africa, took up communal living in the Powelton Village neighborhood of West Philadelphia and adopted a lifestyle that aimed at self-reliance, scavenging for supplies and eating raw foods. However, they soon also began to annoy their neighbors with the large numbers of animals being kept on the property, generally filthy conditions, violation of weapons laws, excessive noise (principally via a bullhorn used to broadcast the MOVE teachings) and refusal to pay utility bills. On August 8, 1978, the police, pursuant to a court order, arrived to evict MOVE from its premises, and a shootout ensued in which a police officer was killed and eighteen persons (police officers, firefighters, MOVE members, and others) were injured. Nine MOVE members were convicted of third-degree murder and sentenced to long prison terms.

MOVE then relocated to a different part of West Philadelphia in a house the members turned into a fortress. They broadcast their message, now including a demand that their nine imprisoned compatriots be freed, by bullhorn around the clock. They continued to keep large numbers of animals, not only dogs and cats but also wild rats. After several years of complaints the police obtained warrants for the arrest of four members on charges ranging from parole violation to possession of illegal weapons. After evacuating neighbors they tried to force the MOVE members from the house in several ways, including by insertion of tear gas, but had no success. A shootout resulted in which the police fired over ten thousand rounds of ammunition. The police commissioner then ordered that two dynamite-like bombs be dropped on a fortified bunker on the roof of the building; the explosion ignited gasoline that was inside. Those in charge of the siege, saying they feared gunfire from the MOVE members still in the house, ordered that the fire be allowed to burn. John Africa, five other adults, and five children died in the fire, and more than 250 of their neighbors were left homeless. One adult, Ramona Africa, and one child survived the fire. Ramona Africa was subsequently convicted of riot and conspiracy charges, for which she spent seven years in prison. She and two surviving relatives of MOVE members later sued the city and won a $1.5 million civil judgment, after the jury found that the police had used excessive force and violated their constitutional rights.

Philadelphia mayor Wilson Goode appointed a commission to investigate the bombing. The commission's report found the police "grossly negligent" in their actions and declared that "dropping a bomb on an occupied row house was unconscionable." Ramona Africa has continued to be the spokesperson for MOVE and to advocate the release of the "MOVE Nine," the still-incarcerated members who were convicted of murder in the 1978 shootout between MOVE and the police.[5]

The Branch Davidian Fire and Massacre

One of the most vivid and violent communal crises of the late twentieth century was the siege of and fire at the communal home of a congregation known as Branch Davidians outside Waco, Texas. On February 28, 1993, the federal Bureau of Alcohol, Tobacco, Firearms, and Explosives (BATF) mounted an armed raid on the property of this offshoot of the Seventh-Day Adventists; the Branch Davidians resisted, and the siege became a fifty-one-day standoff. On April 19, a fire of uncertain origin engulfed the communal buildings, resulting in the deaths of some seventy-six Branch Davidians, both adults and children.

The roots of the story could be found nearly two centuries ago, in the millennial excitement aroused by William Miller and associates in the 1830s and 1840s that preceded the founding of the Seventh-day Adventist Church by Ellen G. White and others in 1863. Although Miller's prediction of the Second Coming of Christ in 1844 had failed, some of his followers kept expecting imminent millennial events and founded a church that now has a worldwide reach.

Into this scene came Victor Houteff, an immigrant from Bulgaria, who joined the church in 1919. He soon became a teacher in a Sabbath

School in Los Angeles, California, and began to propound doctrines not endorsed by the church. Most important, he saw the Kingdom of God that all Adventists anticipated as a literal, earthly kingdom headquartered in Palestine. That restoration of the throne of David would happen soon, and Houteff would lead the 144,000 chosen to be present at Christ's return to Jerusalem. After he was disfellowshipped from the Seventh-day Adventist Church, he organized his own movement, the Davidian Seventh-day Adventists.

In 1935 Houteff moved his small church to Waco, Texas, where the members developed a community Houteff called Mount Carmel. It was designed to be a gathering place from which the faithful would soon depart for the Holy Land. They worked devotedly to gather the 144,000, mailing out enormous quantities of literature and sending missionaries abroad. Then, in 1955, Houteff died and his wife, Florence, assumed the role of leader. She sold the Mount Carmel property for a large profit and moved the believers to a new site, again called Mount Carmel, several miles outside the city. She also announced that the Second Coming would be inaugurated at Passover in 1959, and urged followers to gather at the community's new home. However, when her prediction failed, she withdrew from her leadership role and moved to California.

Ben Roden and his wife Lois Roden emerged as the next leaders of the Davidians, with Ben Roden claiming that he had received a revelation that he was the "Branch" mentioned in the biblical book of Zechariah.[6] After his death in 1978 Lois Roden became the leader of the movement, and like her predecessors introduced some new ideas, in her case feminizing ones (she taught, for example, that the Messiah would have female as well as male qualities). Some Davidians rejected her leadership, forming new Davidian organizations in Missouri and South Carolina, both of which continue. But other adherents came along as well, among them, in 1981, Vernon Howell, a young man passionate about the Bible and steeped in Seventh-day Adventist theology. He quickly became attracted to Lois Roden and developed a sexual relationship with her. Soon he was displacing her as the generally accepted leader of the Branch Davidians.

More leadership disputes ensued, but by 1988 David Koresh was in charge at Mount Carmel. He changed his name from Vernon Howell in 1990, reflecting his identification with a biblical messianic figure called "Koresh," which is the Hebrew form of Cyrus, the Persian king who conquered the Babylonians and freed the Jews from captivity. His spellbinding Bible teaching continued to draw followers, the enduring ones firmly enough that they could overlook what most would have considered erratic or dysfunctional behavior, such as decreeing a rule of celibacy for all except himself, who would marry any and all of the women of the colony, some as young as twelve years old, and have children by several of them. However, it was not the sexual deeds of the "Sinful Messiah," as a local newspaper labeled him, but allegations of amassing an arsenal that led to the fateful raid on Mount Carmel.[7]

That firearms were present at Mount Carmel is a matter of record. In fact, one of the businesses conducted by some members of the group was the buying and selling of guns. In planning its raid, the BATF relied on allegations that some of the weapons were illegal. But why the agency's agents mounted a military-style assault on the movement's communal home is less clear, especially in light of the fact that members came and went freely. What is clear is that agents stormed the main Mount Carmel building on the morning of February 28, 1993, and that gunfire resulting in deaths on both sides ensued. Later that day the BATF called in the Federal Bureau of Investigation. A fifty-one-day standoff ensued. In the early morning of April 19 tanks began to punch holes in the building and inject CS gas intended to force the occupants out. Around noon the building was consumed in a fire whose origin has never been firmly determined. Seventy-six Branch Davidians, including twenty-one small children, died.[8]

The public perception of the entire event is stereotypical: a deranged leader stockpiles weapons, sexually abuses followers, and leads them, either innocent or coconspiring, to their deaths. Media accounts of the movement and raid largely overlook the biblically based millennial and apocalyptic theological views of Koresh and his congregation. Millions of Americans say they anticipate millennial events that will involve a great war between the righteous and the forces of Satan. Moreover, they believe the forces of the adversary will probably be disguised as good people, just to deceive unwary believers. How many of the faithful would refuse to yield to the army of the slippery, devious Antichrist when he came blasting into their homes? And how long will media outlets and government agencies decline to even try to understand a message preached in thousands of churches every weekend—that the Great Tribulation is poised to begin any minute?

Heaven's Gate

In 1972 Marshall Herff Applewhite and Bonnie Lu Nettles met at a hospital in Houston, Texas, and the following year began the first of many road trips spreading a message that came to center on UFOs, closely tied to a fascination with what they called the Evolutionary Level Above Human. It seems that humans were required to leave earth to get to that higher level, and the way to do it was with the assistance of UFOs. Applewhite and Nettles told their audiences that they were visitors to earth from the higher level, to which they would return soon. They traveled extensively, speaking in town after town, and began to attract members to a movement that became known as Human Individual Metamorphosis. The leaders, downplaying their human identities, called themselves, at different times, by such complementary names as Ti and Do, and Bo and Peep. They taught that the earth was about to be "recycled"—that is, wiped clean and then recreated. The only way humans could survive this cataclysmic cleansing was to get off the planet.

In 1976 the movement began to adopt communal living. Ti and Do, who had been in seclusion for several months, emerged and instructed their followers to meet them at a camp near Laramie, Wyoming. Several marks of group identity emerged: uniform clothing styles, simplicity in appearance (no jewelry, and no beards on men), and mandatory celibacy. Members with marketable skills undertook various jobs to support the group. Over time several members developed expertise in the emerging world of computer technology.

In the 1980s Nettles's health declined as she battled cancer, and she died in 1985. Applewhite explained to the group that Nettles had left her body to return to the next level, where she would await the rest of them. Then, in the 1990s, the group surged forward again, preparing for the ascent to the level above human. Some members had not been able to eliminate their sexual urges, and took medical hormone suppressors. A few, including Applewhite, went farther, undergoing castration. The message became increasingly fervent: that we were near the end of the time we had on earth before ascension. But the setting was not heavily emotional. Members who did not join the mass suicide describe the movement not as a religion but as a class—a schoolroom where they learned powerful truths.

In 1996 the group rented a large house in Rancho Santa Fe, near San Diego. And then, the following March, it became known that a comet, called Hale-Bopp, was nearing earth. Applewhite announced that a spacecraft was hiding behind the comet, and on board was a being from the level above human. Here, finally, was the moment for which they had all been waiting. On March 24 email messages to the group from absent members and others were suddenly not answered. Two days later one member returned to the mansion and found thirty-nine bodies, neatly arrayed and wearing the group's uniform clothing and footwear.

The mass suicide confounds some popular ideas about "cults." Those who joined the final exit were from a wide range of ages; they were by and large intelligent and well-educated individuals. They were not commanded to end it all; some members chose to leave before the final drama occurred. The farewell videos that some created were upbeat and cheerful.[9]

Maybe they became angels? To most this group and its departure were sheer madness. But who can know that the spaceship did not in fact carry them away? A few months after the suicides, Lorraine Snelson, the mother of departed member Judi Rowland, told the world she was proud of her daughter: "I was *happy* for her. She completed her lifetime." Snelson had been a member of Heaven's Gate herself for five years, and afterward continued to provide support to members when they stopped by to visit her—a place to sleep, meals, gasoline for their cars, and cash. "Is it evil if someone wants to be with God? As far as I'm concerned, there was nothing but good. . . . So they had to leave their human bodies here and take their minds with them and prepare a place for us. Do people ever stop and think about that?"[10]

And the movement survives. Surviving members who chose not to depart the planet answer email, fill orders, and maintain the website heavensgate.com. This message was, at recent notice, front and center on that website:

> Whether Hale-Bopp has a "companion" or not is irrelevant from our perspective. However, its arrival is joyously very significant to us at "Heaven's Gate." The joy is that our Older Member in the Evolutionary Level Above Human (the "Kingdom of Heaven") has made it clear to us that Hale-Bopp's approach is the "marker" we've been waiting for—the time for the arrival of the spacecraft from the Level Above Human to take us home to "Their World"—in the literal Heavens. Our 22 years of classroom here on planet Earth is finally coming to conclusion—"graduation" from the Human Evolutionary Level. We are happily prepared to leave "this world" and go with Ti's crew.
>
> If you study the material on this website you will hopefully understand our joy and what our purpose here on Earth has been. You may even find your "boarding pass" to leave with us during this brief "window."
>
> We are so very thankful that we have been recipients of this opportunity to prepare for membership in Their Kingdom, and to experience Their boundless Caring and Nurturing.[11]

Twelve Tribes

In 1972 Elbert and Marsha Spriggs opened a Christian coffeehouse in Chattanooga, Tennessee, and from the young people who gathered there came a group of intentional communities now known as the Twelve Tribes. At various times in their history they have been known as the Vine Church, the Commonwealth of Israel, the Messianic

Communities, the Community Apostolic Order, and sometimes the Northeast Kingdom Community Church or Island Pond communities, after their once-preeminent community in northern Vermont. The group took up communal living rather informally early on, and for a time they attended the First Presbyterian Church in Chattanooga. However, when that church canceled a Sunday service to give members leisure time to watch the Super Bowl in 1975, they pulled away and began worshiping separately. To support themselves they developed several small businesses, especially restaurants, each known as the Yellow Deli.

The movement began to arouse controversy in Chattanooga in 1978, when three local colleges forbade their students to patronize the Yellow Deli. In that year a second community was opened in Island Pond, where members established a restaurant called Common Sense. The group proceeded to sell its properties in Chattanooga and by 1979 all its members were located in Island Pond. It continued to develop a distinctive theology and a set of distinctive practices, seeing itself as the latter-day manifestation of the early Christian church, which retained Jewish traditions and which adopted a practice of holding all earthly possessions in common, as prescribed in the second and fourth chapters of the biblical book of Acts.[12] Twelve Tribes members observe a Jewish Sabbath (sundown Friday to sundown Saturday), celebrate some Jewish holidays, and adhere to Jewish dietary laws. Community members celebrate the Sabbath in part by joining in Israeli folk dances. They use a Hebrew form of the name of Jesus, Yashua. Similarly, each member upon joining is given a Hebrew name. The group believes that today's world is hopelessly sinful, an indication that the coming of the Messiah is at hand.

Controversies have dogged the Twelve Tribes since their early days in Chattanooga. Several deprogrammings, in which members are forcibly removed and subjected to intense "reeducation" have occurred, especially in the movement's early years. The group has been accused of exploiting its children by forcing them to work; it responds that children should help their families, as is common on farms and in gardens and cottage industries. The group has been criticized for spanking its children for wayward acts; it responds that it is not physically abusing children, but providing a traditional punishment for bad behavior. The movement homeschools its children, a practice whose legality varies from one jurisdiction to another.

Some of the Twelve Tribes' strict treatment of children has occasioned government raids. The first major raid occurred on June 22, 1984, when ninety state troopers, accompanied by fifty Social Rehabilitation Services workers, descended on Island Pond. On the basis of allegations of child abuse by anticult activists and ex-members of the group (some of the allegations rooted in child-custody disputes), 112 children were taken into protective state custody. They were returned to their homes the same day, however, when Judge Frank Mahady ruled that no evidence of abuse existed.[13] At the postraid detention hearings, he remarked, "The term 'child abuse' cannot be invoked as a talismanic invocation to support the exercise of State power which egregiously violates both First and Fifth Amendment Rights."[14]

Several other smaller raids have taken place in the United States, and raids both large and small have occurred in other countries—for example, Canada, Germany, and France. Germany outlaws homeschooling entirely, and its removal of children from the Klosterzimmern, Bavaria, community in 2002 was sweeping and long-lasting. A second raid on Klosterzimmern and one at the nearby Wörnitz Twelve Tribes community in 2013 once again swept children from their homes. The cycle of raids seems not to be over yet.[15]

The Twelve Tribes have continued to grow despite their vocal opposition and now have more than forty communities in the United States, Canada, Germany, Spain, France, Czechia, Brazil, England, Argentina, and Australia. One can expect that more raids are on the horizon.

And Many More

Other crises and disasters have afflicted hundreds of communities. Sometimes they involve serious crimes, as when Chris Turgeon, the leader of a Christian survivalist commune called Gatekeepers in

California who began calling himself the prophet Elijah, started punishing the errors of his followers violently, and eventually was convicted of murdering a former follower.[16] Sexual abuse and other violent crimes have taken place in many communities, just as they have in so many other places in our society. Communal living aims to bring peace, harmony, and a satisfying life to its participants, and by and large it does an excellent job of that, but intentional communities finally seem unable to escape entirely the depredations of contemporary life.

Conclusion and Afterword

Into the Twenty-First Century

As the curtain came down on the twentieth century, hundreds of intentional communities, mostly small, were alive and well in the United States. The great communal flowering of the 1960s era was withering into history, the massive energy that fueled the creation of thousands of communes dissipating. A new communal generation had arrived, with better organizational skills, leading to greater communal longevity and, in many cases, a more stable, even prosperous, financial base. For over four hundred years intentional communities have been in our midst, sometimes quietly, sometimes boisterously, and at century's end they were still with us.

How, in the twentieth century, did communities change, and how did they stay the same? Why are so many of them short-lived? Why is there often high turnover of membership among communitarians, even in a community that lasts for many decades? What patterns can we detect in the establishment and dissolution of communities? Are there certain types of communities that are in favor at certain times but not at others? When have intentional communities had the largest and smallest presence in our society—in other words, is the existence of communities a cyclical phenomenon, is their waxing and waning random, or is it connected to some external causal factor?

American life is gradually becoming more secular, and communitarian life seems to reflect that trend.[1] The communal societies best known in American history have been predominantly religious, and certainly most of the long-lasting ones have been strongly based in one or another faith tradition. The Shakers, for well over two centuries in the United States, were firmly grounded in a distinctive variety of Christianity that was strictly regimented. Several notable communities of Radical Pietists, especially the Harmonists, the Amana Society, and the Separatists of Zoar, all had long nineteenth-century life spans. The Hutterites, the largest of all North American communitarian movements apart from the religious orders of the Catholic Church, have been communal for most of their five-hundred-year history, including nearly a century and a half in the United States and Canada.

That is not to say that secular communities have not made their own strong imprint on the American communitarian saga. Robert Owen, the Scottish industrialist who came to the United States with great fanfare in the 1820s to found a secular community at New Harmony, Indiana, was a nonbeliever whose communitarian ideals appear to have had no notable religious roots. One of the most popular communal movements of the nineteenth century was that of the devotees of the French social philosopher Charles Fourier, and although their communal experiments were mostly short-lived, the vision energized thousands of Americans. The Owenites and Fourierists, however, were well outnumbered in their day by the community builders whose feet were firmly planted in Pietist or Shaker conviction.

By definition (my definition, anyway), intentional communities are constituted on the basis of some common purpose. In earlier times that purpose, Owenites and Fourierists notwithstanding, was most often some kind of common religious commitment, but now secular (yet still passionate) concerns are increasingly the focal points of communities. Perhaps the most important of these are related to environmental concerns. It does not take a lot of insight to realize that we have major environmental problems that are on the verge of overwhelming us. As James Lovelock observes, it is not that the earth is fragile; it will survive whatever comes, and will be all the healthier if we can eliminate the humans who are wreaking havoc with their lifestyle choices.[2]

Thus in the latter years of the twentieth century a new, or perhaps refurbished, type of intentional community appeared: the ecovillage. As we noted in an earlier chapter, “Ecovillages are communities of people who strive to lead a sustainable lifestyle in harmony with each other, other living beings and the earth."[3] Those who flock to the new ecovillages are as passionate about their environmental convictions as were medieval monks and nuns about their spiritual beliefs. At the same time another secular communitarian movement also began to spread rapidly: cohousing. The focal point here was partly environmental (cohousers have smaller carbon footprints than most middle-class Americans) and partly social, a sort of nostalgic longing for the kinds of neighborhood and kinship ties that once served as social glue for the larger society. By the end of the century, these two related movements had taken a major role on the American communal stage. Something of a variant of cohousing began to take shape at the end of the century and gathered speed a bit later, by around 2010: coliving, also known as cohouseholding. Coliving, as opposed to cohousing, tends to be urban and often high-rise. Exact configurations vary widely, but generally a coliving community offers private bedrooms, usually with bathrooms, and common spaces, including kitchens. Residents, who are often young professionals, frequently socialize together. The longing for community can find expression in ever-changing ways.

One puzzling phenomenon that has persisted through much of American communal history is the relatively short life of a great many American communities. That said, trying to calculate average communitarian longevity is a formidably difficult task, for the simple reason that accurate information is so hard to collect. We have founding dates, or at least approximate dates, for a great many communities, but finding accurate dates of dissolution is much harder. Many communities seem to fade away; eventually someone notices that a community is gone, but no one has noted the date. It is safe to estimate, however, that the average lifespan of American communities would be measured in years, not decades or centuries. Some groups practicing communal living, such as the Shakers and Hutterites, are powerfully long-lived, but a community that celebrates its fiftieth anniversary is the exception, not the rule.

So if there is a natural, innate human desire for community, as some would argue, why have the intentional communities of the last four hundred years on the whole been short-lived? Developing an answer to that question tends to be anecdotal, but I will endeavor to provide a few generalized explanations.

Explanation one: building is fun, maintenance is not. Communal memoirs that recount the spirit of the founding years usually bristle with energy. Starting a new community is full of great excitement. Such a venture is a daunting undertaking, given the challenges of acquiring property, financing the project, selecting and evaluating members, and many more. These pioneers are traveling to a new land and new way of life. There are buildings to erect, a food supply to establish, and other essential tasks. But maintaining what has been started seems to be less exciting than building it in the first place. That sentiment echoes a lament endemic among those who raise money for charitable causes: donors like to support new initiatives and shy away from paying for routine operations.

Explanation two: community founders are typically fairly young, and as they age, they and their communities become less attractive to new young seekers of community. As I have suggested above, the young energy that seems ideally suited to the building of community will not endure forever. And age discrimination is a reality in our culture. We no longer live in traditional tribes that value their elders; a great many young people simply do not want to move into a community with an aging population. I had a student who became a novice sister in a Catholic religious order. Her fervor was great, and she had excellent contributions to make to that community. But before long she left, and when I asked her why, she said that the other members were simply too old—she had few peers, and thus she felt adrift. Perhaps she could have joined others in creating a new community—but then what would happen to the old one?

Explanation three: too many leaders, not enough followers. People interested in community are often cultural visionaries, with strong personalities and leadership instincts. Simply put, they often have a fairly specific vision of community and want other people to unite on the basis of that vision. Sometimes that works well, as people find themselves drawn to a particular communal vision or to the person expounding it, but in many cases it doesn't work out, because those who might join a community are busy promoting their own visions. The back pages of *Communities* magazine are testimony to this problem: every issue has listings of proposed new communities that could take off and fly if only people would unite around the vision.

So what is the shape of communitarianism as we move forward? No one answer seems to fit. The largest communal movement of all, that of the Catholic religious orders, has been declining in numbers for many years for a variety of reasons, and, barring major reforms in the Catholic Church (specifically, allowing its clerical and monastic members to marry), the decline seems likely to continue. On the other hand, our second-largest communal movement, the Hutterites, is thriving, with some fifty thousand members in North America (the majority of them in Canada) living in five hundred colonies. Our longest-lived American communal movement, apart from the Catholic monasteries, is that of the Shakers, which seems inescapably near its end, although it is possible that one or two members may survive to see the 250th anniversary of the arrival of their forebears from England in 1774.

So I am reluctant to generalize or to offer any summary wisdom. I do have confidence that, while many communities have short life spans, the communal impulse and form are not about to disappear. As long as people dream of a better world, some of them will try to create it.

I am also reluctant to predict just what that future communal world will look like, however. Although the basics remain the same—people living together on the basis of a common purpose, practicing some level of economic sharing—the details are elastic. Such innovations, or at least modifications of earlier communal patterns, as cohousing and ecovillages seem poised to become a prominent public face for the intentional communities movement well into the future. And, in a society that is aging as never before, communal retirement housing was growing substantially as the twenty-first century dawned. A full-scale cohousing project or even a shared house with just a few people is far more attractive than a typical nursing home, and that fact seems unlikely to change.

In the early years of the twenty-first century some other variations on the old theme seemed to have some promise. The largely Protestant movement known as the New Monasticism has captured much of the sacrificial spirit of the great monastic institutions of the past, but with adjustments suited to the times: members can be married, and they do not have to pledge to stay for a lifetime. The plague of homelessness in the most prosperous societies in history is finding a communal response in little villages of the homeless living in tiny houses. That will not end homelessness, but it will help. There is no reason not to think that other such innovations will continue to arise.

In short, communitarianism has proved attractive to a small but highly dedicated group of Americans throughout our common history. It does not seem destined to become America's standard form of economic and residential organization, but neither does it appear to be disappearing. As long as idealists arise among us, communes will be in our midst.

Appendixes

Notes

Bibliography

Index

Appendix A

A Reflection on 400 Years of American Communes

Does Communal Activity Come in Waves? If So, When Have They Occurred?

In 1984 Michael Barkun published an article in the journal *Communal Societies* arguing that communal societies are "cyclical phenomena" that have "experienced four periods of unusually intense" activity: the early nineteenth century, the late nineteenth century, the Great Depression, and the 1960s. He found that the surges in the founding of communes corresponded to a fair degree with surges of millennialism, sometimes religious, sometimes secular—the Millerite Adventists in the 1840s, the progressive movements of the late nineteenth century (the Single Tax movement of Henry George and the populist uprising, to name only two), reform proposals and projects during the Depression, and diverse movements with millennial overtones during the 1960s era (the new religions, resurging fundamentalism that pushed aside the mainline denominations, and the rise of a new doom-predicting environmental movement).[1]

Following in Barkun's wake, historian Brian J. L. Berry, in his book published in 1992, argued that the founding of communes intensified during times of economic depression. People who were hurting economically, he contended, turned to communal living—a very sensible move, in fact, given that communal living is typically a low-cost endeavor. Drawing from the work of the Russian economist Nikolai D. Kondratiev, Berry saw major economic downturns approximately every fifty-five years, and lesser ones more or less halfway between the major downturns.[2]

The influence of Barkun's article and Berry's book has been considerable. Others have claimed, usually without specific examination of the evidence, that the early to mid-nineteenth century and the 1960s era were the two major high points of communal activity. Howard Segal has gone so far as to state that "most students of American utopian communities" have seen things that way.[3]

Both Barkun and Berry depend heavily on Otohiko Okugawa's enumeration of American intentional communities founded between 1787 and 1919.[4] Okugawa found 270 communities within his parameters, one-third of which, Barkun calculates, were founded during two seven-year periods, 1842 to 1848 and 1894 to 1900. The earlier period saw the later phase of Owenism, the briefly explosive arrival of Fourierism, Perfectionists, and a few ethnic immigrant groups. The latter period was smaller, but had visible prophets in Henry George and Edward Bellamy. Barkun's third wave came after the period Okugawa had studied, but was easy to identify with the rise of about one hundred government-sponsored communities founded by the New Deal for Depression relief. And his fourth wave, the 1960s era, is self-evident.

Both Barkun and Berry have presented interesting and useful hypotheses about periodic surges of interest in communal living, but more can be done. For example, Berry's hanging of his analysis on economic cycles ignores many other things that could spur people to head for communes—domestic and international politics, weather and climate, immigration, and agricultural conditions and economics, among others. (Berry's book is problematic in other ways as well; see my review of it published in 1994.[5]) And both authors limit their counting of communal groups by examining only starting dates of movements and individual communes. Could we not get a more complete reading of the communal presence in American life by looking at communities during their entire existence, not just their founding dates? And would it not be useful to consider counts of people living communally rather than just numbers of communes? A Shaker village with hundreds of members, or a Hutterite colony with around a hundred, should count for more than a three-family enclave when we examine the impact of American communitarianism.

The possibility of taking a broader measure of the communal presence in America has long intrigued me, and as I was winding up this third volume of my history of American communal living in the twentieth century I set out to see if I could quantify that presence. What I propose is a stab at answering the first limitation of the earlier studies: How great was the overall presence of communal living in America, measured not just by looking at founding dates, but at the entire lifetime of a community? The second, involving counts of people, is beyond my reach at this time, and probably will remain that way. Even when one can find membership statistics or estimates for a given community—which, often, is not easy—hardly ever are those numbers tracked over time.

My main source for this enumeration is my own *Encyclopedic Guide to American Intentional Communities*, supplemented by materials I have examined since its publication. That earlier publication also provides, at length, a definition of "intentional community" and discussions of my rationale for including or excluding from consideration certain communities and categories of communities. I only wish that this study could be truly comprehensive, but in the nature of things that seems unlikely ever to happen.[6]

Table 1
American communities in operation, by decade

1600s	1	1740s	11	1880s	142
1610s	1	1750s	18	1890s	153
1620s	2	1760s	20	1900s	169
1630s	1	1770s	13	1910s	161
1640s	1	1780s	13	1920s	145
1650s	1	1790s	24	1930s	229
1660s	2	1800s	31	1940s	194
1670s	1	1810s	39	1950s	245
1680s	2	1820s	56	1960s	628
1690s	4	1830s	50	1970s	1378
1700s	3	1840s	103	1980s	1126
1710s	2	1850s	122	1990s	1190
1720s	3	1860s	78	2000s	1252
1730s	4	1870s	116	2010s	1184

Certainly the numbers of communities have grown enormously over time, and especially since the 1960s. I have identified over three thousand communities active since the beginning of English and Dutch settlement in the seventeenth century. Here is a count of communities that were in operation for each decade from that time forward:

In fact growth of the numbers of communities, relatively speaking, was not as dramatic as those numbers make it appear. Over those four hundred years the American population was growing dramatically as well. In 1610 the American population (excluding American Indians, who were not counted in any government census or estimate until 1860) is estimated to have been 350.[7] By 1790, the date of the first official census, there were fewer than four million Americans. But by 2017 we had some 325 million.[8] The number of people living communally, as a percentage of the population, has never been large, but it is more stable than uncontextualized numbers suggest.

Table 2 shows official census counts of the American population (or, for the earlier years, estimates).

Table 2
Ratio of communes to population

Decade	*Number of communes active*	*US population*	*Ratio of communes to population*	*Notes*
1600s	1	104	1:104	Original population of Jamestown, 1607
1610s	1	325	1:325	Persons in the colonies
1620s	2	2,302	1:1,151	
1630s	1	4,646	1:4,646	
1640s	1	26,634	1:26,634	
1650s	1	50,368	1:50,368	
1660s	2	75,058	1:37,529	
1670s	1	111,935	1:111,935	
1680s	2	151,507	1:75,754	
1690s	4	210,372	1:52,593	
1700s	3	250,888	1:83,629	
1710s	2	331,711	1:165,855	
1720s	3	466,185	1:155,395	
1730s	4	629,445	1:157,361	
1740s	11	905,563	1:82,323	
1750s	18	1,170,760	1:65,042	
1760s	20	1,593,625	1:79,681	
1770s	13	2,148,076	1:165,236	
1780s	13	2,780,369	1:213,874	
1790s	24	3,929,214	1:163,717	Persons in the US
1800s	31	5,308,483	1:171,241	
1810s	39	7,239,881	1:185,638	
1820s	56	9,638,453	1:172,115	
1830s	50	12,860,702	1:257,214	
1840s	103	17,063,353	1:165,664	

Table 2 (*Cont.*)
Ratio of communes to population

Decade	*Number of communes active*	*US population*	*Ratio of communes to population*	*Notes*
1850s	122	23,191,876	1:190,097	
1860s	78	31,443,321	1:403,120	
1870s	116	38,558,371	1:332,380	
1880s	142	50,189,209	1:353,445	
1890s	153	62,979,766	1:411,632	
1900s	169	76,212,168	1:450,960	
1910s	161	92,228,496	1:572,848	
1920s	145	108,021,537	1:744,976	
1930s	229	123,202,624	1:538,003	
1940s	194	132,164,589	1:681,260	
1950s	245	151,325,798	1:617,656	
1960s	628	179,323,175	1:285,546	
1970s	1378	203,302,031	1:147,534	
1980s	1126	226,542,199	1:201,192	
1990s	1190	248,709,873	1:209,000	
2000s	1252	281,421,906	1:224,778	
2010s	1184	308,745,538	1:260,765	

So by my estimates the heaviest concentration of communities in relation to population came with the establishment of Jamestown in 1607 (Jamestown, like Plymouth Colony a few years later, initially had a communal economy, a requirement imposed by the backers of the colony). Once the population of the colonies reached one million, the highest number of communities relative to the total population was 1 per 65,042 Americans (in the decade of the 1750s), and that "market penetration" was never reached again. The lowest came in the 1920s, with one community for every 744,976 people. The 1970s saw more communes, both absolutely and by percentage of population, than the 1960s, with (in the 1970s) one commune for every 147,534 Americans. That was the highest ratio of communes to the American population since the 1760s.

But how many people were living communally? Let us take a huge leap into the unknown and declare that each community had an average of twenty members. On that basis, in Table 3, in the last column, is an estimate of the number of people living communally as a portion of the whole population.

Table 3
Ratio of people living communally to population

Decade	Number of communes active	US population	Ratio of communes to populations	Ratio of people living communally to population	Percentage of population living communally
1600s	1	104	1:104	104:104	100%
1610s	1	325	1:325	1:16	6.250%
1620s	2	2,302	1:1,151	1:58	1.738%
1630s	1	4,646	1:4,646	1:232	0.431%
1640s	1	26,634	1:26,634	1:1,331	0.075%
1650s	1	50,368	1:50,368	1:2,518	0.040%
1660s	2	75,058	1:37,529	1:1,876	0.053%
1670s	1	111,935	1:111,935	1:5,597	0.018%
1680s	2	151,507	1:75,754	1:3,788	0.026%
1690s	4	210,372	1:52,593	1:2,630	0.038%
1700s	3	250,888	1:83,629	1:4,181	0.024%
1710s	2	331,711	1:165,855	1:8,293	0.012%
1720s	3	466,185	1:155,395	1:7,770	0.013%
1730s	4	629,445	1:157,361	1:7,868	0.013%
1740s	11	905,563	1:82,323	1:4,116	0.024%
1750s	18	1,170,760	1:65,042	1:3,252	0.031%
1760s	20	1,593,625	1:79,681	1:3,984	0.025%
1770s	13	2,148,076	1:165,236	1:8,262	0.012%
1780s	13	2,780,369	1:213,874	1:10,694	0.009%
1790s	24	3,929,214	1:163,717	1:8,186	0.012%
1800s	31	5,308,483	1:171,241	1:8,562	0.012%
1810s	39	7,239,881	1:185,638	1:9,282	0.011%
1820s	56	9,638,453	1:172,115	1:8,606	0.012%
1830s	50	12,860,702	1:257,214	1:12,861	0.008%
1840s	103	17,063,353	1:165,664	1:8,283	0.012%
1850s	122	23,191,876	1:190,097	1:9,505	0.011%
1860s	78	31,443,321	1:403,120	1:20,156	0.005%
1870s	116	38,558,371	1:332,400	1:16,619	0.006%
1880s	142	50,189,209	1:353,445	1:17,672	0.006%
1890s	153	62,979,766	1:411,632	1:20,582	0.005%
1900s	169	76,212,168	1:450,960	1:22,548	0.004%
1910s	161	92,228,496	1:572,848	1:28,642	0.003%
1920s	145	108,021,537	1:744,976	1:37,249	0.003%

Table 3 (*Cont.*)
Ratio of people living communally to population

Decade	*Number of communes active*	*US population*	*Ratio of communes to populations*	*Ratio of people living communally to population*	*Percentage of population living communally*
1930s	229	123,202,624	1:538,003	1:26,900	0.004%
1940s	194	132,164,589	1:681,260	1:34,063	0.003%
1950s	245	151,325,798	1:617,656	1:30,883	0.003%
1960s	628	179,323,175	1:285,546	1:14,277	0.007%
1970s	1378	203,302,031	1:147,534	1:7,377	0.014%
1980s	1126	226,542,199	1:201,192	1:10,060	0.010%
1990s	1190	248,709,873	1:209,000	1:10,450	0.010%
2000s	1252	281,421,906	1:224,778	1:11,239	0.009%
2010s	1184	308,745,538	1:260,765	1:13,038	0.008%

In 1840, the Shaker heyday, the national population was 17 million. Today it is 325 million. Figuring the Shakers as a percentage of population, the 5000 Shakers of 1840, about .03 percent of the population, would have been over 97,000 today—far more than today's communal powerhouse, the Hutterites. In other words, the American communal presence looks as if it had been stronger in 1840 than it has been since, and that is largely true. But it has gone up and down, making trends or patterns difficult to identify.

So, to return to my original question, were there waves of communal activity, and, if so, when did they occur? In terms of simple numbers of communities, there was a surge in the 1840s and 1850s and then another in the 1960s and 1970s, the latter largely continuing ever since, although it is now in decline. There was a bit of a surge at the end of the nineteenth century, but it was not a wave that crested and passed; communities remained at similar numbers for the next half century. There was a small surge in the 1930s, but after a dip in the 1940s, numbers stayed above the 1930s level permanently.

In terms of numbers of communities in relation to the nation's population, the strongest communal presence was clearly in the seventeenth century. Until the 1710s there was only one decade (the 1670s) that failed to reach one commune per 100,000 citizens. Of course that reflects a small number of communities in a sparsely populated set of colonies. There was a bit of a surge in the 1740s through 1760s, a major dip in communal presence in the 1860s during the civil war, and then a mild rebound in the 1870s and 1880s (although the prewar communal presence was not achieved again), but thereafter ups and downs that presented at best mild surges. The next real surge waited until the 1960s. That one seems to be slowing in the 2010s, but there have been more communities, relative to population, every decade than at any time since the 1850s.

As for numbers of participants in communal living in relation to the nation's population, with my rather wild postulate of an average of twenty members per commune, it's hard to see any strong waves at all. Overall, the pattern here resembles the one just above. Again, the strongest communal penetration of the culture was in the seventeenth century. In the eighteenth century, there was a modest communal surge in the 1740s, 1750s, and 1760s, but the numbers of communitarians did not reach those, proportionately, of the century before. The early twentieth century had the lowest numbers of all, with the communal population hovering at about 0.003 percent of the national population for half a century. Then in the late 1960s there was an upswing that crested in the 1970s and has been declining ever since, although we still have twice as many people living communally, proportionately, as we did in the early twentieth century.

I don't really have any quarrel with Barkun except that his database, the only one available at the time, was too small. He and Berry were looking at the founding of communes, a useful enterprise. Looking at numbers that reflect a growing national population, however, I believe that the communal presence in the country has been more stable than we have heretofore tended to think, and, unfortunately, quite marginal.

A Final Disclaimer

This attempt at understanding the true presence of communes and communitarians is filled with methodological problems. I will enumerate the most important of them:

1. The parameters I have placed on my counting constitute methodological limitations. One is that I have only counted by decades—that is, in my enumeration I have tried to count every community that was operating at any point in a given decade. That can produce

misleading results; if one is checking a box for every decade a community was known to have been active, conceivably a community that only operated for a few weeks or months at the end of, say, 1969, and the beginning of 1970 would get the same notice as a community that operated for a whole twenty-year span. The picture would be much clearer if a count could be taken by year rather than by decade. But that makes the whole task much more complex. We simply don't have enough detailed information to be that precise in our counting. As it is, I have made many estimates of founding and ending decades (based on as many data points as I could discern), and narrowing those estimates down to a year would make them much more error-prone.

2. A related limitation is that we just don't have enough documentation to make a thorough and reliable study of these thousands of communities. Most communal historical scholarship has focused on a relatively few well-known communitarian groups—preeminently the Shakers, but also the Harmonists (and other Radical Pietists), Oneida, the Hutterites, and a few others—and has hardly noticed the vast majority of the thousands of communities this country has seen. It is hard to study the whole if a great many parts are not included.
3. The count of communities is based on entries in my *Encyclopedic Guide*. But in addition to the 3,000 or so communities that have entries in that work, I have an appendix with some 1,400 communities that I believe existed but about which I have not had enough information to write even a brief entry. Further, and most important, there are a great many communities—thousands of them, almost certainly—that have escaped my notice. I learn of new communities, past and present, on a nearly weekly basis. In other words, the database here, while much larger than Okugawa's, remains woefully incomplete.
4. I have not counted any early American settlements of Spain or France—that is, those that pre-dated the beginning of English settlement in 1607. I believe that all or most of them did not fit my definition of intentional community. I also have not counted American Indian tribes, because their admittedly communal culture did not withdraw from, or stand in opposition to, the larger society, but *was* the larger society in which they lived.

5. Generally, I have identified individual communities, not networks of communities. Thus Shaker villages and Hutterite colonies are listed individually, and I do not include in my count Owenites, Fourierists, New Monasticism, Bruderhof, Movement for a New Society, Shakers, Hutterites, Dariusleut, or other such groupings. In each of these cases I have listed the individual communities within the larger movement. But then I have listed Amana only once, because the villages were in fairly close proximity and the landholding was in one large parcel. On the other hand, I have included each Harmonist village, even though the group involved was essentially the same each time, moving from place to place; similarly I have counted each Brotherhood of the New Life location separately. Not much consistency there, but, as Emerson said, "Consistency is the hobgoblin of little minds."
6. I have not counted subcommunities separately. I did not include such "pods" or "homesteads" as Dandelion or Yarrow at Red Earth Farms or Skyhouse at Dancing Rabbit in my count. But I do include those that were freestanding at one point, but that later (or earlier) were not.
7. I have not included individual Catholic Worker houses; they are too diffuse (they are self-identified), their dates can be hard to find, and lists of them are incomplete. (I have a list of 469 Worker houses past and present in the United States, but I'm fairly sure it's not complete, nor is it probably entirely accurate.)
8. I have not included Catholic, Eastern Orthodox, Episcopalian, or Lutheran religious communities, except noncanonical ones. I have excluded them only to make my work easier, since they fit my definition of intentional community. There are well over a thousand Catholic monasteries and convents in the United States, as well as (probably) around one hundred Orthodox monasteries, and smaller numbers of Episcopal and Lutheran ones. Including them all would greatly increase my task. Help!
9. I have not included cohousing communities. Some cohousers eschew labels such as "commune" or "communal"; some do not. I have identified about 190 cohousing communities in the United States, and, as with other categories, I am sure my list is incomplete.

10. I have ducked out of cases in which specific details are hard to find. For example, by my standards the Morehouses, which may have numbered more than one hundred, should have individual listings—but I can't find anything like a list, so I have just one Morehouse entry. That skews things—there should be at least one hundred entries. Similarly several religiously based communal networks (Gospel Outreach, Move of the Spirit) had multiple locations, and the Shiloh Youth Revival Centers had as many as 175 local communal houses at the movement's peak.

Adding all of those "not included" categories together, they represent more communities than I have used in my database. And no one can estimate the number of communities that have escaped notice. This work is far from complete.

Appendix B

American Intentional Communities, 1900–2000

Herewith I list intentional communities active in twentieth-century America. For economy of space, only names are provided here. For dates, places, and other information on each of them, see my *Encyclopedic Guide to American Intentional Communities*, 2nd ed. (Clinton, NY: Richard W. Couper, 2015). Other lists of communities active during various time periods in American history have been published; I have had the advantage of using those lists, since they preceded my own publication, and they have helped make my own list as comprehensive as possible. Readers may want to refer to such works as Robert Fogarty's *Dictionary of American Communal and Utopian History* (Westport, CT: Greenwood, 1980); Donald Pitzer's edited volume *America's Communal Utopias* (Chapel Hill: Univ. of North Carolina Press, 1997); Foster Stockwell's *Encyclopedia of American Communes, 1663–1963* (Jefferson, NC: McFarland, 1998); and James Morris and Andrea Kross's *Historical Dictionary of Utopianism* (Lanham, MD: Scarecrow, 2004).

In an effort to keep this list under control, I have not included Catholic monasteries or convents (except for noncanonical ones), Catholic Worker communities, or cohousing communities; those three categories together have numbers of local communities approaching two thousand. Lists covering the latter two categories are included in an appendix in my *Encyclopedic Guide*. Hutterite colonies in the United States are listed here, but are presented separately following the main list.

Many communities change their names over time; the communities listed here are presented by the names by which they are or were best known.

Communities Founded Earlier, Still in Operation in 1900

Alfred Shakers
Almondale
Bellamy Colony
Bookwalter Colony
Brotherhood of the New Life
Bryn Athyn (Pennsylvania)
Burley
Burning Bush
Canterbury Shakers
Cassadaga
Chi Theta Chi
Christian Commonwealth Colony
Christian Cooperative Colony
Christian Social Association
Church of the Living God (Shiloh)
Church Triumphant
Clitherall
Colonia Chuichupa
Colonia Diaz
Colonia Dublan
Colonia Garcia
Colonia Juarez
Colonia Morelos
Colonia Oaxaca
Colonia Pacheco
Colorado Co-operative Company
Commonwealth of Israel
Cooperative Industrial Colony
Duke Colony
Dunlap
Enfield Shakers (Connecticut)
Enfield Shakers (New Hampshire)
Equality (Washington)
Esoteric Fraternity
Fairhope
Fort Amity
Fort Herrick
Fort Romie
Fountain Grove
Freedom Colony
Freeland (Bellingham, Washington)
Friedheim
Friendswood
Glenmore
Hancock Shakers
Harvard Shakers
Home
Home Employment Co-operative Community
Iosepha
Israel Hill
Jan Hus Residence
Kinder Lou
Koreshan Unity
Lake Pleasant
Leclaire
Lily Dale
Lord's Farm
Lystra
Megiddo Mission
Mount Lebanon Shakers
Narcosee Shakers
New Clairvaux
Niksur
North Union Shakers
Olive Branch
Palestine
Penington Friends House
Philadelphia Shakers

Pleasant Hill Shakers
Point Loma
Preston
Ralston Heights
Roycroft
Ruskin (Georgia)
Sabbathday Lake Shakers
Shalam
Shirley Shakers
Socialist Valley
Societas Fraternia
South Union Shakers
Straight Edge Industrial Settlement
Sunnyside (Arizona)
Union Village Shakers
Watervliet Shakers
White Oak Shakers
Whitewater Shakers
Willard Co-operative Colony
Winters Island
Woman's Commonwealth
Woodbine (New Jersey)
Zion Home

Communities Founded 1900–2000

17th Street Collective
21st Street Commune (New York)
21st Street House (Texas)
25 to 6 Baking and Trucking Society
23rd Psalm House
23rd Street Collective
34 Delmar
507 Atlanta Avenue
611 EcoVillage
924 Howard Street
1000 Small Pharmablisters
1090 Page Street
1616 22nd Street, NW
1801 Woolsey Street
1957 Biltmore Street NW
AAA
Abba's Way
Aberdeen Gardens
Abhayagiri Buddhist Monastery
Abhedananda Acres
Abode of the Message
Abundant Dawn
Acorn
Active Acres
Ad Astra Coop
Adawehi
Adelphi
Adidam
Adirondack Herbs
Adobeland
Aerious
African American Theme House
African Hebrew Israelites
Agahpay
Agape Community
Agape Family
Agape Fellowship
Agape Fellowship House
Agape House
Agape Inn (Oregon)
Agape Inn (Texas)
Agape Lay Apostolate
Aggressive Christianity Missions Training Corps

Ahimsa
Ahimsa Farm
Ahimsa House
Ahupuaa Village
Airplane House
Akwenasa
Alamo Christian Foundation
Alapine Village
Alcuin
Alcyone Light Center
Aliya Community
Alleluia Community
Almanac House
Almost Heaven
Aloe
Alpha Colony
Alpha Farm
Alta
Alta Vista House
Alternative Community
Alternative Futures
Alternative LifeStyles
Alton Colony
Altruist
Alvastra
Amalgamated Housing Cooperative
Amana Colonies
Amata Community
Am Chai
American Brotherhood
American Buddhist Shim Gum Do
American Colony
American Landuist Society
American Playground Commune
Amitabha Ashram
Amity Experimental Community
Ananda Ashram
Ananda Ashrama
Ananda Center
Ananda Kamalalaya
Ananda Kanan
Ananda World Brotherhood Village
Anathoth Community Farm
Ancient Artisans Village
Andorra II
Andres Castro Arms
Anitya Bhavan
Annwin (or Annwfn)
Ant Farm
Ant Hill Cooperative
Antioch Community
Antioch Group
Any Day Now
Apex Belltown Co-op
Apollo
Apostolic United Brethren
Apple Tree Acres
Appletree Co-op
April Farm
Aprovecho
Aquarian Concepts
Aquarian Foundation
Aquarian Research Foundation
Aquarian Temple
Aquarius Ranch
Arcata House
ARC Ecumenical Retreat Center
Archuletaville
Arco Iris
Arcosanti
Arden
Ardencroft

Ardentown
ARF
Arizona Abode of Love
Ark
Ark of the New Covenant
Arlington Friends House
Army of Industry
Arpin
Arrakis
Arsha Vidya Gurukulam
Art Colony at Eden Falls
Artesia
Arthurdale
Arts and Humanities Cooperative
Arunachala Ashram
Aryaloka Buddhist Retreat Center
Aryan Nations
Ashburnham
Ashby TreeHome
Ashland Vineyard Community
Askov
Assembly, The
Assembly of YHW Yoshua
Assisi Community
Astro
Atherton Stewardship Commty
Atkins Bay Farm Community
Atlanta Fellowship
Atlantis
Atlantis I
Atlantis Rising
Atmaniketan Ashram
Audarya Ashram
Audre Lorde Co-op
Aum Desert Temple Sanctuary
Aurora (Lincoln, California)
Aurora (Mendocino County, California)
Aushet
Austin Community Fellowship
Austin Homesteads
Avalon Co-op (Texas)
Avalon Co-op (Wisconsin)
Baby Farm
Baca Grande-Crestone
Backbench
Baggins End
Baltic Street
Banana Patch
Bankhead Farms
Baring Street Fellowship
Bartimaeus Community Church
Bass Lake Farm
Batavia Community
Bawa Muhaiyaddeen Fellowship Farm
Bayard Lane
Bayland Family
Beacon Hill Friends House
Beal House Co-op
Bear Gulch
Bear Mountain Sanctuary
Bear Tribe Medicine Society
Beaux Arts Village
Beaver Lodge
Bee Farm
Beechtree
Be-Lite Community
Belle Terre
Bellyacres
Bemis Erectus
Ben Israel Fellowship

Benton Farm
Berachah House
Berkeley Town House
Beth Adriel
Bethany Fellowship
Bethel College
Bethel Home
Beth-El Village
Bethlehem Covenant Community
Beyond Jordan
Bhaktivana
Bhavana Society Forest
Bible Way
Big Brother and the Holding Company
Bigfoot
Big House East
Big Indian
Big River Farm
Big Water Colony
Big Wheels Ranch
Bike Republic
Biosphere 2
Birdsfoot Farm
Black Bart
Black Bear Ranch
Blackberry
Black Cat House
Black Elk Co-op
Black Flag
Black Mountain College
Black Oak Ranch
Black Panther Communes
Black Walnut Cooperative
Bliss Wizards
Blossom
Blue Heron Farm
Blue House (Georgia)
Blue House (Washington)
Blue Moon Cooperative Community
Blue Moon Ranch
Blue River Ashram
Bob the House
Bodega Pastures
Bodhi Manda Zen Center
Bodhi Monastery
Body of Christ
Bohemian Cooperative Farming Company
Bonsilene
Bosch Co-op
Bo's Land
Bosque Farms
Boundary Farms
Bower House
Bowers House
Branch Davidians
Brandywine Forest
Brazos de Dios
Bread and Puppet Theatre
Bread and Roses College House
Breitenbush Hot Springs
Bride of Christ (Azalea, Oregon)
Bride of Christ (Corvallis, Oregon)
Bridge Mountain
Briggs and His Devouts
Bright Morning Star
Brigid Collective
Broad Street
Brook House
Brooklyn Commune

Brotherhood Community
Brotherhood of Christ
Brotherhood of Eternal Love
Brotherhood of Light
Brotherhood of the Spirit
Brotherhood of the Sun
Brotherhood of the Way
Brotherhood of the White Temple
Brothers and Sisters of Charity
Brotmanville
Brown House
Brownville
Bryn Athyn (Vermont)
Bryn Gweled
Bubbaland
Buck Rock
Buddhist Society for Compassionate Wisdom
Burch House
Bushville
Butler Green Farm
Butterworth Farm
Byrdcliffe
Cabbage Lane
Cactus Rose
Cadmus Lifesharing Association
Cahaba
Calabash Farm
Calliope
Cambridge Commune
Cambridge Commune (Lewd)
Cambridge Cooperative Club
Cambridge Zen Center
Camelot of the Wood
Campbell Club
Camphill Communities California
Camphill Kimberton Hills
Camphill Minnesota
Camphill Soltane
Camphill Special School
Camphill Village USA
Camp Joy
Camp Sister Spirit
Canaan Farm
Canaan Franciscan Brothers
Canterbury Community
Canyon
Capp Street Collective
Caritas of Birmingham
Carl Street House
Carmel in the Valley
Casa Grande Farms
Casa Zimbabwe
Caspar Point
Castle Hayne
Cat City
Catholic Resistance Commune
Catholic Worker farms and houses
Cedar Grove
Cedar Gulch
Cedar Hollow
Cedarwood
Celo
Centennial Park
Center
Center for Christian Renewal
Center for Feeling Therapy
Center for Peace and Life Studies
Center for Purposeful Living
Center for the Examined Life
Center for the Next Step
Center for Well-Being

Center of the Light
Centers for Change
Central-Page
Cerro Gordo
Cesar Chavez House
Chandler Farms
Chatham Colony
Cheesecake
Chelsea Commune
Cherry Lake Farms
Chester Creek House
Chestnut Hill Farm
Chicago Religious House Commune
Chicot Farms
Children Kansas
Children of God
Children of Light
Children of the Valley of Life
Chinook Learning Community
Christananda Adi Shakti
Christ Brotherhood
Christ Family
Christ House Church
Christian Brothers
Christian Communities Program
Christian Encounter Ranch
Christian Faith and Life Community
Christian Family
Christian Farm
Christian Homesteading Movement
Christian Liberation House
Christian World Liberation Front
Christine Center
Christmas Star
Christ of the Hills
Christ's Church of the Golden Rule
Christ's Community
Christ's Household of Faith
Chrysalis (Indiana)
Chrysalis (Virginia)
Chrysalis Co-op (Colorado)
Church of All Worlds
Church of Bible Understanding
Church of Christ Patriarchal
Church of God and Saints of Christ
Church of Hope
Church of Isla Vista
Church of the Creative
Church of the Divine Birth
Church of the Earth
Church of the Golden Rule
Church of the Lamb of God
Church of the Messiah
Church of the Redeemer
Church of the Risen Christ
Church of the Saviour
Church of the Servant King
Church of the Sojourners
Church of Unlimited Devotion
Church on West Street
Church Universal and Triumphant
Circle of Friends
Circle Pines Center
Circle Springs
City Island Commune
City of Light
City of Love
City of Ten Thousand Buddhas
City of the Sun

Clare's Hermitage
Clarion
Clarkstown Country Club
Claymont Society
Clayton House
Clinton Farm
Clivendon House Club
Close Farm
Cloud Mountain Retreat Center
Cloyne Court
Coagulators
Cockette House
Coe Ridge
Coffee House Commune
Cogslea
Cohasset Ashrama
Cold Comfort Farm
Coldfoot Creek
Cold Mountain Farm
Cold Pond Community Land Trust
CoLibri
Collegiate Living Organization
Colonia LeBaron
Colony, The (California)
Colony, The (Kansas)
Colorado City
Committee for Nonviolent Action Farm
Common Circle
Common Ground (Alabama)
Common Ground (Virginia)
Common Ground Housing
Common Place
Commonterra
Common Threads
Commonwealth College
Commonwealth Farm
Commonwealth Guest House
Commune, The (New York)
Communitarian Village
Community (Virginia)
Community at Cookeville
Community Covenant Fellowship
Community Evolving
Community for Creative Nonviolence
Community for Urban Encounter
Community Frontiers
Community Homestead
Community Homestead Osceola
Community House (New York)
Community House (Virginia)
Community of Celebration
Community of Christian Family Ministry
Community of Hospitality
Community of Jesus
Community of Santa Barbara
Community of St. Luke
Community of the Agape
Community of the Servant
Community of Urbana Cooperative Housing
Community of Zen
Compost College
Compound "I"
Concord
Concord House
Confluence
Consciousness Village
Contemporary Mission
Convent

Cooperative College Community
Cooperative Farm
Cooperative Homesteads
Cooper Street Household
Coop House
Copifawna
COPS Commune
Cornucopia
Cornucopia West
Corvallis Conservation Farm
Cosmotheist Community
Countryside Community
Couples and Grad Girls Co-op
Covenant Community
Covenant House (New York)
Covenant House (Oregon)
Covenantal Community
Covenant, the Sword, and the Arm of the Lord
Crabapple
Crabapple Corners
Crack of Dawn
Craftsman Farms
Crestone Mountain Zen Center
CRO Farm
Crook's Creek
Cropperville
Crosses Creek
Cumberland Homesteads
Cumbres
Currents Community
D Acres
Dai Bosatsu Zendo
Dalworthington Gardens
Dance Hawaii
Dancing Bones
Dancing Rabbit
Dancing Rocks
Dancing Waters Permaculture Co-op
Dandelion Hill
Danevang
Danish Colony
Davidian Seventh Day Adventists
Davis Bend
Davis County Cooperative Society
Davis House
Davis Student Co-op
Dawes Hill
Daybreak
Daybreak Ranch
Dayspring Church
Daystar
Dayton Homesteads
Dayton House
Dearfield
Debs House
Decatur Homesteads
DeCloud Family Commune
Deep Run Farm
Deep Woods Farm
Deer Park Monastery
Deer Rock
Deer Spring Bruderhof
De Graff
Delancy Street Foundation
Delaware Valley Land Trust
Delhi
Delta Cooperative Farm
Denbigh Ecumenical Community
Denver Space Center
Derby House

Desert Ashram
Deshee Farms
Desiderata
Devil's Lake
Dhamma Dena
Diakonia Farm
Diamond Mountain
Diga
Dignity Village
Dinky Universal Church
Disciples of Thunder
Diverse Matrix
Divine Light Mission
Divine Madness
Doe Branch Community
DOE Farm
Dolphin Society
Dome House
Domes, The
Dona Ana Farms
Don Henry Co-op
DooDah
Doreá Peace Community
Dos Pinos
Double Dyke Ranch
Dover Associates
Downeast Friends Community
Downhill Farm
Dragon Belly Farm
Dragonwagon
Dreamers
Dreamtime Village
Drop City
Drug Abuse Preventive Center
Druid Heights
DuBois House
Dudley Co-op
Du-Ma
Dunamis
Dunes Beach
Dunmire Hollow
Durham
Dyess Colony
Eagle Ranch
Earth, Air, Fire, and Water
Earth Cycle Farm
Earthdance
Earth Family Farm and Ecovillage
Earth Garden Community
Earthaven
Earthlands
Earthmind
Earth People's Park
Earth Walkers
Earth's Rising
Earthward Bound
Earthworks
East Blair Housing Cooperative
East Hill Farm (Cherry Valley, New York)
East Hill Farm (Rochester, New York)
East Los Angeles Molokan Community
East Ridge Community
East River Farm
East Street Gallery
East-West House
East Wind
Eater Family
Ecofarm Community
Economy

Ecovillage at Ithaca
Ecumenical Institute
Eden Ministry Center
Eden West
Edges
E-Haus
Eighth Day Faith Community
Ekone Ranch
El Centro
ElDorado Mountain Yoga Ashram
Ella Baker Graduate House
Ella Jo Baker Intentional Community Cooperative
Ellicott City
Ellis Island
Elm Lane Eight
El Monte Homesteads
Elohim City
Eloin
Elsworth Cooperative
Elverhoj
Elysium Fields
Embassy of the Heavens
Emerald City
Emerson Tenants Cooperative
Emma Goldman Finishing School
Emmaus Movement
Enchanted Garden
Enchanted House
Encounter House
Enright Ridge
Entitas
Entropy Acres
Entwood
Equitable Farm
Esalen
Eschatologia
EskDale
Essenes of Kosmon
Establishment
Eternal Cause Society
Ethiopian Coptic Zion Church
Etna House
Euclid Hall
Evangelical Sisterhood of Mary
Evenstar
Expanded Family
Fairfield Bench Farms
Fairview House
Fairview Mennonite House
Fairway Farms
Falsington
Families of St. Benedict
Family (Bronx, New York)
Family (New Mexico)
Family (New York City)
Family Dog
Family Farm
Family of David
Family of Friends
Family of Peace
Family of the Mystic Arts
Family of Three Lights
Family Service Corps
Family Synergy
Fan Lake Brethren
Farband Houses
Fare-Thee-Well Community
Farkle Farm
Farm (Kansas)
Farm (Oregon)
Farm (Tennessee)

Far Valley Farm
Fat Man's Jug Band
Featherfield Farm
Federation of Communities in Service
Fellowship Community
Fellowship Farm (California)
Fellowship Farm (New Jersey)
Fellowship Farm (West Acton, Massachusetts)
Fellowship Farm (Westwood, Massachusetts)
Fellowship House (Illinois)
Fellowship House (Indiana)
Fellowship of Believers
Fellowship of Hope
Felton Guild
Fenway Studios
Ferency House
Ferrer Colony
Festival Church
Fillmore House
Finders
Finlandia
First Baptist Church of Beverly Hills
First Baptist Church of Chula Vista
First Church in Community of the Cosmic Christ
First Street Fellowship
Five Star
Flatrock Community
Flint River Farms
Floating Lotus Opera Company
Flora
Floras Creek
Flow Creek
Floyd's Big House
Fly Away Home
Flying Frog Farm
Food Farm
Footbridge Farm
Forest River Colony
Forgotten Works
Fort Hill Faggots for Freedom
Foundlings
Four Chimneys Farm
Four Winds Community
Four Winds Farm
Four Winds Village Peace Center
Fox Hill Bruderhof
Franciscan Workers
Franklin Farms
Fraternity of Preparation
Free Acres
Free Bakery
Freedom City
Freedom Hill
Freedom Molokan Community
Free Farm
Freefolk
Free Growth
Freeland (Whidbey Island, Washington)
Free Press Commune
Free School Community
Free State of the Ark
Free Vermont
French House
Friendly Homes
Friends Community
Friends' Cooperative House

Friendship House
Friends Lake Cooperative Community
Friends Southwest Center
Frogge Hollow
Frogs Run Farm
Fruit Crest
Fruitvale Housing Cooperative
Full Circle (Vermont)
Full Circle Farm (California)
Full Circle Farm (Pennsylvania)
Fuller House
Fun Family Farm
Furies Collective
Furry Freak Brothers
Gaia Grove
Gaia Sangha
Gaien
Galahad's
Ganas
Ganja Boogie Band
Garberville House
Garden of Joy Blues
Gardner, Tim
Gate Hill Cooperative
Gatekeepers
Gates of Heaven
Gathering (Pennsylvania)
Gathering (Virginia)
Gee's Bend Farms
Gemeinschaft Group
Genesis
Georgeville Trading Post
Gesundheit!
Geysers
Gibbs Co operative Colony
Gila Colony-Llano
Gilbert
Gilman Hot Springs
Gilpin's Point
Ginger Ridge Farms
Gita Nagari
GLAD
Glendale Molokan Community
Glen Eyrie
Glen Ivy
Glen Maples
Glennonville
Glenwood Cooperative House
Global Order
Goat Farm
God's Free Universe
God's Love in Action
Golden
Goldens Bridge Cooperative Colony
Gold Mountain Monastery
Gold Sage Monastery
Gold Summit Sagely Monastery
Gold Wheel Sagely Monastery
Good Earth Commune
Goodenough Community
Goodrich Farm Cooperative
Good Shepherd Tabernacle
Good Times Commune
Goose Pond
Gorda Mountain
Gorg Family
Gorilla Choir House
Gospel Outreach
Gould Farm
Grace Catholic Church

Grace Haven Farm
Grail Community
Grandma's Place
Grand Valley Independent Baptist Church
Granger Homesteads
Graniteville Commune
Grant Street House
Grasmere
Grassroots Community
Grassroots/Dandelion
Grateful Dead
Grateful Union
Great Commission Community
Greater World Earthship
Great Oaks School of Health
Great Pumpkin Commune
Greenbelt
Greenbriar
Greendale
Greenfeel
Greenfield Ranch
Green Gulch Farm
Greenhills
Green House Cooperative
Greenhouse Cooperative (Michigan)
Greenhouse Cooperative (Ohio)
Greening Life
Greenleaf
Green Oaks Community
Green Pastures Estate
Green Tower Community
Green Valley School
Greenwave
Greenwood Forest
Greenwood Homesteads
Gregory House
Grey Gables
Griffin Gorge Commons
Group, Inc.
Group W House
GROW II
Guardians of the Earth
Haidakhandi Universal Ashram
Hale Byodo Corazon
Halidon
Halifax Farms
Hallomas
Halstead House
Hamilton Street Resistance House
Hamsa Community
Happening House
Happyville
Harbinger
Harbin Hot Springs
Hardscrabble Hill
Harkness Co-op
Harlem Ashram
Harlem House Bruderhof
Harman Co-op
Harmon House
Harmony
Harmony Hill
Harmony Hills
Harmony House
Harmony Ranch
Harrad West
Hartford Street Zen Center
Harvest Hills
Harvest House (Costa Mesa, California)

Harvest House (San Francisco, California)
Harvest House (New York)
Harwood House
Hattiesburg Homesteads
Havagoats
Havurat Shalom
Hawk Hill
Hawkwind Earth Renewal Cooperative
Haymarket House
Hayward Heath Little Landeers
Head
Healing Light Foundation
Healing Waters
Healthy, Happy, Holy Organization (3HO)
Heartbeet Lifesharing
Hearthaven
Hearthshire Community
Hearthstone
Hearthwind Farm
Heartland
Heartland Farm
Heartlight Center
Heartsong
Heartwood Institute
Heathcote Community
Heaven City
Heavenly Breakfast
Heaven's Gate
Heckalutz Farm
Hei Wa House
Helicon Home Colony
Helios
Henderson Cooperative House
Henley House
Heraseed
Hickory Farms
Hickory Ridge
Hidden Hill Friends Center
Hidden Springs (Georgia)
Hidden Springs (New Hampshire)
Hidden Springs (New Jersey)
High Flowing
Highland Community
Highlander Folk School
Highland House
High Ridge Farm
High Top
High Valley
Highway Missionary Society
High Wind
Hilden Gibson Co-op
Hill Co-op
Hillegass House
Hillegass-Parker House
Hill Farm
Hillsdale Neighbors Association
Hilltop
Hill Top Farm
Himalayan Academy
Himalayan Institute
His Name Ministry
Hitchcock Hill
Hoedads
Hog Farm
Hogwild
Hohm
Hokyoji
Holden Village
Holiday

Holy City
Holyland
Holy Order of MANS
Holy Protection Gnostic Christian Monastery
HOME
Home Farm
Home of Truth
Homestead at Denison
Homestead Guild Communities
Hong Kong West 1/2 Way House
Hooker House
Hop Brook Commune
Hope Community
Hopewell
Hopkins Hall
House (California)
House (Massachusetts)
Household of Faith
House of Acts
House of Agape
House of Christian Love
House of Commons
House of David
House of Elijah
House of Emmanuel
House of Esther
House of Joy
House of Judah (Alabama)
House of Judah (Georgia)
House of Lavendar
House of Life
House of Love and Prayer
House of Miracles
House of Pergamos
House of Prayer (California)
House of Prayer (Ohio)
House of Psalms
House of Sky
House of the Lord
House of the Seventh Angel
House of Tiny Egos
House of Yahweh
House of Zaccheus
Hoyt Hall
Hsi Lai Temple
Hudgeons Creek Farm
Huggs Family
Human Dancing Company
Human Potential Foundation
Hummingbird Community
Hunters Lodge
Hypatia Cooperative House
IDA Community
Ilarne
Illustrated Farm
Indian Camp
Indralaya
Ingleside
Ink
Inner Life Fellowship
Innisfree
Inn on the Way
In Search of Truth
Insight Meditation Society
Institute for Harmonious Development
Institute for the Development of the Harmonious Human Being
Institute Mountain West
Institute of Mentalphysics
Integral Urban House

International Babaji Yoga Sangam
International Buddhist Meditation Center
International Buddhist Progress Society
International Center for Self-Analysis
International Cooperative House
International Federation for Internal Freedom
Ionia
Iowa City All-Women's Collective
Ironwood Homesteads
Island (California)
Island (Rhode Island)
Island Earth
Island of the Red Hood Commune
Israel Family
Ithaca Project
Ithilien
Jabul Arabiyya
J'Ananda
Janet Smith House
Jayhawk Co-op
JC Light and Power Company
Jersey Homesteads
Jerusalem
Jesuit Volunteer Corps
Jesus Christ Power House
Jesus Christians
Jesus Christ's Community at Hebron
Jesus People Army
Jesus People USA
Jiun
Job Chilaway House
John Moore Co-op
Johnson Pasture
John T. Lyle Center
Jolly Ranchers
Jonah House
Joseph House (Maryland)
Joseph House (Pennsylvania)
Joshua House
Journey Family
Jubilee Church
Jubilee House Community
Jubilee Partners
Judi Cooperative
Julian Pleasants
Julian Woods Community
Jump Off Community Land Trust
Jupiter Hollow
Jupiter's Ridge
Kabbalah Center
Kahumana Farm and Community Center
Kalalau Outlaws
Kalani Oceanside Retreat
Kaliflower
Kanatsiohareke
K'an Ts'ui
Kanzeon Sangha
Karma Dzong
Karma Farm
Karma Triyana Dharmachakra
Karmê Chöling
Karmu
Karum Group
Kashi Ashram
Katharsis
Kaw Koettes Co-op

Kayavarohana
Kearney Street
Keep Cottage
Keetley Farms
Kelly Road House
Ken Keyes College
Kenney Ridge
Kerista
Kerman Molokan Community
Keystone
Keystone Ecological Urban Center
Kiantone
Kibbutz Micah
Kidd Hall
Kid Kolony
Kindness House
Kindred Community
King House
Kingdom of Heaven
Kingman Hall
Kingwood
Kinsey Farms
Kirkridge Retreat
Kitsiookla Group
Kittamaqundi Community
Kneadmore Community
Koinonia Community (California)
Koinonia Community (Kansas)
Koinonia Community (Maryland)
Koinonia Farm
Kopkind Colony
Kripalu Center
Krishna
Kristenstadt
Krotona (Hollywood, California)
Krotona (Ojai, California)
Kunga Ling
La'akea Community
Laetare Partners
Lake Dick
Lake Istokpoga
Lake Village
Lakeview Farms
Lakota Cooperative
La Luz de la Lucha
Lama Foundation
Lamaist Buddhist Monastery
Lamb of God
Lamborn Valley Community
Lampa Mountain Community
The Land
Landlovers
Land of Oz
Lane's End Homestead
Laramie County Jewish Colony
Laramie Street
L'Arche Communities
Last Days Ministries
La Tierra
Laughing Rock Farm
Laurel Canyon
Laurel House
Lavender Hill Womyn's Retreat
LaVita Township
Lay Order of St. Michael
Lazarus House Church
Leatherbark Community Farm
Leavitt Hill Farm
Leicester Commune
LeisureLand!
Lemurian Fellowship
Leslie Community

Lester House
Leyden Society
Libertee World
Liberty Cluster
Libre
Lichen Co-op
LIFE
Lifestyle Associates
Light as Color Foundation
Lighthouse
Lighthouse Ranch
Light Morning
Light of Freedom
Light of the Mountains
LILA
LimeSaddle
Lincoln County Colony
Linden Tree
Linder House
Lindisfarne Association
LION Community
Little River House
Living Communion Association
Living Lightly Village
Living Love Center
Living Love Fellowship
Living Rock Christian Men's Co-op
Living Room
Living Springs
Llano del Rio Colony
Logan Street Covenant House
Log Cabin
Lokelani 'Ohana
Lonaku
Long Branch Environmental Education Center
Long Leaf
Longview Homesteads
Lopez Island
Lorax Manner
Lorien
Lorien Family Land
Los Angeles Eco-Village
Los Torrenitos Little Landers
Lost Valley Educational Center
Lothlorien
Lothlorien Cooperative House
Lothlorien Nature Sanctuary
Love
Love Holy Trinity Blessed Mission
Love Inn
Love Valley
Lower Farm
Lucedale
Lucerne
Lukas Community
Lunasi
Luther Buchele House
Lyle Olsen
Lyman Family
Lystra
M.A. Center
Mabel Dodge Luhan House
Maccabee Farm
MacDowell Colony
Macedonia Cooperative Community
Mad Brook Farm
Madhava Family
Madison House
Madre Grande Monastery
Magdalen Farm
Magic

Magic Animal Farm
Magic Forest Farm
Magic Tape Community
Magic Tortoise
Magnolia Homesteads
Magnolia Street Commune
Mahantongo Spirit Garden
Main Street Gathering
Maitreya Ecovillage
Maitri Therapeutic Community
Makena Beach Colony
Malu 'Aina
Mama Mountain
Ma-Na-Har Cooperative Fellowship
Mankind United
Mann Ranch
Manor
Mansion Messiah
Manson Family
Maple Hill Commune
Maple Ridge Bruderhof
Maple Tree Farm
Maranatha Houses
Maranatha North Church
Marathon
Marathon Co-operative
Marblemount Outlaws
Marcella
Marengo
Marietta
Marion Mennonite Brethren Fellowship
Mariposa Group
Mariposa Grove
Mariposa School
Marpa House
Martha's Housing Cooperative
Martinsville Ministry Center
Mary's City of David
Masala Co-op
Master's House
Matagiri Sri Aurobindo Center
Matanuska Colony
Maud's Land
Maui Zendo
Maverick
Maxwood Institute
May Creek Farm
May Valley Cooperative Community
Maya
Mayday Farm
Ma Yoga Shakti International Mission
McComb Homesteads
McGee's Farm
Meadowlark Farm
Meadowlark Homestead
The Meadows (California)
The Meadows (Oregon)
Medical Opera
Medicine Wheel
Meditation Mount
The Meeting
Meher Spiritual Center
Melbourne Village
Mennonite Voluntary Services
Menominee River Fellowship
Merion
Merry Fox Community
Merry Pranksters

Messiah's World Crusade
Meta Tantay
Mettanokit
Miccosukee Land Cooperative
Michigan Farm
Mid-Mountain
Milarepa Center
Mileston Farms
Milk River Farms
Milkweed Hill
Millay Colony
Millbrook
Millstone Co-op
Mill Valley Commune
Minneapolis Group
Minnesota Commune
Minnie's Co-op
Minton Commune
Mirkwood
Mohegan Colony
Molino Creek Farming Collective
Molly Hare Cooperative
Monan's Rill
Moniteau Farm
Monroe Institute
Montague Farm
Monta Vista Little Landers
Montebello Community
Monteville
Montrose
Moonridge
Moonshadow
Moorish Science Homes
Morehouse Communities
Moriah
Morning Glory Community
Morning Star (New Mexico)
Morning Star (New York)
Morning Star (California)
Morningstar Family
Morningside
Morningside House
Morningtown Pizza Parlor
Mosaic
Mother Earth Church of Opihihale
Motherfuckers
Mother Love's Nature Sanctuary
Mother of God
Mounds Farms
Mountain Drive
Mountain Grove Community
Mountain Homestead
Mount Airy
Mount Angelus Drive Sanctuary
Mount Baldy Zen Center
Mount Ecclesia
Mount Madonna
Mount Olive Homesteads
Mount Zion Overcoming Body of Christ—The True Bride
MOVE
Move of the Spirit Communities
Moy Mell
Mud People
Mu Farm
Mukaki Farm Village Community
Mulberry Family
Mulberry Farm
Mullein Hill
Muslims of America
Mustard Seed
Mustard Tree Co-op

Mutual Township
Nadabrahmananda Ashram
Nada Hermitage
Nahziryah Monastic Commty
Nakamura House
Namaste
Namgyal
Nanish Shontie
Narrow Ridge
Narrow Ridge Earth Literacy Center
Nasalam
Nation of Islam Farms
Nation of Yahweh
Naturalism
Nature Farm
Nature's Spirit Community
Nearing homestead
Neary Lagoon Co-op
Neem Karoli Baba Ashram
Ness Community
Nethers Community
Nevada Colony
Neverland
Newark Ashram
New Beginnings Community
New Berlin
New Buffalo
New Community Church
New Community Cooperative
New Community Farm
New Community I
New Community Projects
New Covenant Fellowship
New Creation
New Era
New Family Community
New Goloka
New Guild
New Hamburger
New Hanover
New Haven Zen Center
New Hope
New House of Israel
New Hrsikesa Foundation
New Jah-rusalem (Wisconsin)
New Jerusalem Community (Ohio)
New Land
New Life (Illinois)
New Life Farm (Missouri)
Newllano Colony
New Meadow Run Bruderhof
New Medinah
New Mexico Farms
New Moon House
New Orleans Zen Temple
New Prairie Fellowship
New Raman Reti
New Skete
New Slant
New South Lifestyles
Newsreel
New Swarthmore
New Talavan
New Vrindaban
Niche
Ninth Street Coop
Nirvana Community
None of the Above Ranch
Norma
North Carolina Biodome
Northeon Forest

North Mountain
Norvelt
Nottingham Cooperative
Nourishing Space
Now House
Nuwaubian Community
Nyingma Institute
Oak Grove
Oakland Elizabeth House
Oakshade
Oak Valley Herb Farm
Oakwood Colony
Oakwood Farm
Obiji
O'Brien Lake Homesteaders
Odiyan
O'Farrell Street House
Ofek Shalom Cooperative House
Ohana Aloha
Ohana Mauka
Ohmega Salvage
Ojai Foundation
O'Keefe House
Old Barrows
Old Day Creek Road Commune
Old McCauley Farm
Old Phoenix Gold Mine
Olema Commune
OLHA
Olive House
Olompali Ranch
Olympia Housing Collective
Omega House (Minnesota)
Omega House (South Dakota)
Om Hollow
Om Lovers
Om Shanti
Oneida II
One Life Family
Onion Farm
Onyx House
Open Door (Texas)
Open Door Community (Georgia)
Open House
Opsis Co-op
Oquitadas Farm
Oracle House
Oracle Tribe
Orange House
Orca Landing
Orchard Street Church
Order:Ecumenical
Order of Christ/Sophia
Order of Christian Workers
Order of St. Michael
Order of Theocracy
Order of Zion
Oregon Farm
Orphalese Foundation
Ortiviz Farm
Oscar Wilde House
Osterweil House
The Other Cheek
Our Father's Family
Outpost
Overcomer Community
Owen House
OWL Farm
Oyotunji Village
Ozarkana Acres
Pacific Family Co-op
Pacific High School

Packer Corners
Padanaram Settlement
Padma Jong
Padma Ling
Pagoda
Paisano Collective
Palmerdale
Pangaia
Papaya
Paradise Valley
Parados
Parishfield
Parker Street Co-op
Park Place Commune
Partners for Global Justice
Partoun
Pasadena House
Patchwork Central
Pax Center
Peace Action Farm
Peace and Liberation Commune
Peace Farm
Peace Gardens
Peace Mission Movement
Peaceful Gardens
Pearl Street Co-op
Pea Soup
Peking Man House
Penderlea Homesteads
Pendle Hill
Penmar
Penn-Craft
People House
People of Hope
People of Joy
People of Praise
People of the Living God
People's Christian Coalition
People's Farm
People's Information Center
Peoples Temple
Perserverance Furthers
Peter Gray's Valley
Phanto Bolo
Philadelphia Fellowship
Philadelphia House
Phillipston Plantation
Phoenicia Pathwork Center
Phoenix Cooperative House
Phoenix Family
Phoenix Homesteads
Physical Culture City
Picknie Farm
Piecemakers
Piedmont Homesteads
Pie in the Sky
Pilar Hill
Pinch of Love
Pinebrook Community
Pine Lake Environmental Campus
Pine Mountain Valley
Pinesdale Community
Pine Street Commune
Pine Terrace Nine
Piñon Ecovillage
Pioneer Cooperative
Pisgah Grande
Pit
Placer County
Platte Cove Bruderhof
Pleiades
Plow Creek Fellowship

Plowshare Community
Plowshare Farm
Plum Bayou
Plum Creek Community
Po-Ahtun
Poiema Community
Point of Infinity Retreat Center and Community
Polarity Institute
Polluck Ferry Mutual Association
Ponderosa Village
Port Centauri
Portland Group
Portugue Ranch
Post-American
Potash Hill Community
Potlatch
Potter's House Church
Potter Valley Molokan Commity
Prag House
Pragtree Farm
Prairie Dog Village
Prana
Prema Dharmasala
Prickly Mountain
Pride Family
Primal Scream Radical Ministry
Process Church of the Final Judgment
Project Artaud
Project One
Project Two
Providence Farm
Providence Zen Center
Prudence Crandall House
Pumpkin Hollow (Tennessee)
Pumpkin Hollow Farm (New York)
Purple Rose
Putney Commune
Pygmy Farm
Quaker City
Quaker House
Quaker Intentional Village-Canaan
Quakerland
Quarry Hill
Quest
Qumbya Cooperative
Rabbity Hill Farm
Rachana Community
Radiance
Raelians
Ragdale
Ragged Mountain
Rainbow Community
Rainbow Family
Rainbow Farm (California)
Rainbow Farm (Michigan)
Rainbow Farm (Vermont)
Rainbow Hearth Sanctuary
Rainbow House
Rainbow Ridge Ecovillage
Rainbow Star Retreat
Rainbow Valley (Washington)
Rainbow Valley Agricultural Cooperative (Texas)
Rainbow's End
Rainbows End Farm
Rainbow's Other End
Raintree Investments
Rajarajeshwari Peetham
Rajneeshpuram
Raj-Yoga Math and Retreat

Ramagiri Ashram
Ramakrishna Monastery
Rancho Linda Vista
Rancho Palomarin
Raphael's House
Ratna Ling
Rattlesnake Gulch
Ravendale
Raven Rocks
REACH Earthship community
Realife Ranch
Reality Construction Company
Reba Place
ReCreation Center
Red Banks Mutual Association
Redbird
Red Clover
Red Dog Saloon
Red Family
Red House
Red House Farms
Red Paint
Red Rockers
Redwood Valley Finnish Colony
Reevis Mountain
Refugio del Rio Grande
Regenerative Cooperative of Pomona
Reina del Cielo
Rejoice Always
Religious Society of Families
REMAR
Renaissance House
Renewal House
Resistance House
Restored Church of Jesus Christ
Restored Israel of Yahweh
Revolutionary Tomato
Rhizome Collective
Richton Homesteads
Ridgefield Colony
Ridge House
Ridge Street Commune
Ridgzin Ling
Righteous Branch of the Church of Jesus Christ of Latter Day Saints
Rinzai-Ji Zen Center
Rio Bonito
Rising Son Ranch
Rising Sun Tribe
Rivendell (Virginia)
Rivendell Cooperative (Michigan)
River City Housing Collective
River Community Homes
River Farm
River Haven
Road #721
Roandoak of God
Roanoke Farms
Robin Hill
Rochdale (Connecticut)
Rochdale Co-op (Kansas)
Rochester Ashram
Rocinante
Rockbottom Farm
Rock Chalk Co-op
Rockridge
Rockridge Ashram
Rootworks
Rose Creek Village
Rose Valley
Roseworth Colony

Rounder Records
Round Mountain Cooperative Community
Rova Farm
Rowe Camp and Conference Center
Royal Co-op
Rudrananda Ashram
Rufus Jones House
Ruggles House
Ruhani Satsang
Running Water Farm
Runnymede Little Landers
Ruskin (Florida)
Russells Mills
Rutabaga House
Ruth's House
Rutland Square House
Sabina's Land
Sacred Heart Community
Saggitarius Rising Tribe
Sai Anantam Ashram
Saints' Christian Retreat
Salal
Salamander Springs
Salem Acres
Saline Valley Farms
Salmonberry Community Land Trust
Salmon Creek Farm
Salmon River House
Sami Mahal
Sanatana Dharma Foundation
Sandhill Farm
Sandstone Retreat
San Fernando Farm
San Fernando Homesteads
San Francisco Zen Center
Sangha
San Jose House
San Luis Valley Farms
San Mateo Ecovillage
Santa Barbara Avenue House
Santa Barbara Student Housing Cooperative
Santa Fe Community School
Santa Rosa Creek Commons
Sant Bani Ashram
San Ysidro Little Landers
Sassafras
Sassafras Ridge Farm
Sattwa
Savitria
SBA Farms Collective
Scatter Creek
School of Living
Scuppernong Farm
Scuppernong Landing
Sea and the East Utopian Mission
SEADS of Truth
Sea Org
Seattle Commune
Seattle Liberation Front
Seattle's Intentional Community Program
Sedgewick Commune
Seed Company
Seekers Church
Self Master Colony
Self-Realization Fellowship Retreat
Seneca Falls Co-op
Seven Middagh Street
Sevenoaks Pathwork Center

Seven Springs Community
Seventh Elect Church in Israel
Seventh Street House
Seven Waves
Shady Grove
Shakerton
Shalom Community
Shalom House
Shamanic Living Center
Shambhala Mountain Center
Shannon Farm
Shanti Ashrama
Shanti Mandir
Shantivanam
Sharing Community
Sharon Springs Zen Center
Shasta Abbey
Sheepfold House
Shekinah
Shenandoah (Idaho)
Shenandoah Homesteads (Virginia)
Shenoa Retreat
Shepherdsfield
Shepherd's Gate
Sherman Hall
Sherwood Co-op
Sherwood Forest Collective
Shiloh (Arkansas)
Shiloh Youth Revival Centers
Shining Waters Ashram
Shivalila (California)
Shivalila (Hawai'i)
Sholem Aleichem Houses
Short Mountain Sanctuary
Shoshoni Yoga Retreat
Shree Hridayam Satsang
Sichlassenfallen
Siddhachalam
Siddha Yoga Dham
Sierra Hot Springs
Silver Circle
Sirius
Sisters for Christian Community
Siva Kalpa
Sivananda Ashram Yoga Ranch
Sivananda Yoga Vedanta Center
Six Points
Skyhouse
Skyview Acres
Sky Woods Cosynegal
Slade Hall
Slaughterhouse Creek
Slaves of the Immaculate Heart of Mary
Society for Ascension Academy
Society for Human Development
Society of Families
Society of St. Pius X monasteries
Sojourners Community
Sojourners' Orchard
Sojourner Truth House (Iowa)
Sojourner Truth House (Michigan)
Songaia
Song of the Morning Ranch
Sonnewald Homestead
Sonoma Mountain Zen Center
Sons Ahmen Israel
Sophia Community
Sophia Cooperative House
Soul Inn
Source Collective
Source Family

South End Commune
Southern Cooperative Association of Apalachicola
Southern Dharma Retreat Center
Southern Rainbow
Southwest Sufi Community
Sowing Circle
Spadefoot
Sparrowhawk Village
Spaulding Unit
Spiral Garden
Spiral Wimmin's Land Trust
Spirit of 76 Realty Trust
Spirit Rock Meditation Center
Spiritual Community, Inc.
Spiritual Dawn Community
Spring Hill Community
Spring Lake Ranch Therapeutic Community
Springtree Community
Spring Valley Bruderhof
Spring Valley Community
Springwater Center
Sri Ram Ashrama
Starcross Monastery
STAR Earthship Community
Starland Retreat
Star Mountain
St. Benedict's Farm
St. Clare's Hermitage
Stebbins Hall
Stelle Community
Stevens House Co-op
Stewart Little Co-op
St. Francis Acres
St. Francis Community
St. Francis River Farms
St. George United Order
St. Helena
St. Herman of Alaska Brotherhood
Still Meadow Community
Still Water Sabbatical
Still Wind Community
Stillpoint
St. James Community
St. John's Order
Stone House
Stone Soup Cooperative
Stonerage Collective
Stoney Mountain Farms
Strange Farm
Strawberry Fields
Strong City
Struggle Mountain
St. Theresa's Village
Suburban Palace
Sugarbush Farm
Sugarloaf Women's Village
Sugar Mountain
Sullivan Institute
Summit Avenue Cooperative
Sunat Center
Sun at Midday
Sunbow
Sundance Extended Commty
Suneidesis Consociation
Sun Farm
Sunflower Cooperative
Sunflower Farm
Sunflower House (Kansas)
Sunflower House (Pennsylvania)
Sunflower Life Center

Sunnyridge Commune
Sunnyside Collective
Sunnyside Farm Christian Community
Sunny Valley
Sunray Peace Village
Sunrise Communal Farm
Sunrise Commune
Sunrise Community Land Trust
Sunrise Co-operative Farm Community (Michigan)
Sunrise Co-operative Farm Community (Virginia)
Sunrise Co-operative Farms (New Jersey)
Sunrise Farm (New York)
Sunrise Hill
Sunrise Ranch
Sunset House (California)
Sunset House (Washington)
Sunshower Farm
Sunstar
SunToads Farm
Sunwise Co-op
Suruban Partners
Susan B. Anthony Memorial Unrest Home
Sweetwater Community
Sweetwater Community Land Trust
Sword of the Spirit
Sycamore Community
Symbionese Liberation Army
Synanon
Synchronicity
Synergia Ranch
Synergy Community
Synergy House
Syntropy Institute
Syracuse Cultural Workers
Table Mountain Ranch
Tahanto
T'Ai Farm
Taliesin Fellowship
Talsalsan Farm
Tanguy Homesteads
Tank House
Taormina
Taos Co-op
Tara
Tara Mandala
Tashi Choling
Tassajara Mountain Center
Taungpulu Kaba-Aye Monastery
Tawapa
Taylor Camp
Teaching Drum Outdoor School
Tekiah
Temenos
Temple of Still Waters
Temple of the Gospel of the Kingdom
Temple of the People
Ten Stones Community
Terra Firma (Oregon)
Terra Firma Commune (New York)
Terra Nova
Terrarium
Terrasquirma
Terrebonne Farms
Thelemic Community
Third Avenue Cooperative
Third Eye Commune

Thomas Merton Peace Community
Threefold Farm
Three Springs
Tiara Street
Tierra Madre
Tierra Verde Fellowship
Tillery
Toad Hall
Toad Lane
Tolstoy Farm
Town Tavern and Café
Trabuco College
Trails End Ranch
Trans-Love Energies
Transylvania Farms
Trapelo
Traprock Peace Center
Tree Frog Farm
Treehouse
Trees Community
Tribe (Arizona)
Tribe (Colorado)
Tri-Cooperatives
Triform Camphill
Trijang Buddhist Institute
Trillium Farm
Trinidad House
Triple Creek
True Farm Community
True House
True Light Beavers
Trumann Farms
Tuolumne Co-operative Farm
Tupelo
Tupelo Homesteads
Tupelo Ridge
Tupumaros Collective
Turkey Ridge Farm
Turtle Creek Farm
Turtles Island
Twelve Tribes
Twin Oaks
Twin Pines Co-op (Kansas)
Twin Pines Cooperative Community (California)
Two D Vegetarian Co-op
Two Rainbows Community
Two Rivers Farm
Tygart Valley Homesteads
Tyler
U & I Community
Ucopia
U-Lab-Three
Unadilla Farm
Unification Church
Union Acres
United Order Family of Christ
United Order of Equality
United Stand
Unity House
Universal Healing Arts & Research
Upaya Zen Center
Upper Applegate Community
Urban Life Center
Urban Stonehenge
USCO
Usonia
Vail House
Vajrapani Institute
Vale
Valley Cooperative School
Valley of Peace

Valley View Christian Fellowship
Valley Zendo
Van Eeden Colony
Van Houten Fields
Varsity House
Vedanta Ashrama
Vedanta Olema Retreat
Vedanta Society Old Temple
Vedic City
Village Design
Village of Arts and Ideas
Village of Harmony
Village Oz
Village Terraces
Villa Sarah
Villa Serena
Vine and Fig Tree
Virgil House
Vivekananda Monastery
Vocations for Social Change
Vocations for Social Change/East
Voice of Elijah
VOL Community
Volksberg
Vrindavan Yoga Farm
Walden House (Connecticut)
Walden House (Washington, DC)
Walden Three
Walker Creek Community
Wall Hill
Walnut House Cooperative
Walnut Street Co-op
Warehouse Family
Washita Farms
Wat Carolina Buddhajakra Vanaram
Water Creek Cooperative Village
Watermargin Cooperative
Watermyn
Wat Lao Buddhavong
Wat Mongkoltempunee
Wawa
Way International
Wayne Produce Association
Weather Underground
Weavers
Webster Street
Wedgwood House
Weed Mine Farm
Weinfeld Group Living Residence
Wellman Road Big House
Wellspring
Wellspring House
We'Moon Land
Wendell Farm
Wesleyan Christian Community
Western Slope Farms
Westside Community
West Wind
Wetumpka Farm
Wheeler's Ranch
Whetstone Community
Whipporwillow
White Buffalo Farm
Whitehall Co-op
White House
White Lotus Study Center
Whole Health Foundation
Wildfair Ranch
WildHeart
Wilfred
Willard Street House

William Street Co-op
Willits House
Willow
Willow Gold
Willow Southwest
Wilmot Center
Windspirit Farm and Community
Windtree Ranch
Windward
Winter Peaches
Wisconsin Family
Wiscoy Valley Community Land Cooperative
Wisteria
Wita Wenton Co-op
WKFL Fountain of the World
Wolf Creek Community
Wolf Creek Sanctuary
Wolf House
Wolf Lake Refuge
Woman's Commonwealth
Woman's Place
WomanShare
Women's Art Colony Farm
Women's Collective
Wonderland Civic Association
Woodbine Community (Florida)
Woodburn Hill Farm
Woodcrest Bruderhof
Wooden Bridge Community
Wooden Shoe
Woodfolk House
Woodlake Community
Woodstock Commune
Woody Hill Co-op
Word of God Community
Word of Life Community
Work of Christ Community
Workers Cooperative Colony
Wormhole House
Wygelia
Xanadu
Yaddo
Yaeger Valley Community Farm
Yahara Linden Coop
Yamato Colony (California)
Yamato Colony (Florida)
Yamato Colony (Texas)
Yana Trails Community
Yea God
Yellow Fire Puppet Theater
Yellow House Commune
Yellow Submarine
Yesss Community
Yoga Anand Ashram
Yoga Society of Rochester
Yogaville
Yonderfamily
York Center Community Co-operative
Your Heritage Church
Youth for Truth
Yronwode
Zami! Housing Coop
Zen Bones Intentional Spirit
Zen Center of Los Angeles
Zen Community of New York
Zen Macrobiotic Retreat
Zen Mountain Center
Zen Mountain Monastery
Zendik Farm
Z Fellowship
Zion (Tennessee)
Zion City (Illinois)

Zion Coptic Church
Zion Harbor
Zion's Inn
Zion Society
Zion's Order of the Sons of Levi
Zion's Retreat
Zuni Mountain Sanctuary

Hutterite Colonies in the United States

Schmiedeleut

Colonies Founded Earlier, Still Operating in 1900

Bon Homme
Milltown

Colonies Founded 1900–2000

Big Stone
Blumengard
Brentwood
Buffalo
Cedar Gove
Claremont
Clark
Clearfield
Cloverleaf
Deerfield
Elmendorf
Evergreen
Fairview
Fordham
Forest River
Glendale
Glendale Farm
Gracevale
Gracevale Farm
Grassland
Grass Ranch
Greenwood
Haven
Heartland
Hillcrest
Hillside
Hillside Farm
Huron (1)
Huron (2)
Hutterville
James Valley
Jamesville
Lake View
Long Lake
Maple River
Maxwell (1)
Maxwell (2)
Mayfield
Millbrook
Millerdale
Neuhof
Newdale
New Elmspring
Newport
Oak Lane
Old Elmspring
Orland
Pearl Creek
Pembrook
Plainview
Platte
Pleasant Valley
Poinsett

Riverside
Rockport
Rolland
Rosedale (1)
Rosedale (2)
Rustic Acres
Shamrock
Spink
Spring Creek
Spring Lake
Spring Prairie
Spring Valley
Starland
Suncrest
Sundale
Sunset
Thunderbird
Tschetter
Upland
White Rock
Willowbank
Wolf Creek

Dariusleut

Colonies Founded Earlier, Still Operating in 1900

Jamesville
King Ranch

Colonies Founded 1900–2000

Ayers Ranch
Beadle
Deerfield
East Malta
Espanola
Fallon
Flat Willow
Fords Creek
Forty Mile
Gilford
Grass Range
Kilby Butte
Kutter
Lamona
Loring
Marlin
Milford
Miller
Mountain View
New Miami
New Rockport
North Harlem
Pleasant Valley
Pondera
Richards
Rimrock
River View
Rockport
Sage Creek
Schoonover
Seville
Spink
Spokane
Spring Creek
Springdale
Stahls
Surprise Creek
Turner
Warden

Warren Range
Wilson Range
Wolf Creek

Lehrerleut

Colony Founded Earlier, Still Operating in 1900

Old Elmspring

Colonies Founded 1900-2000

Big Sky
Big Stone
Birch Creek
Cascade
Duncan Ranch
Eagle Creek
East End
Fairhaven
Glacier
Glendale
Golden Valley
Hartland
Hidden Lake
Hilldale
Hillside
Kingsbury
Martinsdale
Milford
Miller
New Miami
New Rockport
Rockport
Sage Creek
Springdale
Springwater

Notes

Preface

1. Timothy Miller, *The Quest for Utopia in Twentieth-Century America, Volume 1* (Syracuse: Syracuse Univ. Press, 1998), xx–xxii.

2. Perdita Buchan, *Utopia, New Jersey: Travels in the Nearest Eden* (New Brunswick, NJ: Rivergate/Rutgers Univ. Press, 2007), 219.

3. Timothy Miller, *The Encyclopedic Guide to American Intentional Communities*, 2nd ed. (Clinton, NY: Richard W. Couper, 2015), xi–xii.

4. Donald E. Pitzer, "Introduction," in *America's Communal Utopias*, ed. Donald E. Pitzer (Chapel Hill: Univ. of North Carolina Press, 1997), 12–13.

1. The Century Winds Down, and Communities Thrive

1. For an estimate of the numbers of communes active during the 1960s era, see my earlier book, *The 60s Communes: Hippies and Beyond* (Syracuse: Syracuse Univ. Press, 1999), xvii–xx.

2. For a survey history of the Hutterites that includes details of the Schmiedeleut division as well as other problems experienced by the Hutterites in the last several years, see Rod Janzen and Max Stanton, *The Hutterites in North America* (Baltimore: Johns Hopkins Univ. Press, 2010).

3. The best history of the Bruderhof is Iaácov Oved, *The Witness of the Brothers: A History of the Bruderhof* (New Brunswick, NJ: Transaction, 1996).

4. Many histories of the Catholic Worker have been published. See, for example, Dorothy Day, *Loaves and Fishes: The Story of the Catholic Worker Movement* (San Francisco: Harper & Row, 1963).

5. One of several good accounts of the Camphill movement in America is found in Dan McKanan, *Touching the World; Christian Communities Transforming Society* (Collegeville, MN: Liturgical, 2007).

6. L'Arche's founder has provided a good introduction to the movement and its philosophy. See Jean Vanier, *Community and Growth* (New York: Paulist, 1989). Another useful work is Kevin S. Reimer, *Living L'Arche: Stories of Compassion, Love and Disability* (Collegeville, MN: Liturgical, 2009).

7. Tracy Elaine K'Meyer, *Interracialism and Christian Community in the Postwar South* (Charlottesville: Univ. of Virginia Press, 1997); Ann Louise Coble, *Cotton Patch for the Kingdom: Clarence Jordan's Demonstration Plot at Koinonia Farm* (Scottdale, PA: Herald, 2002).

8. On the Peace Mission Movement, see Robert Weisbrot, *Father Divine and the Struggle for Racial Equality* (Urbana: Univ. of Illinois Press, 1983); Jill Watts, *God, Harlem, USA* (Berkeley: Univ. of California Press, 1992). On the House of David, see Clare E. Adkin, *Brother Benjamin: A History of the House of David* (Berrien Springs, MI: Andrews Univ. Press, 1990).

9. On the Fundamentalist Latter Day Saints of Colorado City/Hildale, see Martha Sonntag Bradley, *Kidnapped from That Land: The Government Raids on the Short Creek Polygamists* (Salt Lake City: Univ. of Utah Press, 1993). More information, plus many references, on the communities covered in these three paragraphs can also be found in my two earlier volumes in this series, *The Quest for Utopia in Twentieth-Century America, Volume I* (Syracuse: Syracuse Univ. Press, 1998), and *The 60s Communes: Hippies and Beyond* (Syracuse: Syracuse Univ. Press, 1999).

10. See, for example, Douglas Stevenson, *The Farm Then and Now: A Model for Sustainable Living* (Gabriola Island, BC: New Society, 2014).

11. At this writing no comprehensive history of the Twelve Tribes has been published. For an overview, see Susan J. Palmer, "The Twelve Tribes: Preparing the Bride for Yashua's Return," *Nova Religio* 13, no. 3 (February 2010): 59–80.

12. For a comprehensive survey of the sprawling Jesus Movement, see Larry Eskridge, *God's Forever Family: The Jesus People Movement in America* (New York: Oxford Univ. Press, 2013).

13. On Jesus People USA, see Shawn David Young, *Gray Sabbath: Jesus People USA, the Evangelical Left, and the Evolution of Christian Rock* (New York: Columbia Univ. Press, 2015).

14. B. F. Skinner, *Walden Two* (New York: Macmillan, 1948).

15. Kat Kinkade, *Is It Utopia Yet? An Insider's View of Twin Oaks Community in Its 26th Year* (Louisa, VA: Twin Oaks, 1994).

16. [Ram Dass], *Remember, Be Here Now* (San Cristobal, NM: Lama Foundation, 1971).

17. Miller, *The 60s Communes*, 80–81, 116–18. My earlier account has been supplemented with oral information from current and former members.

2. Cohousing Comes to America

1. Dorit Fromm, "American Cohousing: The First Five Years," *Journal of Architectural and Planning Research* 17 (Summer 2000): 94–109. Fromm found cohousing projects ranging from eight to forty-two units, with an average of twenty-four.

2. Kathryn McCamant, Charles Durrett, and Ellen Hertzman, *Cohousing: A Contemporary Approach to Housing Ourselves*, 2nd ed. (Berkeley: Ten Speed, 1994).

3. Danny Milman, "Where It All Began: Cohousing in Denmark." www.getriil.org/~getriil/cgi-bin/details.php?anum=1505.

4. Timothy Miller, *The Encyclopedic Guide to American Intentional Communities*, 2nd ed. (Clinton, NY: Richard W. Couper, 2015), 502–5.

5. One good account of Doyle Street Cohousing is McCamant, Durrett, and Hertzman, *Cohousing*, chapter 17.

6. Stella Tarnay, "Bringing Life Back to an Urban Neighborhood," in *Reinventing Community: Stories from the Walkways of Cohousing*, ed. David Wann (Golden, CO: Fulcrum, 2005), 144–54.

7. Fromm, "American Cohousing: The First Five Years," 94–109.

8. Mark Oppenheimer, "Soul-Searching in a Christian Community Over Views on How to Live," *New York Times*, September 1, 2012.

9. A.P. Glass, "An Evaluation of an Elder Cohousing Community," *Gerontologist* 51, supplement 2 (2011): 504.

10. Lydia Ferrante-Roseberry, "Living with Integrity: My Experience in Cohousing," *Social Policy* 33, no. 2 (Winter 2002): 18–19.

11. Fromm, "American Cohousing: The First Five Years," 94–109.

12. Graham Meltzer, "Cohousing: Verifying the Importance of Community in the Application of Environmentalism," *Journal of Architectural and Planning Research* 17, no. 2 (Summer 2000): 110–32.

13. David Wann, *Reinventing Community: Stories from the Walkways of Cohousing* (Golden, CO: Fulcrum, 2005), 47.

14. Graham Meltzer. *Sustainable Community: Learning from the Cohousing Model* (Victoria, BC: Trafford, 2005), 38.

15. The most substantial work on cohousing for older persons is Charles Durrett, *Senior Cohousing* (Berkeley: Ten Speed, 2005).

16. Dene Peterson, "ElderSpirit: Living the Spiritual Quest in Later Years," *Communities* no. 121 (Winter 2003): 26–29; Patricia Leigh Brown, "Growing Old Together, in New Kind of Commune," *New York Times*, February 27, 2006.

17. The Urban Homesteading Assistance Board has conducted research on the number of co-op housing projects and individual units; some of its findings can be found at www.uhab.org/coopresearch.

18. Gerald W. Sazama, "Lessons from the History of Affordable Housing Cooperatives in the United States: A Case Study in American Affordable Housing Policy," *American Journal of Economics and Sociology*, 59, no. 3 (October 2000): 573–608.

19. "Marathon Low-Income Co-op," *Communities Directory* (Rutledge, MO: Fellowship for Intentional Community, 2010), 229.

20. For a list of student housing cooperatives, see Miller, *Encyclopedic Guide*, 516–18. Many of the co-ops have entries in various editions of the *Communities Directory*. See also Deborah Altus, "Student Housing Cooperatives: Communitarianism among American Youth," *Communal Societies* 17 (1997): 1–13; Deniz Tuncer, ed., "Student Co-ops: What I Really Learned in College," *Communities* no. 110 (Spring 2001): 30–64.

3. The Ecovillage Revolution

1. Karen Svensson, "What Is an Ecovillage?" in *Ecovillage Living: Restoring the Earth and Her People*, ed. Hildur Jackson and Karen Svensson (Foxhold, England: Green, 2002), 10.

2. Diane Gilman and Robert Gilman, *Eco-Villages and Sustainable Communities: A Report for Gaia Trust by Context Institute* (Bainbridge Island, WA: Context Institute, 1991).

3. Jan Martin Bang, *Ecovillages: A Practical Guide to Sustainable Communities* (Gabriola Island, BC: New Society, 2005).

4. Jonathan Dawson, *Ecovillages: New Frontiers for Sustainability* (White River Junction, VT: Chelsea Green, 2006), 7.

5. William Metcalf, *The Findhorn Book of Community Living* (Forres, Scotland: Findhorn, 2004), 19.

6. Louisa May Alcott, "Transcendental Wild Oats," in *Bronson Alcott's Fruitlands*, compiled by Clara Endicott Sears, 115–56 (Harvard, MA: Fruitlands Museums, [1915] 2004).

7. Richard Francis, *Fruitlands: The Alcott Family and Their Search for Utopia* (New Haven: Yale Univ. Press, 2010), 191.

8. Timothy Miller, *The 60s Communes: Hippies and Beyond* (Syracuse, NY: Syracuse Univ. Press, 1999), 140.

9. Miller, *The 60s Communes*, 140–41.

10. Kropotkin's works have been published in many editions. See, for example, Peter Kropotkin, *Fields, Factories, and Workshops* (Montreal: Black Rose, 1994).

11. A. Whitney Sanford, "Being the Change: Food, Nonviolence, and Self-Sufficiency in Contemporary Communities," *Communal Societies* 34, no. 2 (2014): 29–53.

12. The process of deciding to found the new community is described in Kat Kinkade, *Is It Utopia Yet? An Insider's View of Twin Oaks Community in Its 26th Year* (Louisa, VA: Twin Oaks, 1994), 300–305.

13. Information on the seed business can be found at www.southernexposure.com/index.php as well as at Acorn's website, www.acorncommunity.org.

14. Lois Arkin and Jesse Moorman, "Sustainability in the City of Los Angeles," *Communities* no. 115 (Summer, 2002): 36–41.

15. Jim Schenk, "A Home-Grown Ecovillage on Our Street," *Communities* no. 129 (Winter, 2005): 52–56. Enright Ridge's website is at enrightecovillage.org.

16. Taken from the Maitreya Ecovillage website, www.maitreyaecovillage.org.

17. Rebecca Reider, *Dreaming the Biosphere: The Theater of All Possibilities* (Albuquerque: Univ. of New Mexico Press, 2009).

18. Brian Vanneman, "Searching for Paradise in the Rain: Oregon's Communes and Intentional Communities of the 1960s and 1970s," BA honors thesis, University of Oregon, 1997, 39–51.

19. Albert Bates, "A Training Center for Ecovillagers," *Communities*, no. 91 (Summer 1996): 34–35.

20. Gilman, *Eco-Villages and Sustainable Communities*, 77–79. Information on the Soldiers Grove solar program can also be found on the town's website, www.soldiersgrove.com.

21. For an illustrated depiction of Camphill Kimberton Hills, see Bang, *Ecovillages*, 140–42. For the Camphill movement more generally, see Dan McKanan, *Touching the World: Christian Communities Transforming Society* (Collegeville, MN: Liturgical, 2007; Jan Martin Bang, *A Portrait of Camphill: From Founding Seed to Worldwide Movement* (Edinburgh: Floris, 2010).

22. Paul Hawken, *The Magic of Findhorn* (New York: Harper & Row, 1975), 1, 5.

23. Quoted from the Sirius Community website, www.siriuscommunity.org/Purpose1.html.

24. Statement on the Sirius Community website, www.siriuscommunity.org/our-fourfold-purpose/.

25. Counts of members and residents are reported by the community to the Fellowship for Intentional Community and posted to the FIC's website at directory.ic.org/1075/Sirius_Community.

26. A basic description of Sirius is provided in community founders Corinne McLaughlin and Gordon Davidson, *Builders of the Dawn: Community Lifestyles in a Changing World* (Walpole, NH: Stillpoint, 1985), 128–34. A briefer description is provided in various editions of the *Communities Directory*; see, for example, *Communities Directory: A Comprehensive Guide to Intentional Communities and Cooperative Living* (Rutledge, MO: Fellowship for Intentional Community, 2010), 273.

27. Much of this information comes from "Abundance Ecovillage," *Communities Directory: A Comprehensive Guide to Intentional Communities and Cooperative Living* (Rutledge, MO: Fellowship for Intentional Community, 2010), 124–25. See also the community's website at www.abundance-ecovillage.com.

28. Diana Christian, "Song, Dance, and Celebration," *Communities* no. 107 (Summer 2000): 28–29.

29. "Potash Hill Community," in *Communities Directory* (Rutledge, MO: Fellowship for Intentional Community, 2000), 315.

30. Quoted in Liz Walker, *EcoVillage at Ithaca: Pioneering a Sustainable Culture* (Gabriola Island, BC: New Society, 2005), 7.

31. "Coho Ecovillage," in *Communities Directory* (2010), 158. The community also maintains an informative website at www.cohoecovillage.org.

32. Basic information on Belfast Cohousing and Ecovillage can be found on the community's website, mainecohousing.org.

33. The final quotation is taken from the community's website, www.earthliteracy center.org. The most extended study of Narrow Ridge is Christopher T. Smith, "Go Tell It on the Mountain: A History of Narrow Ridge Earth Literacy Center," BA honors thesis, Carson-Newman College, 2009. The community's outlook is well embodied in a survey of the environmental health of its bioregion that community members were involved in: John Nolt, Athena Lee Bradley, Mike Knapp, Donald Earl Lampard, and Jonathan Scherch, *What Have We Done? The Foundation for Global Sustainability's State of the Bioregion Report for the Upper Tennessee Valley and the Southern Appalachian Mountains* (Washburn, TN: Earth Knows, 1997).

34. Nicholas K. Geranios, "Residents Believe in Being Comfortable While Preparing for the Worst: Homesteaders Will Be in the Hot Tub Awaiting World War III," *Los Angeles Times*, July 31, 1988; Meg Letterman, "Ponderosa Village: A Self-Reliant Lifestyle," *Communities* no. 67 (Summer 1985): 15–21.

35. Brief synopses of these and other similar environmentally oriented communities can be found in my *Encyclopedic Guide to American Intentional Communities, 2nd ed.* (Clinton, NY: Richard W. Couper, 2015).

36. Miller, *The 60s Communes*, 241–42.

4. The Spiritual Search I

1. Lawrence J. McCrank, "Religious Orders and Monastic Communities in America," in *America's Communal Utopias*, ed. Donald E. Pitzer (Chapel Hill: Univ. of North Carolina Press, 1997), 218–19. McCrank notes that Catholic monks were present in North America from the early days of Spanish exploration, but that organized, settled communities of them came later. He identifies the arrival of Ursuline Sisters in New Orleans in 1727 as a possible starting point for the presence of actual monasteries and convents.

2. "Monasticism in the United States." *Bulletin de l'AIM* (Alliance Inter-Monastères) no. 97 (n.d., ca. 2010). www.aimintl.org/index.php?option=com_content &id=466&lang=en.

3. "Monasticism in the United States."

4. On the controversy over accepting women in close association with the men of the monastery, see Simon Romero, "A Ruling on the Status of Its Women Roils a Monastery," *New York Times*, January 7, 2006.

5. David Janzen and John Michael Talbot, "Brothers and Sisters of Charity," in *Fire, Salt, and Peace: Intentional Christian Communities Alive in North America*, ed. David Janzen et al. (Evanston, IL: Shalom Mission Communities, 1996), 49–52; Terry Mattingly, "Ozark Monastery Not Just for Celibate," *Kansas City Star*, October 10, 1992. The monastery's website is at www.littleportion.org.

6. "Agape," in *Communities Directory: A Comprehensive Guide to Intentional Communities and Cooperative Living* (Rutledge, MO: Fellowship for Intentional Community, 2005), 93. The community's website is at www.agapecommunity.org.

7. Jim McIntosh, "Assisi Community Celebrates 25 Years," *HNP Today Newsletter* 54, no. 24 (December 7, 2011). HNP stands for the Holy Name Province of the Franciscan Friars; it is available online at hnp.org/assisi-community-celebrates-25-years. See also Susanne and Vincent Donoghue, "Assisi Community," in *Fire, Salt, and Peace*, 43–44.

8. From the church's website, www.communityofcelebration.com.

9. David Janzen, "Community of Celebration," in *Fire, Salt, and Peace*, 77–82.

10. George Vecsey, "New Group Combines Evangelism and Orthodoxy," *New York Times*, March 11, 1979.

11. Phillip Charles Lucas, *The Odyssey of a New Religion: The Holy Order of MANS from New Age to Orthodoxy* (Bloomington: Indiana Univ. Press, 1995).

12. Tom Heinen, "Mystics Misunderstood? Religious Order Says It's Out of the Mainstream but Not a Cult," *Milwaukee Journal Sentinel*, March 6, 2005.

13. The Monks of New Skete, *In the Spirit of Happiness* (Boston: Little, Brown, 1999).

14. Acts 2:44–47, New Revised Standard Version.

15. Acts 4:32–37, New Revised Standard Version.

16. Luke 14:33, New Revised Standard Version.

17. Jason Byassee, "The New Monastics," *Christian Century* 122, no. 21 (October 18, 2005): 38–47; Dale Gish and Margaret Swink, "Church of the Sojourners," in *Fire, Salt, and Peace*, 58–62.

18. Virgil Vogt, "Hope Community," in *Fire, Salt, and Peace*, 99–103.

19. Byassee, "The New Monastics," 38–47.

20. Lou Hillendahl, "A Community of Counselor Pioneers," *Communities* no. 92 (Fall 1996): 39–41; David Janzen and Lou Hillendahl, "Wesleyan Community," in *Fire, Salt, and Peace*, 160–64.

21. David Janzen, "Church on West Street," in *Fire, Salt, and Peace*, 63–66.

22. David Janzen, "Shepherdsfield Community," in *Fire, Salt, and Peace*, 138–42; "Shepherdsfield," in *Communities Directory: A Comprehensive Guide to Intentional Communities and Cooperative Living* (Rutledge, MO: Fellowship for Intentional Community, 2007), 245.

23. Richard A. Pride, "Elmo Stoll and the Christian Community at Cookeville," *Border States: Journal of the Kentucky Tennessee American Studies Association* 15 (2003): 36–49.

24. Karel Holloway, "Homestead Heritage Combines Farming, Arts, and a Bit of Tourism," *Dallas Morning News*, September 26, 2003; Roger Olson, "Where Community Is No Cliche: Forty-Three Families in Rural Texas Blend Pentecostal Fervor and Anabaptist Simplicity," *Christianity Today* 49, no. 2 (February, 2005): 56–60.

25. Kelly Hertz, "Hutterites: Not the Best of Times," *Yankton Press and Dakotan*, October 7, 1989, 1, 14.

26. "Friends Community," in *New Age Community Guidebook: Alternative Choices in Lifestyles*, 4th. ed., ed. Bobbi Corcoran (Middletown, CA: Harbin Springs, 1989), 74–75.

27. "Oak Grove," in *Communities Directory: A Comprehensive Guide to Intentional Communities and Cooperative Living* (Rutledge, MO: Fellowship for Intentional Community, 2005), 199–200.

28. "Quakerland," in *Communities Directory: A Guide to Cooperative Living* (Rutledge, MO: Fellowship for Intentional Community, 1996), 287.

29. Barry Yeoman, "Rethinking the Commune," *AARP: The Magazine* (March–April, 2006).

30. "Communities with Openings," *Communities* no. 151 (Summer 2011): 68.

31. The network maintains a website at www.swordofthespirit.net.

32. See, for example, Jay Reeves, "Ala. Commune Leader Involved in New Project Despite Past Abuse Claims, Fire Deaths of Children," *Minneapolis Star Tribune*, April 7, 2010.

33. Rick Reha and Mary Richardson, "Wooden Bridge Community," in *Fire, Salt, and Peace*, 138–42.

34. Nadia Christensen, *Action, Reflection, Celebration: The ARC Story* (n.p, n.d.).

35. For an examination of the principal branches of the Latter Day Saints movement, see *Scattering of the Saints: Schism within Mormonism*, ed. Newell G. Bringhurst and John C. Hamer (Independence, MO: John Whitmer, 2007).

36. J. Gordon Melton, *The Encyclopedia of American Religions*, 7th ed. (Detroit: Gale, 2003), 691–92; Steven L. Shields, *Divergent Paths of the Restoration: A History of the Latter Day Saint Movement*, 4th ed. (Independence, MO: Herald House, 2001), 197–202, 258.

37. Steven L. Shields, "Communalism in the Latter Day Saint Movement," *Communal Societies* 28, no. 2 (2008): 37.

38. Shields, "Communalism in the Latter Day Saint Movement," 37.

39. John R. Llewellyn, *Polygamy Under Attack: From Tom Green to Brian David Mitchell* (Scottsdale, AZ: Agreka, 2004), 33; Andrea Moore-Emmett, *God's Brothel* (San Francisco: Pince-Nez, 2004), 28, 184–90, 230; Steven L. Shields, "Communalism in the Latter Day Saint Movement," 37.

40. Anne Wilde, "Fundamentalist Mormonism: Its History, Diversity and Stereotypes, 1886–Present," in *Scattering of the Saints*, 270–71.

41. See the two volumes of *The Sealed Portion of the Brother of Jared* (Leawood, KS: Leathers, 2001, 2002).

42. Leland Mark Searles, "Returning to Babylon: Processes of Social Change and the Characteristics of Former Participants in a New Religious Movement," MA thesis, Iowa State University, 1993; William D. Russell, "The Fundamentalist Schism, 1958–Present," in *Let Contention Cease: The Dynamics of Dissent in the Reorganized Church of Jesus Christ of Latter Day Saints*, ed. Roger D. Launius and W. B. "Pat" Spillman (Independence, MO: Graceland/Park, 1991), 144–45.

43. Pete Early, *Prophet of Death: The Mormon Blood-Atonement Killings* (New York: William Morrow, 1991); Cynthia Stalter Stassé and Peggy Murphy Widder, *The Kirtland Massacre: The True and Terrible Story of the Mormon Cult Murders* (New York: Donald I. Fine, 1991).

44. Jody Myers, *Kabbalah and the Spiritual Quest: The Kabbalah Centre in America* (Westport, CT: Praeger, 2007).

45. Laurie Zimmerman and Ranee Zaporski, "Kashrut and Compromise at Ofek Shalom," *Communities*, no. 96 (Fall 1997): 38–40.

46. "Center for Well-Being," in *New Age Community Guidebook*, 85. On the earlier Sunrise Co-operative Farm Community, see Christina Lemieux, "The Sunrise Co-operative Farm Community: A Collectivist Utopian Experiment," *Communal Societies*, no. 10 (1990): 39–67.

47. James E. Landing, *Black Judaism: Story of an American Movement* (Durham, NC: Carolina Academic, 2002), 378–82.

48. Joel Rothschild, ["Ravenna Kibbutz, USA."] *C.A.L.L.: Communes at Large Letter*, no. 32 (Summer 2010): 24–25; Fred A. Bernstein, "The Four-Bedroom Kibbutz," *New York Times*, February 11, 2010.

49. "For Orthodox Jews, an Experiment in Farming and Faith," *New York Times*, November 1, 2002; Uriel Heilman, "The Frum Farm," *Jerusalem Post*, March 6, 2003.

5. The Spiritual Search II

1. Alexandra Avakian, *Windows of My Soul: My Journeys in the Muslim World* (Washington, DC: National Geographic, 2008), 164–65; Katy Reckdahl, "Mississippi Muslim," *Gambit* (New Orleans), July 8, 2003, www.bestofneworleans.com/gambit/mississippi-muslim/Content?oid=1241688.

2. The multifaceted story of York's ever-changing operation has been best recounted by Susan J. Palmer in her book *The Nuwaubian Nation: Black Spirituality and State Control* (Farnham, England: Ashgate, 2010).

3. Jo Thomas with Ralph Blumenthal, "Rural Muslims Draw New, Unwanted Attention," *New York Times*, January 3, 2002.

4. Gisela Webb, "Tradition and Innovation in Contemporary American Islamic Spirituality: The Bawa Muhaiyaddeen Fellowship." In *Muslim Communities in North America*, ed. Yvonne Yazbeck Haddad and Jane Idleman Smith (Albany: State Univ. of New York Press, 1994), 96–97.

5. Corinne McLaughlin and Gordon Davidson, *Builders of the Dawn: Community Lifestyles in a Changing World* (Walpole, NH: Stillpoint, 1985), 356.

6. Daniel Atesh Sonneborn, "Music and Meaning in American Sufism: The Ritual of *Dhikr* at Sami Mahal, a Chistiyya-derived Sufi Center," PhD diss., Univ. of California, Los Angeles, 1995, chapter 4.

7. "Southwest Sufi Community," *Communities*, no. 118 (Summer 2003): 67.

8. E. Burke Rochford Jr. has written two books that together provide a narrative of the twists and turns that ISKCON has experienced. See Rochford, *Hare Krishna in America* (New Brunswick, NJ: Rutgers Univ. Press, 1985), and Rochford, *Hare Krishna Transformed* (New York: New York Univ. Press, 2007). Little has been written on Audarya Ashram; one newspaper account is Bob Welch, "East Meets West at Audarya Ashram," *Eugene Register-Guard*, August 8, 1993.

9. Karen Pechilis, "Gurumayi, the Play of Shakti and Guru," in *The Graceful Guru: Hindu Female Gurus in the United States*, ed. Karen Pechilis (New York: Oxford Univ. Press, 2004), 219–43; Gene R. Thursby, "Siddha Yoga: Swami Muktananda and the Seat of Power," in *When Prophets Die: The Postcharismatic Fate of New Religious Movements*, ed. Timothy Miller (Albany: State Univ. of New York Press, 1991), 165–81; Lola Williamson, *Transcendent in America: Hindu-Inspired Meditation Movements as New Religion* (New York: New York Univ. Press, 2010), 106–33.

10. Several books and a multitude of articles have been written on Rajneeshpuram. See, for example, James S. Gordon, *The Golden Guru: The Strange Journey of Bhagwan Shree Rajneesh* (Lexington, MA: Stephen Greene, 1987); Frances Fitzgerald, *Cities on a Hill: A Journey Through Contemporary American Culture* (New York: Simon & Schuster, 1986), 247–381; Marion S. Goldman, *Passionate Journeys: Why Successful Women Joined a Cult* (Ann Arbor: Univ. of Michigan Press, 1999).

11. "Rachana Community," in *Communities Directory* (Rutledge, MO: Fellowship for Intentional Community, 2000), 318.

12. Katharine Webster, "The Case of Swami Rama of the Himalayas," *Yoga Journal* 95 (November–December, 1990): 59ff.

13. Philip Goldberg, *American Veda: From Emerson and the Beatles to Yoga and Meditation—How Indian Spirituality Changed the West* (New York: Harmony Books/Random House, 2010), 203–4; Gene R. Thursby, "Hindu Movements Since Mid-Century: Yogis in the States," in *America's Alternative Religions*, ed. Timothy Miller (Albany: State Univ. of New York Press, 1995), 195–98; Pandit Rajmani Tigunait, *At the Eleventh Hour: The Biography of Swami Rama* (Honesdale, PA: Himalayan Institute, 2001).

14. Sita Bordow, *Sri Swami Satchidananda: Apostle of Peace* (Yogaville, VA: Integral Yoga, 1986); Goldberg, *American Veda*, 198–201; Thursby, "Hindu Movements Since Mid-Century," 198–201.

15. For a general survey of both the TM presence in the town of Fairfield and the nearby Maharishi Vedic City, see Joseph Weber, *Transcendental Meditation in America: How a New Age Movement Remade a Small Town in Iowa* (Iowa City: Univ. of Iowa Press, 2014).

16. Ma and Kashi Ashram are mentioned in several books and articles, but no major study of either the person or the institution has appeared to date. Perhaps the fullest treatment is Vasudha Narayanan, "Gurus and Goddesses, Deities and Devotees," in *The Graceful Guru*, ed. Karen Pechilis, 149–78.

17. Judith Cornell, *Amma: Healing the Heart of the World* (New York: William Morrow, 2001); Selva J. Raj, "Ammachi, the Mother of Compassion," in *The Graceful Guru*, ed. Karen Pechilis, 203–18; David Amsden, "The Big Squeeze," *Rolling Stone* (August 16, 2012): 56–61.

18. Andrew Rawlinson, *The Book of Enlightened Masters* (Chicago: Open Court, 1997), 575–78.

19. Dundas, Paul. *The Jains* (London: Routledge, 2002), 254.

20. Information, with references, on all of these groups is available in my *Encyclopedic Guide to American Intentional Communities* (Clinton, NY: Richard W. Couper, 2015).

21. Rick Fields, *How the Swans Came to the Lake: A Narrative History of Buddhism in America* (Boulder, CO: Shambhala, 1981), 341–42.

22. "Abhayagiri Monastery," in Don Morreale, *The Complete Guide to Buddhist America, 2nd ed.* (Boston: Shambhala, 1998), 32–33. The monastery's website is at www.abhayagiri.org.

23. Charles S. Prebish, *Luminous Passage: The Practice and Study of Buddhism in America* (Berkeley: Univ. of California Press, 1999), pp. 46–47.

24. Fields, *How the Swans Came to the Lake*, 1, 2; Morreale, *The Complete Guide to Buddhist America*, 179.

25. Prebish, *Luminous Passage*, 97–107.

26. Morreale, *The Complete Guide to Buddhist America*, 189–90.

27. "American Buddhist Shim Gum Do Association," in *Communities Directory* (Rutledge, MO: Fellowship for Intentional Community, 2010), 130; see also the organization's website at www.shimgumdo.org.

28. James William Coleman, *The New Buddhism: The Western Transformation of an Ancient Tradition* (New York: Oxford Univ. Press, 2001), 165–66.

29. "Heartlight Center," in *Communities Directory* (Rutledge, MO: Fellowship for Intentional Community, 2000), 261. The community itself does not appear to have a website, but the angel project does: www.theangelworkshop.com.

30. Sandy Boucher, *Turning the Wheel: American Women Creating the New Buddhism* (Boston: Beacon, 1993), 165–74.

31. Timothy Miller, *The Encyclopedic Guide to American Intentional Communities*, 2nd ed. (Hamilton, NY: Richard W. Couper, 2015), xi.

32. Timothy Miller, *The 60s Communes: Hippies and Beyond* (Syracuse, New York: Syracuse Univ. Press, 1999), 153, 272; see also Miller, *The Encyclopedic Guide to American Intentional Communities*, 36, 287–88.

33. "Kanatsiohareke (Gana Jo Haleke)," in *Communities Directory* (Rutledge, MO: Fellowship for Intentional Community, 2000), 273. The community's website is at www.mohawkcommunity.com.

34. "Coldfoot Creek," *Communities* no. 56 (December 1982–January 1983): 60. See also "Coldfoot Creek Community," in *New Age Community Guidebook: Alternative Choices in Lifestyles*, ed. Bobbi Corcoran (Eugene, OR: Community Referral Service, 1985), 14–15.

35. Information about Annwfn is on the community's website, http://annwfn.org/.

36. Lucinda Carspecken, *An Unreal Estate: Sustainability and Freedom in an Evolving Community* (Bloomington: Indiana Univ. Press, 2011).

37. Carol E. Parrish, "Two Decades of Community Experience," *Communities* no. 87 (Summer 1995): 19–21.

38. Anastasia Galadriel Mashacek, *Growing Up Hippie* (n.p.: author, 2012), 87.

39. Brad C. Whitsel, *The Church Universal and Triumphant: Elizabeth Clare Prophet's Apocalyptic Movement* (Syracuse: Syracuse Univ. Press, 2003).

6. Communities on Purpose

1. Pat Freeman, "Five Families Pursue Peace, a Better Life," *St. Paul Pioneer Press and Dispatch*, April 14, 1985; Sue Sondreal, "Dorea Continues Growth," *Amery Free Press* (WI), May 15, 1984.

2. Jonathan R. Wilson, *Living Faithfully in a Fragmented World: Lessons for the Church from MacIntyre's After Virtue* (Harrisburg, PA: Trinity Press International, 1997).

3. Several books and many articles have been published on the New Monasticism. See, for example, Shane Claiborne, *The Irresistible Revolution: Living as an Ordinary Radical* (Grand Rapids, MI: Zondervan, 2006); Scott Bessenecker, *The New Friars: The Emerging Movement Serving the World's Poor* (Downers Grove, IL: InterVarsity, 2006); Jason Byassee, "The New Monastics," *Christian Century* 122, no. 21 (October 18, 2005): 38–47.

4. David Janzen, Don Mosley, and Josie Winterfeld, "Jubilee Partners," in *Fire, Salt, and Peace: Intentional Christian Communities Alive in North America*, ed. David Janzen et al. (Evanston, IL: Shalom Mission Communities, 1996), 106–11; Don Mosley,

With Our Own Eyes: The Dramatic Story of a Christian Response to the Wounds of War, Racism, and Oppression (Scottdale, PA: Herald Press, 1996).

5. David Janzen and Ed Loring, "The Open Door," in *Fire, Salt, and Peace*, 117–21; Peter R. Gathje, *Christ Comes in The Stranger's Guise* (n.p.: author, 1991); Peter R. Gathje, *Sharing the Bread of Life: Hospitality and Resistance at the Open Door Community* (Atlanta: Open Door Community, 2006).

6. Clarence E. Shuler, *Winning the Race to Unity: Is Racial Reconciliation Really Working?* (Chicago: Moody, 1998), 234.

7. The most complete published account of the Antioch Community is a memoir: Chris P. Rice, *Grace Matters: A True Story of Grace, Friendship, and Faith in the Heart of the South* (San Francisco: Jossey-Bass, 2002).

8. Brief synopses of all of these communities, together with references, can be found in my *Encyclopedic Guide to American Intentional Communities*, 2nd ed. (Clinton, NY: Richard W. Couper, 2015).

9. Joseph Bear Wilner, "All My Sisters and Brothers: Redefinitions of Family in Oregon Intentional Communities During the Late Twentieth Century," MA thesis, University of Oregon, 2000, 46–48.

10. Dan McKanan, *Touching the World: Christian Communities Transforming Society* (Collegeville, MA: Liturgical, 2007), 20. For this detail McKanan credits Anke Weihs, *Fragments from the Story of Camphill, 1939/40* (Llangadog, Wales: Coleg Elidyr, 1992); Karl König Archive, cited in Hans Müller-Wiedemann, *Karl König: A Central-European Biography of the Twentieth Century*, trans. Simon Blaxland-de Lange (Botton Village, England: Camphill, 1996), 174–75.

11. McKanan, *Touching the World*, 25–29.

12. Description on the community's website, apexcoop.org.

13. Diana Leafe Christian, *Creating a Life Together: Practical Tools to Grow Ecovillages and Intentional Communities* (Gabriola Island, BC: New Society, 2003).

14. The community's principal founder recounted the community's struggle with its neighbors and the state as well as its longer history: Graham Ellis, "My Struggle to Legalize Sustainable Living," *Communities* no. 168 (Fall 2015): 22–25. The conflict was reported in a newspaper article: Colin M. Stewart, "State: Group in Seaview Estates Broke Law," *Hawaiʻi Tribune-Herald*, June 26, 2014.

15. "Compound 'i,'" in *Communities Directory: A Guide to Cooperative Living* (Rutledge, MO: Fellowship for Intentional Community, 1996), 234.

16. "Art Colony at Eden Falls," *Communities* no. 83 (Summer 1984): 50.

17. Information on Ganas has been in several editions of the *Communities Directory* (see, for example, *Communities Directory* [Rutledge, MO: Fellowship for Intentional Community, 2010], 191). The community has also received ongoing popular media attention; see, for example, Andrew Jacobs, "Yes, It's a Commune. Yes, It's on

Staten Island," *New York Times*, November 29, 1998. The community's website is at ganas.org.

18. Ayla Heartsong, "Why We Still Need Women-Only Space," in *Shewolf's Directory of Wimmin's Lands and Lesbian Communities* (Melrose, FL: JRB, 2007), 5.

19. Priscilla Frank, "Look Inside Some of the Last Remaining All-Female Communes," *Huffington Post*, June 30, 2015, http://www.huffingtonpost.com/2015/06/30/leah-devun_n_7690580.html.

20. Joyce Cheney, *Lesbian Land* (Minneapolis: Word Weavers, 1985), 12.

21. Jeanne Tetrault and Sherry Thomas, *Country Women: A Handbook for the New Farmer* (Garden City, NY: Anchor/Doubleday, 2016), 9.

22. Billie Miracle, Jo Olszewska, and Jennifer Weston, *Country Lesbians: The Story of the WomanShare Collective* (Grants Pass, OR: WomanShare Press, 1976).

23. Catherine B. Kleiner, "Doin' It for Themselves: Lesbian Land Communes in Southern Oregon, 1970–1995," PhD diss., Univ. of New Mexico, 2003, 47, 111–14.

24. Kleiner, "Doin' It for Themselves," 105–8; Pelican Lee, "Nozama Tribe," in *Lesbian Land*, ed. Joyce Cheney, 157–63.

25. Catriona Sandilands, "Lesbian Separatist Communities and the Experience of Nature," *Organization and Environment* 15, no. 2 (June 2002): 131–63; La Verne Gagehabib and Barbara Summerhawk, *Circles of Power: Shifting Dynamics in a Lesbian-Centered Community* (Norwich, VT: New Victoria, 2000), 57–59, 122–23; Kleiner, "Doin' It for Themselves," 115–16.

26. Martin Duberman, *A Saving Remnant: The Radical Lives of Barbara Deming and David McReynolds* (New York: New Press, 2011), 217–29.

27. Katharine Parker Riddle, *A Nourishing Life* (Raleigh, NC: Pentland, 1999), 161–80; Martha Courtot, "Nourishing Space," in *Lesbian Land*, ed. Joyce Cheney, 103–4. Riddle's papers, including the plans for Nourishing Space, are archived at the Univ. of Texas at San Antonio library.

28. "Susan B. Anthony Women's Land Trust," in *Communities Directory* (Rutledge, MO: Fellowship for Intentional Community, 2007), 256.

29. John A. Stover III, "When Pan Met Wendy: Gendered Membership Debates Among the Radical Faeries," *Nova Religio* 11, no. 4 (May 2008): 37–38.

30. Alex Halberstadt, "Out of the Woods," *New York Times Magazine*, August 6, 2015. The Winter 2011 (38, no. 2), issue of *RFD*, edited at Short Mountain Sanctuary, was a special issue featuring the community.

31. MaxZine Weinstein, Tom Seidner, and K. Hass, "Radical Faeries in Rural Tennessee," *Communities* no. 87 (Summer 1995): 46.

32. Joseph Bear Wilner, "All My Sisters and Brothers: Redefinitions of Family in Oregon Intentional Communities During the Late Twentieth Century," MA thesis, Univ. of Oregon, 2000, 73–85. See also the Nomenus website, www.nomenus.org.

33. Ben Haggard, "Zuni Mountain Sanctuary: From Habit to Habitat," *Communities* no. 95 (Summer 1997): 29–30, 50; Jay Hasbrouck, "Utopian Imaginaries and Faerie Practice: Mapping Routes of Relational Agency," in *Gay Religion*, ed. Scott Thumma and Edward R. Gray (Walnut Creek, CA: Alta Mira, 2005), 239–58.

34. Basic information on Starland can be found in "Starland Retreat Center/Campground," in *Communities Directory: The Guide to Intentional Communities and Cooperative Living* (Rutledge, MO: Fellowship for Intentional Community, 2016), 355.

35. Christian Zinzendorf and Johannes Zinzendorf, "The Challenge of Finding New Community Members," *Communities* no. 122 (Spring 2004): 55–57; Johannes Zinzendorf, "Infilling with the Spirit at Christiansbrunn Cloister," *Communities* no. 87 (Summer 1995): 49.

36. James A. Aho, *The Politics of Righteousness: Idaho Christian Patriotism* (Seattle: Univ. of Washington Press, 1990), passim; Jeffrey Kaplan and Leonard Weinberg, *The Emergence of a Euro-American Radical Right* (New Brunswick, NJ: Rutgers Univ. Press, 1998), 146–50.

37. David A. Neiwert, *In God's Country: The Patriot Movement and the Pacific Northwest* (Pullman: Washington State Univ. Press, 1999), chapter 7; Rebecca Boone, "Almost Heaven, Idaho, Is Almost Silent Now," *Salt Lake Tribune*, August 30, 2004.

38. I Kings 17:8–16.

39. Jonathan Ford, "Covenant, the Sword, and the Arm of the Lord," in *The Encyclopedia of Arkansas History and Culture*, www.encyclopediaofarkansas.net/encyclopedia/entry-detail.aspx?entryID=4031; Kerry Noble, *Tabernacle of Hate: Why They Bombed Oklahoma City* (Prescott, ON: Voyageur, 1998).

40. Noble, *Tabernacle of Hate*, 111–12.

41. Somer Shook, Wesley Delano, and Robert W. Balch, "Elohim City: A Participant-Observer Study of a Christian Identity Community," *Nova Religio* 2, no. 2 (April 1999): 245–65.

7. Communities in the Media Spotlight

1. John R. Hall, *Gone from the Promised Land: Jonestown in American Cultural History* (New Brunswick, NJ: Transaction, 1987); Jeff Guinn, *The Road to Jonestown: Jim Jones and the Peoples Temple* (New York: Simon & Schuster, 2017). The Jonestown Report, an extensive archive of material on Jonestown, is online at http://jonestown.sdsu.edu.

2. The references on Rajneeshpuram in chapter 5, above, remain pertinent here: James S. Gordon, *The Golden Guru: The Strange Journey of Bhagwan Shree Rajneesh* (Lexington, MA: Stephen Greene, 1987); Frances Fitzgerald, *Cities on a Hill: A Journey through Contemporary American Culture* (New York: Simon & Schuster, 1986),

247–381; Marion S. Goldman, *Passionate Journeys: Why Successful Women Joined a Cult* (Ann Arbor: Univ. of Michigan Press, 1999).

3. Cynthia Stalter Sassé and Peggy Murphy Widder, *The Kirtland Massacre: The True and Terrible Story of the Mormon Cult Murders* (New York: Donald I. Fine, 1991); Pete Earley, *Prophet of Death: The Mormon Blood-Atonement Killings* (New York: Morrow, 1991). A detailed four-part series of retrospective newspaper articles by David Glasier for the *News-Herald* of northeastern Ohio provides a concise overview of the Lundgren story. The first, "Kirtland Cult Killings: Looking Back at Lake County's Worst Mass Murder, 25 Years Later," posted on December 31, 2014, is online at www.news-herald.com/article/HR/20141231/NEWS/141239955. The other parts of the series are linked to the first.

4. Jon Krakauer, *Under the Banner of Heaven: A Story of Violent Faith* (New York: Doubleday, 2003), 196–97.

5. John Anderson and Hilary Hevenor, *Burning Down the House: MOVE and the Tragedy of Philadelphia* (New York: Norton, 1987); Michael Boyette, *"Let It Burn!" The Philadelphia Tragedy* (Chicago: Contemporary, 1989).

6. Zechariah 3:8 and 6:12.

7. Mark England and Darlene McCormick, "The Sinful Messiah," *Waco Tribune-Herald*, February 27, 1993.

8. James D. Tabor and Eugene V. Gallagher, *Why Waco? Cults and the Battle for Religious Freedom in America* (Berkeley: Univ., of California Press, 1995); Stuart Wright, ed., *Armageddon in Waco: Critical Perspectives on the Branch Davidian Conflict* (Chicago: Univ. of Chicago Press, 1995).

9. Benjamin E. Zeller, *Heaven's Gate: America's UFO Religion* (New York: New York Univ. Press, 2014).

10. James A. Fussell, "Two Sides of Heaven: A Heaven's Gate Grandmother Is Proud Her Daughter Made It to 'the Next Level,'" *Kansas City Star*, November 9, 1997.

11. www.heavensgate.com.

12. Acts 2:44–47 and 4:32–37.

13. Jean Swantko and Ed Wiseman, "Messianic Communities, Sociologists, and the Law," *Communities: Journal of Cooperative Living* no. 88 (Fall 1995): 34–35.

14. Quoted in Susan Palmer, "Frontiers and Families: The Children of Island Pond," in *Children in New Religions*, ed. Susan J. Palmer and Charlotte E. Hardman (New Brunswick, NJ: Rutgers Univ. Press, 1999), 153.

15. Susan J. Palmer, "The Twelve Tribes," in *Storming Zion: Government Raids on Religious Communities*, ed. Stuart A. Wright and Susan J. Palmer (New York: Oxford Univ. Press, 2016), 47–72.

16. David Fisher, "A Cult Leader's 'Visions' Result in Murder Trial," *Seattle Post-Intelligencer*, May 11, 2001.

Conclusion and Afterword

1. Several surveys conducted by the Pew Forum have documented a rapid growth in numbers of Americans who are religiously unaffiliated. See, for example, "A Closer Look at America's Rapidly Growing Religious 'Nones,'" at http://www.pewresearch.org/fact-tank/2015/05/13/a-closer-look-at-americas-rapidly-growing-religious-nones/.

2. William K. Stevens, "Evolving Theory Views Earth as a Living Organism," *New York Times*, August 29, 1989.

3. Karen Svensson, "What Is an Ecovillage?" in *Ecovillage Living: Restoring the Earth and Her People*, ed. Hildur Jackson and Karen Svensson (Foxhold, Dartington, Totnes, Devon, England: Green, 2002), 10.

Appendix A

1. Michael Barkun, "Communal Societies as Cyclical Phenomena," *Communal Societies* 4 (1984): 35–48.

2. Brian J. L. Berry, *America's Utopian Experiments: Communal Havens from Long-Wave Crises* (Hanover: Dartmouth College/Univ. Press of New England, 1992).

3. Howard P. Segal, *Utopia: A Brief History from Ancient Writings to Virtual Communities* (Chichester, England: Wiley-Blackwell, 2012), 25. Segal does not name any of the "most students" and his bibliography provides no further clues.

4. Otohiko Okugawa, "Annotated List of Communal and Utopian Societies, 1787–1919," in *The Dictionary of Communal and Utopian History*, by Robert S. Fogarty (Westport, CT: Greenwood, 1980), 172–233.

5. *Journal of American History* 81, no. 2 (September, 1994), 691.

6. Timothy Miller, *The Encyclopedic Guide to American Intentional Communities*, 2nd ed. (Clinton, NY: Richard W. Couper, 2015). My definitions and discussions of communities and categories included or excluded are on pp. xi–xvi.

7. All of these census statistics have been gathered from the official U. S. Census website, www2.census.gov/prod2/statcomp/documents/CT1970p2-13.pdf.

8. The census totals apparently do not reflect French or Spanish people in early post–European-settlement North America.

Bibliography

Adkin, Clare E. *Brother Benjamin: A History of the House of David.* Berrien Springs, MI: Andrews Univ. Press, 1990.

Aho, James A. *The Politics of Righteousness: Idaho Christian Patriotism.* Seattle: Univ. of Washington Press, 1990.

Alcott, Louisa May. "Transcendental Wild Oats." In *Bronson Alcott's Fruitlands,* compiled by Clara Endicott Sears, 145–74. Harvard, MA: Fruitlands Museums, 2004.

Altus, Deborah. "Student Housing Cooperatives: Communitarianism among American Youth." *Communal Societies* 17 (1997): 1–13.

Amsden, David. "The Big Squeeze." *Rolling Stone* (August 16, 2012): 56–61.

Anderson, John, and Hilary Hevenor. *Burning Down the House: MOVE and the Tragedy of Philadelphia.* New York: Norton, 1987.

Arkin, Lois, and Jesse Moorman. "Sustainability in the City of Los Angeles." *Communities* no. 115 (Summer 2002): 36–41.

"Art Colony at Eden Falls." *Communities* no. 83 (Summer 1984): 50.

Avakian, Alexandra. *Windows of My Soul: My Journeys in the Muslim World.* Washington, DC: National Geographic, 2008.

Bang, Jan Martin. *Ecovillages: A Practical Guide to Sustainable Communities.* Gabriola Island, BC: New Society, 2005.

———. *A Portrait of Camphill: From Founding Seed to Worldwide Movement.* Edinburgh: Floris, 2010.

Barkun, Michael. "Communal Societies as Cyclical Phenomena." *Communal Societies* 4 (1984): 35–48.

Bates, Albert. "A Training Center for Ecovillagers." *Communities* no. 91 (Summer 1996): 34–35.

Belluck, Pam. "For Orthodox Jews, an Experiment in Farming and Faith." *New York Times,* November 1, 2002.

Bernstein, Fred A. "The Four-Bedroom Kibbutz." *New York Times*, February 11, 2010.

Berry, Brian J. L. *America's Utopian Experiments: Communal Havens from Long-Wave Crises.* Hanover: Dartmouth College/Univ. Press of New England, 1992.

Bessenecker, Scott. *The New Friars: The Emerging Movement Serving the World's Poor.* Downer's Grove, IL: IVP, 2006.

Boone, Rebecca. "Almost Heaven, Idaho, Is Almost Silent Now." *Salt Lake Tribune*, August 30, 2004.

Bordow, Sita. *Sri Swami Satchidananda: Apostle of Peace.* Yogaville, VA: Integral Yoga, 1986.

Boucher, Sandy. *Turning the Wheel: American Women Creating the New Buddhism.* Boston: Beacon, 1993.

Boyette, Michael. *"Let It Burn!" The Philadelphia Tragedy.* Chicago: Contemporary, 1989.

Bradley, Martha Sonntag. *Kidnapped from That Land: The Government Raids on the Short Creek Polygamists.* Salt Lake City: Univ. of Utah Press, 1993.

Bringhurst, Newell G., and John C. Hamer, ed. *Scattering of the Saints: Schism within Mormonism.* Independence, MO: John Whitmer, 2007.

Brown, Patricia Leigh. "Growing Old Together, in New Kind of Commune." *New York Times*, February 27, 2006.

Buchan, Perdita. *Utopia, New Jersey: Travels in the Nearest Eden.* New Brunswick, NJ: Rivergate /Rutgers Univ. Press, 2007.

Byassee, Jason. "The New Monastics." *Christian Century* 122, no. 21 (October 18, 2005): 38–47.

Carspecken, Lucinda. *An Unreal Estate: Sustainability and Freedom in an Evolving Community.* Bloomington: Indiana Univ. Press, 2011.

Cheney, Joyce, ed. *Lesbian Land.* Minneapolis: Word Weavers, 1985.

Christian, Diana. *Creating a Life Together: Practical Tools to Grow Ecovillages and Intentional Communities.* Gabriola Island, BC: New Society, 2003.

Claiborne, Shane. *The Irresistible Revolution: Living as an Ordinary Radical.* Grand Rapids: Zondervan, 2006.

Coble, Ann Louise. *Cotton Patch for the Kingdom: Clarence Jordan's Demonstration Plot at Koinonia Farm.* Scottdale, PA: Herald, 2002.

"Coldfoot Creek." *Communities* no. 56 (December 1982–January 1983): 60.

"Coldfoot Creek Community." In Corcoran, *New Age Community Guidebook* (1985), 14–15.

Coleman, James William. *The New Buddhism: The Western Transformation of an Ancient Tradition*. New York: Oxford Univ. Press, 2001.

Communities Directory. Rutledge, MO: Fellowship for Intentional Community, 2000.

Communities Directory: A Comprehensive Guide to Intentional Communities and Cooperative Living. Rutledge, MO: Fellowship for Intentional Community, 2005.

Communities Directory: A Comprehensive Guide to Intentional Communities and Cooperative Living. Rutledge, MO: Fellowship for Intentional Community, 2007.

Communities Directory: A Comprehensive Guide to Intentional Communities and Cooperative Living. Rutledge, MO: Fellowship for Intentional Community, 2010.

Communities Directory: A Guide to Cooperative Living. Rutledge, MO: Fellowship for Intentional Community, 1996.

Communities Directory: The Guide to Intentional Communities and Cooperative Living. Rutledge, MO: Fellowship for Intentional Community, 2016.

"Communities with Openings." *Communities* no. 151 (Summer 2011): 68.

Corcoran, Bobbi, ed. "Center for Well-Being." In Corcoran, *New Age Community Guidebook* (1989), 85.

———. *New Age Community Guidebook: Alternative Choices in Lifestyles*, edited by Bobbi Corcoran. Eugene, Oregon: Community Referral Service, 1985.

———. *New Age Community Guidebook: Alternative Choices in Lifestyles*. 4th ed. Middletown, CA: Harbin Springs, 1989.

Cornell, Judith. *Amma: Healing the Heart of the World*. New York: William Morrow, 2001.

Courtot, Martha. "Nourishing Space." In Cheney, *Lesbian Land*, 103–4.

Curl, John. *For All the People: Uncovering the Hidden History of Cooperation, Cooperative Movements, and Communalism in America*. 2nd ed. Oakland, CA: PM, 2009.

Dawson, Jonathan. *Ecovillages: New Frontiers for Sustainability*. White River Junction, VT: Chelsea Green, 2006.

Day, Dorothy. *Loaves and Fishes: The Story of the Catholic Worker Movement*. (San Francisco: Harper & Row, 1963).

Donoghue, Susanne, and Vincent Donoghue. "Assisi Community." In Janzen et al., *Fire, Salt, and Peace*, 43–44.

Duberman, Martin. *A Saving Remnant: The Radical Lives of Barbara Deming and David McReynolds*. New York: New Press, 2011.

Durrett, Charles. *Senior Cohousing*. Berkeley: Ten Speed, 2005.

Earley, Pete. *Prophet of Death: The Mormon Blood-Atonement Killings*. New York: William Morrow, 1991.

Ellis, Graham. "My Struggle to Legalize Sustainable Living." *Communities* no. 168 (Fall 2015): 22–25.

England, Mark, and Darlene McCormick. "The Sinful Messiah." *Waco Tribune-Herald*, February 27, 1993.

Eskridge, Larry. *God's Forever Family: The Jesus People Movement in America*. New York: Oxford Univ. Press, 2013.

Fallon, D'Arcy. *So Late, So Soon: A Memoir*. Portland, OR: Hawthorne, 2004.

Ferrante-Roseberry, Lydia. "Living with Integrity: My Experience in Cohousing." *Social Policy* 33, no. 2 (Winter 2002), 17–22.

Fields, Rick. *How the Swans Came to the Lake: A Narrative History of Buddhism in America*. Boulder, CO: Shambhala, 1981.

Fisher, David. "A Cult Leader's Visions Result in Murder Trial." *Seattle Post-Intelligencer*, May 11, 2001.

Fitzgerald, Frances. *Cities on a Hill: A Journey through Contemporary American Culture*. New York: Simon & Schuster, 1986.

Fogarty, Robert S. *Dictionary of American Communal and Utopian History*. Westport, CT: Greenwood, 1980.

Ford, Jonathan. "Covenant, the Sword, and the Arm of the Lord." *The Encyclopedia of Arkansas History and Culture*. http://www.encyclopediaofarkansas.net/encyclopedia/entry-detail.aspx?entryID=4031.

Francis, Richard. *Fruitlands: The Alcott Family and Their Search for Utopia*. New Haven: Yale Univ. Press, 2010.

Frank, Priscilla. "Look Inside Some of the Last Remaining All-Female Communes." *Huffington Post*, June 30, 2015. www.huffingtonpost.com/2015/06/30/leahdevun_n_7690580.html.

Freeman, Pat. "Five Families Pursue Peace, a Better Life." *St. Paul Pioneer Press and Dispatch*, April 14, 1985.

"Friends Community." In Corcoran, *New Age Community Guidebook* (1989), 74–75.

Fromm, Dorit. "American Cohousing: The First Five Years." *Journal of Architectural and Planning Research* 17 (Summer 2000): 94–109.

Fussell, James A. "Two Sides of Heaven: A Heaven's Gate Grandmother Is Proud Her Daughter Made It to the Next Level." *Kansas City Star*, November 9, 1997.

Gagehabib, La Verne, and Barbara Summerhawk. *Circles of Power: Shifting Dynamics in a Lesbian-Centered Community*. Norwich, VT: New Victoria, 2000.

Geranios, Nicholas K. "Residents Believe in Being Comfortable While Preparing for the Worst: Homesteaders Will Be in the Hot Tub Awaiting World War III." *Los Angeles Times*, July 31, 1988.

Gilman, Diane, and Robert Gilman. *Eco-Villages and Sustainable Communities: A Report for Gaia Trust by Context Institute*. Bainbridge Island, WA: Context Institute, 1991.

Gish, Dale, and Margaret Swink. "Church of the Sojourners." In Janzen et al., *Fire, Salt, and Peace*, 58–62.

Glasier, David. "Kirtland Cult Killings: Looking Back at Lake County's Worst Mass Murder, 25 Years Later." *News-Herald* [Lake County, OH], December 31, 2014. www.newsherald.com/article/HR/20141231/NEWS/141239955.

Glass, A. P. "An Evaluation of an Elder Cohousing Community." *Gerontologist* 51, supplement 2 (2011): 504.

Goldberg, Philip. *American Veda: From Emerson and the Beatles to Yoga and Meditation: How Indian Spirituality Changed the West*. New York: Harmony /Random House, 2010.

Goldman, Marion S. *Passionate Journeys: Why Successful Women Joined a Cult*. Ann Arbor: Univ. of Michigan Press, 1999.

Gordon, James S. *The Golden Guru: The Strange Journey of Bhagwan Shree Rajneesh*. Lexington, MA: Stephen Greene, 1987.

Haddad, Yvonne Yazbeck, and Jane Idleman Smith, eds. *Muslim Communities in North America*. Albany: State Univ. of New York Press, 1994.

Haggard, Ben. "Zuni Mountain Sanctuary: From Habit to Habitat." *Communities* no. 95 (Summer 1997): 29–30, 50.

Halberstadt, Alex. "Out of the Woods." *New York Times Magazine*, August 6, 2015.

Hall, John R. *Gone from the Promised Land: Jonestown in American Cultural History*. New Brunswick, NJ: Transaction, 1987.

Hasbrouck, Jay. "Utopian Imaginaries and Faerie Practice: Mapping Routes of Relational Agency." In *Gay Religion*, edited by Scott Thumma and Edward R. Gray, 239–58. Walnut Creek, CA: Alta Mira, 2005.

Hawken, Paul. *The Magic of Findhorn*. New York: Harper & Row, 1975.

Heartsong, Ayla. "Why We Still Need Women-Only Space." In *Shewolf's Directory of Wimmin's Lands and Lesbian Communities*. 5th ed. Melrose, FL: JRB, 2007.

Heilman, Uriel. "The Frum Farm." *Jerusalem Post*, March 6, 2003.

Heinen, Tom. "Mystics Misunderstood? Religious Order Says It's Out of the Mainstream but Not a Cult." *Milwaukee Journal Sentinel*, March 6, 2005.

Hertz, Kelly. "Hutterites: Not the Best of Times." *Yankton Press and Dakotan*, October 7, 1989.

Hillendahl, Lou. "A Community of Counselor Pioneers." *Communities* no. 92 (Fall 1996): 39–41.

Hollenbach, Margaret. *Lost and Found: My Life in a Group Marriage Commune*. Albuquerque: Univ. of New Mexico Press, 2004.

Holloway, Karel. "Homestead Heritage Combines Farming, Arts, and a Bit of Tourism." *Dallas Morning News*, September 26, 2003.

Jackson, Dave. *Coming Together: All Those Communities and What They're Up To*. Minneapolis: Bethany Fellowship, 1978.

Jacobs, Andrew. "Yes, It's a Commune. Yes, It's on Staten Island." *New York Times*, November 29, 1998.

Janzen, David. "Church on West Street." In Janzen et al., *Fire, Salt, and Peace*, 63–66.

———. "Community of Celebration." In Janzen et al., *Fire, Salt, and Peace*, 77–82.

———. "Shepherdsfield Community." In Janzen et al., *Fire, Salt, and Peace*, 138–42.

Janzen, David, and John Michael Talbot. "Brothers and Sisters of Charity." In Janzen et al., *Fire, Salt, and Peace*, 49–52.

Janzen, David, and Lou Hillendahl. "Wesleyan Community." In Janzen et al., *Fire, Salt, and Peace*, 160–64.

Janzen, David et al., eds. *Fire, Salt, and Peace: Intentional Christian Communities Alive in North America*. Evanston, IL: Shalom Mission Communities, 1996.

Janzen, David, Don Mosley, and Josie Winterfeld. "Jubilee Partners." In Janzen et al., *Fire, Salt, and Peace*, 106–11.

Janzen, Rod, and Max Stanton. *The Hutterites in North America*. Baltimore: Johns Hopkins Univ. Press, 2010.

Kaplan, Jeffrey, and Leonard Weinberg. *The Emergence of a EuroAmerican Radical Right.* New Brunswick, NJ: Rutgers Univ. Press, 1998.

Kinkade, Kat. *Is It Utopia Yet? An Insider's View of Twin Oaks Community in Its Twenty-Sixth Year.* Louisa, VA: Twin Oaks, 1994.

Kleiner, Catherine B. "Doin' It for Themselves: Lesbian Land Communes in Southern Oregon, 1970–1995." PhD diss., Univ. of New Mexico, 2003.

K'Meyer, Tracy Elaine. *Interracialism and Christian Community in the Postwar South.* Charlottesville: Univ. of Virginia Press, 1997.

Krakauer, Jon. *Under the Banner of Heaven: A Story of Violent Faith.* New York: Doubleday, 2003.

Landing, James E. *Black Judaism: Story of an American Movement.* Durham, NC: Carolina Academic, 2002.

Lee, Pelican. "Nozama Tribe." In Cheney, *Lesbian Land,* 157–63.

Letterman, Meg. "Ponderosa Village: A Self-Reliant Lifestyle." *Communities* no. 67 (Summer 1985): 15–21.

Llewellyn, John R. *Polygamy Under Attack: From Tom Green to Brian David Mitchell.* Scottsdale, AZ: Agreka, 2004.

Lockyer, Joshua. "Sustainability and Utopianism: An Ethnography of Cultural Critique in Contemporary Intentional Communities." PhD diss., Univ. of Georgia, 2007.

Lucas, Phillip. *The Odyssey of a New Religion: The Holy Order of MANS from New Age to Orthodoxy.* Bloomington: Indiana Univ. Press, 1995.

Mashacek, Anastasia Galadriel. *Growing Up Hippie.* N.p.: author, 2012.

Mattingly, Terry. "Ozark Monastery Not Just for Celibate." *Kansas City Star,* October 10, 1992.

McCamant, Kathryn, Charles Durrett, and Ellen Hertzman. *Cohousing: A Contemporary Approach to Housing Ourselves.* 2nd ed. Berkeley, CA: Ten Speed, 1994.

McCrank, Lawrence J. "Religious Orders and Monastic Communities in America." In *America's Communal Utopias,* edited by Donald E. Pitzer, 204–52. Chapel Hill: Univ. of North Carolina Press, 1997.

McIntosh, Jim. "Assisi Community Celebrates 25 Years." *HNP Today Newsletter* 54, no. 24 (December 7, 2011). hnp.org/assisicommunitycelebrates 25years.

McKanan, Dan. *Touching the World: Christian Communities Transforming Society.* Collegeville, MN: Liturgical, 2007.

McLaughlin, Corinne, and Gordon Davidson. *Builders of the Dawn: Community Lifestyles in a Changing World.* Walpole, NJ: Stillpoint, 1985.

Melton, J. Gordon. *The Encyclopedia of American Religions.* 7th ed. Detroit: Gale, 2003.

Meltzer, Graham. "Cohousing: Verifying the Importance of Community in the Application of Environmentalism." *Journal of Architectural and Planning Research* 17, no. 2 (Summer 2000): 110–32.

———. *Sustainable Community: Learning from the Cohousing Model.* Victoria, BC: Trafford, 2005.

Metcalf, William. *The Findhorn Book of Community Living.* Forres, Scotland: Findhorn, 2004.

Miller, Timothy, ed. *America's Alternative Religions.* Albany: State Univ. of New York Press, 1995.

———. *The Encyclopedic Guide to American Intentional Communities.* 2nd ed. Clinton, NY: Richard W. Couper 2015.

———. *The Quest for Utopia in Twentieth-Century America, Volume I.* Syracuse: Syracuse Univ. Press, 1998.

———. *The 60s Communes: Hippies and Beyond.* Syracuse: Syracuse Univ. Press, 1999.

———, ed. *When Prophets Die: The Postcharismatic Fate of New Religious Movements.* Albany: State Univ. of New York Press, 1991.

Milman, Danny. "Where It All Began: Cohousing in Denmark." www.getriil.org/~getriil/cgibin/details.php?anum=1505.

Miracle, Billie, Jo Olszewska, and Jennifer Weston. *Country Lesbians: The Story of the WomanShare Collective.* Grants Pass, OR: WomanShare, 1976.

"Monasticism in the United States." *Bulletin de l'AIM* (Alliance Inter-Monastères) no. 97 (n.d., ca. 2010). www.aimintl.org/index.php?option=com_content&id=466&lang=en.

The Monks of New Skete. *In the Spirit of Happiness.* Boston: Little, Brown, 1999.

Moore-Emmett, Andrea. *God's Brothel.* San Francisco: Pince-Nez, 2004.

Morreale, Don. *The Complete Guide to Buddhist America.* 2nd ed. Boston: Shambhala, 1998.

Morris, James M., and Andrea L. Kross. *Historical Dictionary of Utopianism.* Lanham, MD: Scarecrow, 2004.

Mosley, Don. *With Our Own Eyes: The Dramatic Story of a Christian Response to the Wounds of War, Racism, and Oppression.* Scottdale, PA: Herald, 1996.

Myers, Jody. *Kabbalah and the Spiritual Quest: The Kabbalah Centre in America.* Westport, CT: Praeger, 2007.

Narayanan, Vasudha. "Gurus and Goddesses, Deities and Devotees." In Pechilis, *The Graceful Guru*, 149–78.

Neiwert, David A. *In God's Country: The Patriot Movement and the Pacific Northwest.* Pullman: Washington State Univ. Press, 1999.

Noble, Kerry. *Tabernacle of Hate: Why They Bombed Oklahoma City.* Prescott, ON: Voyageur, 1998.

Nolt, John, Athena Lee Bradley, Mike Knapp, Donald Earl Lampard, and Jonathan Scherch. *What Have We Done? The Foundation for Global Sustainability's State of the Bioregion Report for the Upper Tennessee Valley and the Southern Appalachian Mountains.* Washburn, TN: Earth Knows, 1997.

Okugawa, Otohiko. "Annotated List of Communal and Utopian Societies, 1787–1919." In Robert S. Fogarty, *Dictionary of Communal and Utopian History*, 172–233. Westport, CT: Greenwood, 1980.

Olson, Roger. "Where Community Is No Cliche: Forty-Three Families in Rural Texas Blend Pentecostal Fervor and Anabaptist Simplicity." *Christianity Today* 49, no. 2 (February 2005): 56–60.

Oppenheimer, Mark. "Soul-Searching in a Christian Community Over Views on How to Live." *New York Times*, September 1, 2012.

Oved, Iaácov. *The Witness of the Brothers: A History of the Bruderhof.* New Brunswick, NJ: Transaction, 1996.

Palmer, Susan J. "Frontiers and Families: The Children of Island Pond." In *Children in New Religions*, edited by Susan J. Palmer and Charlotte E. Hardman, 153–71. New Brunswick, NJ: Rutgers Univ. Press, 1999.

———. *The Nuwaubian Nation: Black Spirituality and State Control.* Farnham, England: Ashgate, 2010.

———. "The Twelve Tribes." In *Storming Zion: Government Raids on Religious Communities*, edited by Stuart A. Wright and Susan J. Palmer, 47–72. New York: Oxford Univ. Press, 2016.

Parrish, Carol E. "Two Decades of Community Experience." *Communities* no. 87 (Summer 1995): 19–21.

Pechilis, Karen, ed. *The Graceful Guru: Hindu Female Gurus in the United States.* New York: Oxford Univ. Press, 2004.

———. "Gurumayi, the Play of Shakti and Guru." In Pechelis, *The Graceful Guru*, 219–43.

Peterson, Dene. "ElderSpirit: Living the Spiritual Quest in Later Years." *Communities* no. 121 (Winter 2003): 26–29.

Pitzer, Donald E., ed. *America's Communal Utopias.* Chapel Hill: Univ. of North Carolina Press, 1997.

Popenoe, Cris, and Oliver Popenoe. *Seeds of Tomorrow: New Age Communities That Work.* San Francisco: Harper & Row, 1984.

Prebish, Charles S. *Luminous Passage: The Practice and Study of Buddhism in America.* Berkeley: Univ. of California Press, 1999.

Pride, Richard A. "Elmo Stoll and the Christian Community at Cookeville." *Border States: Journal of the Kentucky Tennessee American Studies Association* 15 (2003): 36–49.

Raj, Selva J. "Ammachi, the Mother of Compassion." In Pechelis, *The Graceful Guru,* 201–18.

[Ram Dass]. *Remember, Be Here Now.* San Cristobal, NM: Lama Foundation, 1971.

Rawlinson, Andrew. *The Book of Enlightened Masters.* Chicago: Open Court, 1997.

Reckdahl, Katy. "Mississippi Muslim," *Gambit* (New Orleans), July 8, 2003. www.bestofneworleans.com/gambit/mississippimuslim/Content?oid=1241688.

Reeves, Jay. "Ala. Commune Leader Involved in New Project Despite Past Abuse Claims, Fire Deaths of Children." *Minneapolis Star Tribune,* April 7, 2010.

Reha, Rick, and Mary Richardson. "Wooden Bridge Community." In Janzen et al., *Fire, Salt, and Peace,* 138–42.

Reider, Rebecca. *Dreaming the Biosphere: The Theater of All Possibilities.* Albuquerque: Univ. of New Mexico Press, 2009.

Reimer, Kevin S. *Living L'Arche: Stories of Compassion, Love and Disability.* Collegeville, MN: Liturgical, 2009.

Rice, Chris P. *Grace Matters: A True Story of Grace, Friendship, and Faith in the Heart of the South.* San Francisco: Jossey-Bass, 2002.

Riddle, Katharine Parker. *A Nourishing Life.* Raleigh, NC: Pentland, 1999.

Rochford, E. Burke. *Hare Krishna in America.* New Brunswick, NJ: Rutgers Univ. Press, 1985.

———. *Hare Krishna Transformed.* New York: New York Univ. Press, 2007.

Romero, Simon. "A Ruling on the Status of Its Women Roils a Monastery." *New York Times,* January 7, 2006.

Rothschild, Joel. ["Ravenna Kibbutz, USA."] *C.A.L.L.: Communes at Large Letter*, no. 32 (Summer 2010): 24–25.

Russell, William D. "The Fundamentalist Schism, 1958–Present." In *Let Contention Cease: The Dynamics of Dissent in the Reorganized Church of Jesus Christ of Latter Day Saints*, edited by Roger D. Launius and W. B. "Pat" Spillman. Independence, MO: Graceland/Park, 1991.

Sandilands, Catriona. "Lesbian Separatist Communities and the Experience of Nature." *Organization and Environment* 15, no. 2 (June 2002): 131–63.

Sanford, A. Whitney. "Being the Change: Food, Nonviolence, and Self-Sufficiency in Contemporary Communities." *Communal Societies* 34, no. 2 (2014): 28–53.

———. *Living Sustainably: What Intentional Communities Can Teach Us about Democracy, Simplicity, and Nonviolence.* Lexington: Univ. Press of Kentucky, 2017.

Sassé, Cynthia Stalter, and Peggy Murphy Widder. *The Kirtland Massacre: The True and Terrible Story of the Mormon Cult Murders.* New York: Donald I. Fine, 1991.

Sazama, Gerald W. "Lessons from the History of Affordable Housing Cooperatives in the United States: A Case Study in American Affordable Housing Policy." *American Journal of Economics and Sociology* 59, no. 4 (October 2000): 573–608.

Schenk, Jim. "A Home-Grown Ecovillage on Our Street." *Communities* no. 129 (Winter 2005): 52–56.

The Sealed Portion of the Brother of Jared. 2 vols. Leawood, KS: Leathers, 2001, 2002.

Searles, Leland Mark. "Returning to Babylon: Processes of Social Change and the Characteristics of Former Participants in a New Religious Movement." MA thesis, Iowa State Univ., 1993.

Segal, Howard P. *Utopia: A Brief History from Ancient Writings to Virtual Communities.* Chichester, England: Wiley-Blackwell, 2012.

Shields, Steven L. "Communalism in the Latter Day Saint Movement." *Communal Societies* 28, no. 2 (2008): 37.

———. *Divergent Paths of the Restoration: A History of the Latter Day Saint Movement.* 4th ed. Independence, MO: Herald House, 2001.

Shook, Somer, Wesley Delano, and Robert W. Balch. "Elohim City: A Participant-Observer Study of a Christian Identity Community." *Nova Religio* 2, no. 2 (April 1999): 245–65.

Shuler, Clarence E. *Winning the Race to Unity: Is Racial Reconciliation Really Working?* Chicago: Moody, 1998.

Skinner, B. F. *Walden Two*. New York: Macmillan, 1948.

Smith, Christopher T. "Go Tell It on the Mountain: A History of Narrow Ridge Earth Literacy Center." BA honors thesis, Carson-Newman College, 2009.

Sondeal, Sue. "Dorea Continues Growth." *Amery Free Press* (WI), May 15, 1984.

Sonneborn, Daniel Atesh. "Music and Meaning in American Sufism: The Ritual of *Dhikr* at Sami Mahal, a Chistiyya-derived Sufi Center." PhD diss., Univ. of California, Los Angeles, 1995.

"Southwest Sufi Community." *Communities* no. 118 (Summer 2003): 67.

Stevens, William K. "Evolving Theory Views Earth as a Living Organism." *New York Times*, August 29, 1989.

Stevenson, Douglas. *The Farm Then and Now: A Model for Sustainable Living*. Gabriola Island, BC: New Society, 2014.

Stewart, Colin M. "State: Group in Seaview Estates Broke Law." *Hawai'i Tribune-Herald*, June 26, 2014.

Stockwell, Foster. *Encyclopedia of American Communes, 1663–1963*. Jefferson, NC: McFarland, 1998.

Stover, John A. III. "When Pan Met Wendy: Gendered Membership Debates Among the Radical Faeries." *Nova Religio* 11, no. 4 (May 2008): 313–55.

Sutton, Robert P. *Modern American Communes: A Dictionary*. Westport, CT: Greenwood, 2005.

Svensson, Karen. "What Is an Ecovillage?" In *Ecovillage Living: Restoring the Earth and Her People*, edited by Hildur Jackson and Karen Svensson, 10–12. Foxhold, England: Green, 2002.

Swantko, Jean, and Ed Wiseman. "Messianic Communities, Sociologists, and the Law." *Communities* no. 88 (Fall 1995): 34–35.

Tabor, James D., and Eugene V. Gallagher. *Why Waco? Cults and the Battle for Religious Freedom in America*. Berkeley: Univ. of California Press, 1995.

Tarnay, Stella. "Bringing Life Back to an Urban Neighborhood." In *Reinventing Community: Stories from the Walkways of Cohousing*, edited by David Wann, 144–54. Golden, CO: Fulcrum, 2005.

Tetrault, Jeanne, and Sherry Thomas. *Country Women: A Handbook for the New Farmer*. Garden City, New York: Anchor/Doubleday, 1976.

Thomas, Jo, with Ralph Blumenthal. "Rural Muslims Draw New, Unwanted Attention." *New York Times*, January 3, 2002, 18.

Thursby, Gene R. "Hindu Movements Since Mid-Century: Yogis in the States." In *America's Alternative Religions*, edited by Timothy Miller, 195–98. Albany: State Univ. of New York Press, 1995.

———. "Siddha Yoga: Swami Muktananda and the Seat of Power." In *When Prophets Die: The Postcharismatic Fate of New Religious Movements*, edited by Timothy Miller, 165–81. Albany: State Univ. of New York Press, 1991.

Tigunait, Pandit Rajmani. *At the Eleventh Hour: The Biography of Swami Rama*. Honesdale, PA: Himalayan Institute, 2001.

Tuncer, Deniz, ed. "Student Co-ops: What I Really Learned in College." *Communities* no. 110 (Spring 2001): 30–64.

Vanier, Jean. *Community and Growth*. New York: Paulist, 1989.

Vanneman, Brian. "Searching for Paradise in the Rain: Oregon's Communes and Intentional Communities of the 1960s and 1970s." BA honors thesis, Univ. of Oregon, 1997.

Vecsey, George. "New Group Combines Evangelism and Orthodoxy." *New York Times*, March 11, 1979.

Vogt, Virgil. "Hope Community." In Janzen et al., *Fire, Salt, and Peace*, 99–103.

Walker, Liz. *EcoVillage at Ithaca: Pioneering a Sustainable Culture*. Gabriola Island, BC: New Society, 2005.

Wann, David, ed. *Reinventing Community: Stories from the Walkways of Co-housing*. Golden, CO: Fulcrum, 2005.

Watts, Jill. *God, Harlem, U.S.A.* Berkeley: Univ. of California Press, 1992.

Webb, Gisela. "Tradition and Innovation in Contemporary American Islamic Spirituality: The Bawa Muhaiyaddeen Fellowship." In *Muslim Communities in North America*, edited by Yvonne Yazbeck Haddad and Jane Idleman Smith, 96–97. Albany: State Univ. of New York Press, 1994.

Weber, Joseph. *Transcendental Meditation in America: How a New Age Movement Remade a Small Town in Iowa*. Iowa City: Univ. of Iowa Press, 2014.

Webster, Katharine. "The Case of Swami Rama of the Himalayas." *Yoga Journal* 95 (November–December, 1990): 59ff.

Weinstein, MaxZine, Tom Seidner, and K. Hass. "Radical Faeries in Rural Tennessee." *Communities* no. 87 (Summer 1995): 46.

Weisbrot, Robert. *Father Divine and the Struggle for Racial Equality.* Urbana: Univ. of Illinois Press, 1983.

Welch, Bob. "East Meets West at Audarya Ashram." *Eugene Register-Guard* [OR], August 8, 1993.

Whitsel, Brad C. *The Church Universal and Triumphant: Elizabeth Clare Prophet's Apocalyptic Movement.* Syracuse: Syracuse Univ. Press, 2003.

Wilde, Anne. "Fundamentalist Mormonism: Its History, Diversity and Stereotypes, 1886–Present." In *Scattering of the Saints,* edited by Newell G. Bringhurst and John C. Hamer, 270–71. Independence, MO: John Whitmer, 2007.

Williamson, Lola. *Transcendent in America: Hindu Inspired Meditation Movements as New Religion.* New York: New York Univ. Press, 2010, 106–31.

Wilner, Joseph Bear. "All My Sisters and Brothers: Redefinitions of Family in Oregon Intentional Communities during the Late Twentieth Century." MA thesis, Univ. of Oregon, 2000.

Wilson, Jonathan R. *Living Faithfully in a Fragmented World: Lessons for the Church from MacIntyre's After Virtue.* Harrisburg, PA: Trinity, 1997.

Wright, Stuart, ed. *Armageddon in Waco: Critical Perspectives on the Branch Davidian Conflict.* Chicago: Univ. of Chicago Press, 1995.

Yeoman, Barry. "Rethinking the Commune." *AARP: The Magazine* (March–April 2006).

Young, Shawn David, *Gray Sabbath: Jesus People USA, the Evangelical Left, and the Evolution of Christian Rock.* New York: Columbia Univ. Press, 2015.

Zeller, Benjamin E. *Heaven's Gate: America's UFO Religion.* New York: New York Univ. Press, 2014.

Zimmerman, Laurie, and Ranee Zaporski. "Kashrut and Compromise at Ofek Shalom." *Communities* no. 96 (Fall 1997): 38–40.

Zinzendorf, Johannes. "Infilling with the Spirit at Christiansbrunn Cloister." *Communities* no. 87 (Summer 1995): 49.

Zinzendorf, Christian, and Johannes Zinzendorf. "The Challenge of Finding New Community Members." *Communities* no. 122 (Spring 2004): 55–57.

Index

Timothy Miller is professor of religious studies at the University of Kansas. He is the author of the two previous books in this series, and of other books on intentional communities, new religious movements, and American religious history.